STUDIES IN ENVIRONMENT AND HISTORY

A new face on the countryside

STUDIES IN ENVIRONMENT AND HISTORY

Editors

Donald Worster   *Brandeis University*
Alfred Crosby   *University of Texas at Austin*

Advisory Board

Reid Bryson   *Institute for Environmental Studies, University of Wisconsin*
Raymond Dasmann   *College Eight, University of California, Santa Cruz*
E. Le Roy Ladurie   *Collège de France*
William McNeill   *Department of History, University of Chicago*
Carolyn Merchant   *College of Natural Resources, University of California, Berkeley*
Thad Tate   *Institute of Early American History and Culture, College of William and Mary*

Other Books in the Series

Donald Worster   *Nature's Economy: A History of Ecological Ideas*
Kenneth F. Kiple   *The Caribbean Slave: A Biological History*
Alfred W. Crosby   *Ecological Imperialism: The Biological Expansion of Europe, 900–1900*
Arthur F. McEvoy   *The Fisherman's Problem: Ecology and Law in the California Fisheries, 1850–1980*
Robert Harms   *Games Against Nature: An Eco-Cultural History of the Nunu of Equatorial Africa*
Warren Dean   *Brazil and the Struggle for Rubber: A Study in Environmental History*
Samuel P. Hays   *Beauty, Health, and Permanence: Environmental Politics in the United States, 1955–1985*
Donald Worster   *The Ends of the Earth: Perspectives on Modern Environmental History*
Michael Williams   *Americans and Their Forests*

A new face on the countryside

Indians, colonists, and slaves in South Atlantic forests, 1500–1800

TIMOTHY SILVER

Appalachian State University

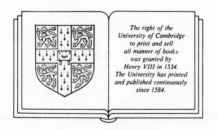

The right of the
University of Cambridge
to print and sell
all manner of books
was granted by
Henry VIII in 1534.
The University has printed
and published continuously
since 1584.

CAMBRIDGE UNIVERSITY PRESS

Cambridge

New York   Port Chester   Melbourne   Sydney

Published by the Press Syndicate of the University of Cambridge
The Pitt Building, Trumpington Street, Cambridge CB2 1RP
40 West 20th Street, New York, NY 10011, USA
10 Stamford Road, Oakleigh, Melbourne 3166, Australia

First published 1990
Reprinted 1990

Printed in the United States of America

Library of Congress Cataloging-in-Publication Data
Silver, Timothy. 1955–
A new face on the countryside: Indians, colonists, and slaves in
South Atlantic forests, 1500–1800 / Timothy Silver.
p.   cm. – (Studies in environment and history)
ISBN 0–521–34374–7. – ISBN 0–521–38739–6 (pbk.)
1. Man – Influence on nature – South Atlantic States – History.
2. Forest ecology – South Atlantic States.   3. Indians of North
America – South Atlantic States – History.   4. South Atlantic States
– History.   5. Slaves – South Atlantic States – History.   I. Title.
II. Series.
GF504.S67S55   1990
304.2'0975 – dc20   89–27263
                                               CIP

British Library Cataloguing in Publication Data
Silver, Timothy
A new face on the countryside: Indians, colonists, and
slaves in South Atlantic forests, 1500–1800. – (Studies in
environment and history)
1. Man. Ecology, history
I. Title   II. Series
304.2'09

ISBN 0–521–34374–7 hardback
ISBN 0–521–38739–6 paperback

For Sharon

Contents

List of figures   *page* viii

Preface   ix

Acknowledgments   xi

1.   Prologue: Images and boundaries   1

2.   Perspectives on the land   7

3.   Perspectives on the people, 1500   35

4.   Europeans going thither   67

5.   An accessible desert   104

6.   The price of civility   139

7.   Conclusion: Perspectives on the land and people, 1800   186

Index   199

Figures

1.1 Sassafras leaves   *page* 20

2.1 Representation of an opossum   27

2.2 Eighteenth-century print of an alligator   29

3.1 Indians roasting fish   47

3.2 Indians burning trees for canoes   58

4.1 Indians working in New World tobacco fields   75

4.2 Ginseng plant and whippoorwill   85

4.3 An Indian hunting camp   95

5.1 "An overseer doing his duty"   109

5.2 Techniques used to extract resin or crude turpentine from
     longleaf pines   125

5.3 Log dam   136

6.1 Tobacco plant   143

6.2 Drawings of birds   150

6.3 A pair of bobolinks   151

6.4 A wolf   178

Preface

I suppose forests have always held a certain fascination for me. From the time I first went camping in the summer before my second birthday until I wore ecology T-shirts and celebrated Earth Day with fellow high-school students, I spent much of my early life either in or thinking about the woodlands. For a time I considered a career in forestry. When I finally got to graduate school as a student of American history, I was captivated by the accounts of the earliest explorers and their descriptions of the New World environment.

Even so, I might not have guessed what could be done with such sources had I not read two important books. Alfred W. Crosby's *The Columbian Exchange: Biological and Cultural Consequences of 1492*[1] convinced me that human history is inevitably intertwined with the history of plants, animals, and microorganisms. Later, I read William Cronon's *Changes in the Land: Indians, Colonists, and the Ecology of New England.*[2] Like many others, I found his interdisciplinary treatment of human impact on New England's landscape compelling. Since I am a Southerner by birth and student of the colonial South by choice, Cronon's book also started me thinking about settlement and environmental change in the warm climes of North America. When my mentors agreed that the peculiarities of southern ecology might justify a similar volume, I set out to write it, taking Cronon's work as my structural and methodological model. From that point, my study evolved into a doctoral dissertation at the College of William and Mary and finally this book.

One of the many things I learned over that period is that those who write history sometimes need to make compromises. Early on I made a big one. Originally, I thought my book would survey the colonial South. Then I discovered that historians disagree about the historical boundaries of the South and that any study, which claimed to cover all of it, should include, at a minimum, all the land east of Texas and south of Pennsylvania. An environmental historian trying to examine such a huge chunk of territory confronts

1. Westport, Conn.: Greenwood Press, 1972.   2. New York: Hill & Wang, 1983.

special problems. Environmental change is frequently a local phenomenon; its scope and scale vary with topography, climate and settlement patterns. Indeed, it might be argued that those who seek accuracy should stick to describing human impact on tiny parcels of land, perhaps a single field.

Unwilling to write a history of a southern field, but believing that tackling the entire colonial South in a short volume would not allow for much detail about anything, I elected to narrow my focus to the principal area of English settlement. In so doing, I went against my training, for I have been taught to ignore political boundaries and think of colonial North America as a single geographic entity, where various groups of people interacted with each other and their environment. To atone for my sin, I have tried throughout to remain conscious of important changes that preceded English colonization. And I have tried to be aware of developments in other parts of North America and to show how they affected the environment of the English South. The payoff for my compromise, I trust, is a book that measures human impact on a large area, allows for significant detail, and seeks to avoid overgeneralizing about environmental change.

When one compromise is made, others come more easily. Like most historians who venture into other disciplines, I have become painfully aware that one cannot become an instant expert in disciplines as diverse as medicine, plant and animal ecology, geography, geology, and anthropology. I and the reader will have to be content with my textbook treatment of those fields. For the sake of clarity, I have chosen, whenever possible, to avoid specialized terminology. I usually refer to plants, animals, and microorganisms by their common names, except when a scientific term is necessary to illustrate important distinctions, as in the case of mosquito-borne diseases and the insects that carry them. Likewise, when describing soils, I focus on common traits, such as color and consistency, instead of mineral and organic content.

The same general rules apply when I write of more familiar subjects. Most readers will know that Columbus made a mistake when he described American natives as Indians. But the name has been used for so long by scholars and by natives themselves that it is no longer so ethnically loaded. I sense no overwhelming need to avoid it. For similar reasons, I refer to Europeans simply as "colonists," "settlers," or "whites," and I use "Africans," "blacks," or "slaves" to describe those who came involuntarily to England's southern colonies. When quoting my human subjects, I have attempted to keep the historical record intact, including haphazard and obsolete spellings and capitalization. I have, however, ignored random italics that did not alter or add to an author's meaning. One other note to clear up possible confusion: Until about 1783, most colonists knew the South Carolina city of Charleston as "Charles Town." In the interest of authenticity, I use Charles Town to describe the city before 1783 and Charleston thereafter. At least on this final and somewhat picky point, there will be no compromise.

Acknowledgments

I often hear that writing a book is a lonely task. I think "solitary" might be a better way to describe it. For although I have been alone – in libraries, at microfilm readers, over legal pads and computer keyboards – during the past few years, I have seldom felt lonely. Many people have freely given their time and wisdom to help smooth the road for a first-time author.

Two teachers started me down that road. When I was a college senior, Judith Pulley made me take my work seriously and convinced me that one could make a career of history. Later, James Axtell introduced me to the techniques of ethnohistory and directed the dissertation that became this book. He gave me the freedom to pursue my ideas and constantly reminded me that history should be written with clarity and style. I am pleased to call him both mentor and friend.

A number of other intellectual companions guided my forays into South Atlantic forests. William Cronon provided inspiration and a how-to manual. Anyone familiar with his book will recognize its impact on my work. Peter H. Wood generously shared information on the population of the colonial South; Jack Temple Kirby did the same with his ideas about soil exhaustion. Stewart Ware tutored me in ecology, proving in the process that a scientist can also be a humanist. Throughout the course of the work I was blessed with toughminded critics who read parts or all of the manuscript at various stages. For their interest, time, and many helpful suggestions, I thank James Merrell, Thad Tate, James Whittenburg, Richard White, Peter Petschauer, Michael Moore, Alfred Crosby, Thomas Dunlap, and Donald Worster.

Along with intellectual guidance, I received invaluable assistance with the practical problems of research. During the initial phase of my study, I relied on the staff and resources of Swem Library at the College of William and Mary. John Ingram, James Garrett, and Susan Berg of the Colonial Williamsburg Foundation's Research Library were also helpful, both during my early research and when I returned later to look for illustrations. At Appalachian State University's Belk Library, Martha Kreszock knew me for two years as her best interlibrary loan customer; she, Dianna Moody, and Lisa Rhodes labored tirelessly to process my endless requests for books and articles. In addition, Gregory Reck and Appalachian State's Office of Graduate Studies and Research found funds for a trip to the Library of Congress.

When it was time to write, others helped ease the way. George Antone did what he could to lighten my teaching load. When I needed to use a computer, Raymond Pulley, Patricia Wellborn, and Nancy Hopper showed me how. Most important, when I grew tired and discouraged, I had friends to lift my spirits. All my colleagues in the history department at Appalachian State heard more than they wanted to about this book. I particularly appreciate the moral support I received from David White and Mike Wade, who always seemed to know when I needed to talk about writing and when my sanity would be better served by watching a ballgame. About a dozen or so colleagues from other departments insisted that I put my work aside every Wednesday and Friday at noon so that I could join them on the basketball court. More than once the distraction of this friendly competition helped renew my creative energy, sending me back to the desk with my body tired, but my mind refreshed.

I also found plenty of encouragement at Cambridge University Press. My editor, Frank Smith, offered constant reassurance and exhibited infinite patience when certain revisions took longer than expected. Herbert Gilbert's meticulous work as copy editor saved me from numerous mistakes.

Finally, I thank my family. My parents and in-laws have been unwavering in their support of my work. But I owe the largest debt to my wife, Sharon. She has endured my absence when I stole away to write; she has endured my presence on those occasions when I returned frustrated and disillusioned. She has made me laugh at my subject matter. And she has at least feigned interest when I droned on for the thousandth time about rice birds, pine trees, or ginseng. Above all, her unfailing belief in the book and my ability to complete it gave me the courage to stay at the task. For these and other reasons, her investment in the following pages truly equals my own.

1

Prologue: Images and boundaries

For most Americans the term "South" or "southern states" immediately calls to mind certain environmental images. A palmetto tree graces South Carolina's state flag. Moonlight and pine trees are recurring themes in Georgia's official state song. Literature, too, reflects similar images. Who can imagine Rhett Butler and Scarlett O'Hara apart from cotton fields and magnolias? And in the first pages of Robert Penn Warren's *All the King's Men*, the reader meets not only hard-boiled southern politicians, but also a hapless "possum" which wanders from the "blackness of the cypresses" to meet its fate under the wheels of a speeding Cadillac. Such typical (scholars prefer "stereotypical") images are largely products of the more recent southern past, drawn from the Civil War and Reconstruction or, to use Warren's phrase, a time when "the smell of gasoline and burning brake bands and red eye [was] sweeter than myrrh."[1]

There was, however, an earlier southern landscape, occupied first by Cherokees, Creeks, and Westos and later by planters and slaves. Its writers were not novelists, but naturalists, travelers, and traders such as John Banister, John Lawson, and James Adair. That landscape, too, had moonlight and magnolias, pines, palmettos, and possums. And then, as in later times, plants and animals figured prominently in the daily lives of the human inhabitants.

What of this earlier landscape, the so-called colonial South? Anyone seeking to unravel the changing relationships between its humans, plants, and animals runs headlong into a problem: where to begin. For if the nineteenth- and twentieth-century South was a land whose people exhibited some cohesiveness and regional character, the colonial South was remarkable for its diversity. Unlike New England, where religion and politics allowed for something of a common bond between colonists, the huge area south of Pennsylvania and east of Texas was a kaleidoscope of dissimilar peoples. Depending on when and where he journeyed, an eighteenth-century traveler in the South might hear European settlers speaking Spanish, French, English, German, or several other languages. Southern Indians also spoke a variety of dialects drawn from at least four major language groups. Black slaves accompanied some of the earliest Spanish expeditions and as English colonists began to use slave labor in their

---

1. Robert Penn Warren, *All the King's Men* (San Diego, Calif.: Harcourt Brace Jovanovich, 1982), 49, 2.

fields, Africans, with their own wide range of cultural and linguistic backgrounds unwillingly, became part of the human population.[2]

One way to begin to understand the relationships of these various peoples to the natural environment is to focus on one part of this huge multicultural area: the portion of the Atlantic seaboard first settled permanently by English colonists. Although this area of English influence was only one piece of a larger landscape, it does have certain boundaries that can be used to delineate it from the rest of the South. Those boundaries are both natural and man made, evident in the physical features of the land and in the settlement patterns of those who occupied it.[3]

Using man-made political boundaries, it is easy to identify the region of the principal British colonies, the southern half of that Atlantic strip so familiar to schoolchildren: Maryland, Virginia, North and South Carolina, and Georgia. Florida became a British possession in 1763, but for much of the colonial period and again after the American Revolution, it officially belonged to Spain, whose goals for the New World differed from those of her antagonist to the north. If imperial borders were not sufficient reason to exclude Florida, environmental boundaries might be. Its warmer climate and longer growing season make Florida substantially different from the rest of the Atlantic seaboard. The natural vegetational border (like most ecological divisions) is indistinct. Trees and plants common to Florida do not suddenly stop growing at the Georgia line. But as Georgia colonists who tried unsuccessfully to export oranges found out, the northern reaches of Florida do mark an agricultural boundary of sorts. A better southern boundary is the Okefenokee Swamp, a tract of wetland spanning more than six hundred square miles. Indeed, the Okefenokee gives rise to the St. Mary's River, which now forms the northeastern section of the political boundary between Florida and Georgia.[4]

2. Two of the more recent works that point up the difficulty of defining the colonial South as a region are Aubrey C. Land, "The American South: First Epiphanies," *Journal of Southern History* 50 (1984), 3–14; and Thad W. Tate, "Defining the Colonial South," in Winthrop D. Jordan and Sheila L. Skemp, eds., *Race and Family in the Colonial South* (Jackson: University Press of Mississippi, 1987), 3–19. See also Clarence L. Ver Steeg, *Origins of a Southern Mosaic: Studies of Early Carolina and Georgia* (Athens: University of Georgia Press, 1975), xi–xiii.

3. Setting boundaries is one of the most difficult tasks confronting the environmental historian. See William Cronon, *Changes in the Land: Indians, Colonists, and the Ecology of New England* (New York: Hill & Wang, 1983), 14–15. I have relied primarily on cultural and political boundaries, electing to study one region in which one group of European colonists carried out their subsistence activities. But as will become clear, the region can also be delineated on the basis of climate and topography.

4. Ann Sutton and Myron Sutton, *Eastern Forests*, The Audubon Society Nature Guides (New York: Knopf, 1986), 123; Stetson Kennedy, *Palmetto Country*, American Folkways, gen. ed. Erskine Caldwell (New York: Duell, Sloane, & Pearce, 1942), 18.

The Okefenokee is significant for another reason. It also marks the southern limits of what – for want of a better term – can be called colonial "plantation agriculture." Even if they found it difficult to grow tropical fruit, colonists north of the Okefenokee were able to cultivate other crops not grown in Europe. Settlers cashed in on that opportunity by developing a system of export agriculture that eventually came to be based on African slave labor.[5] For the northern boundary of that agricultural system, scholars look to Maryland, which was part of the slave-based tobacco economy, and also a transitional colony "between southern plantations and middle colony farms."[6] A suitable northern natural boundary can probably be pinpointed at the confluence of the Susquehanna River and the Chesapeake Bay. Settlers north of that point held slaves, and the specific nature of southern slavery varied widely from Maryland to Georgia.[7] But the general practice of using African labor to produce exotic commodities was perhaps the most distinguishing factor of the region between the lower Susquehanna and the Okefenokee Swamp.

To the west, a hard and fast boundary is more difficult to discern. The Appalachian Mountains are the most obvious natural feature, and the English government believed their peaks made a suitable boundary. Once Britain laid claim to all of eastern North America in 1763, the Crown's Proclamation Line theoretically curtailed settlement beyond the mountains' eastern slopes. But as George III and Parliament discovered, certain boundaries are destined to be ignored. Indeed by 1763 colonists had been traversing the mountains for about a hundred years. In the second half of the seventeenth century, traders and explorers from Virginia and South Carolina went into, around, and beyond the Appalachians to survey the land and to seek commercial contacts with Indians. Despite the Crown's directive, bands of settlers took up residence west of the Proclamation Line in the years before the American Revolution, eventually forcing royal officials to adjust and extend their man-made border. The Appalachians, then, can serve only as a flexible western boundary. Much of

5. The Okefenokee marks the southern limits of rice culture in colonial America and can be considered the southern boundary of those parts of North and South Carolina collectively known as "Lowcountry." See Duncan Clinch Heyward, *Seed From Madagascar* (Chapel Hill: University of North Carolina Press, 1937), 5; and St. Julian Ravenel Childs, *Malaria and Colonization in the Carolina Low Country, 1526–1696*, The Johns Hopkins University Studies in Historical and Political Science, series 58, no. 1 (Baltimore: Johns Hopkins University Press, 1940), 32.
6. Carville V. Earle, *The Evolution of a Tidewater Settlement System: All Hallow's Parish, Maryland, 1650–1783* (University of Chicago Department of Geography Research Paper no. 170, 1975), 3.
7. For a brief discussion of differences, see Tate, "Defining the Colonial South," in Jordan and Skemp, *Race and Family*, 11–14.

white settlement was confined east of the mountains, but colonial influence extended farther and continued to spread west in the decades after 1750.[8]

Is it any easier to find an eastern boundary? Maybe. All the colonies bordered the Atlantic; the shoreline is the obvious easternmost feature. Or is it? All the American colonies – Spanish, English, French – might be said to lie on the "periphery" of European settlement, tiny outposts on the Atlantic's western shore. On the other side of the ocean, Europe stood as the core of occupation and influence. Not only did colonists come from Europe, but the European market frequently dictated how colonists used the land and resources of America.[9] The needs of Caribbean settlements, other outposts with which England's southern colonies developed commercial ties, also helped define which products colonists took from American fields and forests. And then there is Africa. As a significant (in some areas the most significant) component of the human population, slaves did much of the actual work on the land. If it is essential to look across the Appalachians, it is equally crucial to see beyond the east coast, to take some account of what historian K. G. Davies has labeled the "North Atlantic World."[10]

Historical boundaries must be temporal as well as spatial. English coloniz-ation of the southern coast began in 1584 with reconnaissance of northern North Carolina and Virginia. But given the heterogeneous character of the South as a whole, that date cannot serve as a point of departure. Spanish and French explorers arrived north of Florida much earlier, sailing along the coast and establishing small short-lived settlements. Roughly a half century before the English arrived, Spanish explorers ventured farther north to pass between the mountains and the coast, overland probes that had important implications for the natural environment. Looking into the past from the present and knowing that England eventually came to dominate the region, it is easy to see that takeover as inevitable. But the English were relative latecomers to the southern coast and their mastery of the region (despite what the Crown might

8. D. W. Meinig, *The Shaping of America: A Geographical Perspective on 500 Years of History,* vol. 1, *Atlantic America, 1492–1800* (New Haven, Conn.: Yale University Press, 1986), 284–8. In setting this flexible western boundary, I have relied on Meinig's definition of the southern English colonies. Meinig identifies two major subregions, Greater Virginia and Greater Carolina, both of which extended their influence into the interior (Meinig, *Atlantic America,* 153–160, 172–90).

9. Immanuel Wallerstein, *The Modern World System: Capitalist Agriculture and the Origins of the European World Economy in the Sixteenth Century* (New York: Academic Press, 1964), see especially 101–3; Tate, "Defining the Colonial South," in Jordan and Skemp, *Race and Family,* 18; Cronon, *Changes in the Land,* 14.

10. K. G. Davies, *The North Atlantic World in the Seventeenth Century* (Minneapolis: University of Minnesota Press, 1974).

have thought) was by no means guaranteed.[11]

Moreover, the land Europeans saw was actually the product of much earlier settlement, of human migrations that began when the ancestors of the southern Indians walked into America from Asia.[12] For several millennia before Europeans thought about staking imperial claims, Indians had lived and traveled widely along the Atlantic seaboard, more concerned with boundaries of villages, fields, and hunting territories than with prominent rivers, swamps, and mountains. Like Indians elsewhere in North America, southern natives had altered the landscape to suit their needs, adapting techniques and technology known across the continent to the peculiarities of local climates and topography.[13] Because this initial human occupation transformed the landscape, it must be taken into account when establishing a beginning date. It may not be necessary to retreat all the way to the first human migrations, but it will be important to focus on those environmental changes wrought by Indians before European colonization. Perhaps an arbitrary date of A.D. 1,500 will suffice for a beginning.

Politically speaking, the colonial period ended either in 1776, 1783, or 1789, depending on whether one accepts a declaration, victory in war, or a new government as irrefutable proof of independence. Those dates mean little within an environmental context. A better specific date, one connected to southern land use, is 1793, the year Eli Whitney invented a gin for cleaning the seeds from short-staple cotton fibers. Growing cotton for export was a longstanding dream in the South. Jamestown colonists experimented with the crop as did the French in Louisiana. In the 1780s planters along the Georgia and South Carolina coasts also began to grow "sea-island" cotton, a variety with long fibers that are relatively easy to separate from the seeds. But it took Whitney's gin to make large-scale cultivation of short-staple cotton a reality, first in central South Carolina and Georgia and later (after displacement of the Indians) in the "black belt" of Alabama and Mississippi.[14]

The Cotton Kingdom did not emerge overnight, nor did it dominate the entire South. Wheat and tobacco, important colonial staples, remained prominent from Maryland to North Carolina. And the most common crop throughout the first half of the nineteenth century was still corn, that grain of

---

11. The notion that historians sometimes "must imaginatively ignore our knowledge of the denouement" is neatly expressed in James Axtell, *The Invasion Within: The Contest of Cultures in Colonial North America* (New York: Oxford University Press, 1985), 5.

12. Brian M. Fagan, *The Great Journey: The Peopling of Ancient America* (London: Thames & Hudson, 1987), 106–7.

13. Cronon, *Changes in the Land*, 12.

14. Lewis Cecil Gray, *History of Agriculture in the Southern United States to 1860*, 2 vols. (1932; reprint, Gloucester, Mass.: Peter Smith, 1958), vol. 2; 691–720.

American origin so crucial to the subsistence of both Indians and colonists.[15] Nonetheless, the shift to cotton in the lower South stands as a significant watershed, a point after which some southern farmers faced new problems and challenges. Allowing for the significance of Whitney's gin and its implications for the nineteenth-century South, perhaps 1800 can serve as a convenient date to mark the end of colonial agriculture and the beginning of antebellum agriculture.

These inevitably fluid and somewhat arbitrary boundaries in space and time suggest another problem. What should this region be called? Before colonization, it might be useful to label it the "South Atlantic region." That name can serve to distinguish it from the larger "South," or "Southeast," and from Florida, which, although it borders the Atlantic, also has a "Gulf coast" and a southern tip pointing toward the Caribbean. After permanent settlement, "southern colonies," "English colonies," or "English South" will do. Such terms are not perfect. As one slice of a larger landscape with a variegated population, this strip of land inevitably became home to many white settlers whose ethnic heritage was non-English. In addition to Indians and Africans, many immigrants from other parts of Europe eventually took up residence along the South Atlantic.

But the various peoples who lived between the lower Susquehanna and the Okefenokee, the Atlantic and the Appalachians shared one important trait. Whether male or female, Indian, African, or European, each person came into contact with the natural world every day. Colonists who wrote about that world usually took note of such encounters: an outbreak of smallpox or "fever," the difficulty of clearing new fields, a hunt for deer or other game. However, for Indians, colonists, and slaves – as for humans everywhere – such occurrences were only small manifestations of larger and more complex relationships with nature. What were those relationships? How did these humans alter their environment? How did their environment change them? How did they change each other? For answers to those questions it is first necessary to turn to the land itself.

15. Ibid., chs. 31–5.

2

Perspectives on the land

If somehow we (I the writer and you the reader)[1] could be transported back in time to view the South Atlantic region before European colonization, what would we see? The answer would depend on a number of variables: where we happened to touch down, how and in which direction we traveled, and which particulars attracted our attention. A team of a hundred observers, each set down in a different locale, could probably describe a hundred different landscapes. To a large extent we would be sharing the perspectives of the earliest European explorers: Giovanni da Verrazzano, who reconnoitered the Atlantic coast for France in 1524; Lucas Vásquez de Ayllon, a Spaniard who explored the eastern Carolinas in 1526 and founded a comparatively short-lived colony in the South Carolina sea islands; or Hernando de Soto and Juan Pardo, both of whom led sixteenth-century expeditions through the south-eastern interior. Each of these explorers provided descriptions of the land they saw: Verrazzano, the coastline and what his party observed while foraging for provisions inland; Ayllon, the flat terrain of the eastern Carolinas inhabited by a wide variety of fish, birds, and mammals; de Soto and Pardo, rolling hills and mountains that rose several thousand feet above the surrounding terrain. Like those Europeans who witnessed it first hand, our imaginary team of observers would be able to describe only random fragments of a large and topographically diverse land.[2]

Suppose, however, we had at our disposal a bit of space-age technology in the form of a satellite capable of producing large-scale land photographs. If, instead of immediately trekking off at random, we carefully calibrated the camera and then positioned the satellite some miles up and just off the east coast

---

1. This noneditorial use of "we" is drawn from Alfred Crosby, *Ecological Imperialism: The Biological Expansion of Europe, 900–1900* (New York: Cambridge University Press, 1986), 21.
2. Lawrence C. Worth, ed., *The Voyages of Giovanni da Verrazzano, 1524–1528* (New Haven Conn.: Yale University Press, 1970), 134–5; David B. Quinn, ed., *New American World: A Documentary History of North America to 1612*, 5 vols. (New York: Arno Press and Hector Bye, Inc., 1979), vol. 1, 263–8; A Fidalgo of Elvas, "True Relation of the Vicissitudes that Attended the Governor Don Hernando de Soto," in Edward Gaylord Bourne, ed., *Narratives of the Career of Hernando de Soto*, 2 vols. (New York: Barnes, 1904), see, for example, vol. 1, 223. On the limited experience of European explorers, see William Cronon, *Changes in the Land: Indians, Colonists, and the Ecology of New England* (New York: Hill & Wang, 1983), 20–5.

(on a clear day, of course), it would offer a sweeping overview of the region, a perspective that would allow us to note much more than the European explorers were able to see. Such a photograph would not resemble a modern road map, for it would show no highways, cities, county lines, or state boundaries; one could not tell where North Carolina ended and Virginia or South Carolina began. Instead the view would be more akin to standing over a relief map, with the various landforms and physical features thrown into sharp focus. It could tell us much about the region that Verrazzano, Ayllon, de Soto, and Pardo could not know.[3]

The South Atlantic coastline would look familiar – jutting eastward in its northern reaches near the top right of the photograph and curving progressively southwest in the lower portion of the picture.[4] It was and is a ragged coastline, punctuated throughout with numerous offshore islands, inlets, sounds, and bays. To the north, the largest of the bays, the one colonists would know by the Indian term "Chesapeake," would be easily recognizable as a long finger of water stretching north and slightly west into the interior. About 195 miles long and 10 to 20 miles wide, the bay has approximately forty-eight principal tributaries that now bear a hodgepodge of Indian and European names. Looking north to south on the western side of the bay, we can recognize the narrow slip of the Susquehanna River entering the northern end of the bay, the wider Potomac near the bay's midpoint, and the Rappahannock, York, and James rivers at the broad, southern end of the Chesapeake. On the bay's eastern side, the tributaries are smaller and less well defined, a labyrinth of rivers and creeks creating myriad small peninsulas or "necks" of land, islands, and estuaries. All these tributaries feel the effects of the Atlantic tides so that even as far as two hundred miles inland water levels rise and recede with every flux of the ocean.[5]

Immediately south of Chesapeake Bay, the character of the coast changes. One distinctive feature is the line of wave-built sand reefs easily recognizable as the Carolina Outer Banks. West of this long, sandy spit are two large sounds; to the east, lies the open Atlantic. Protected somewhat from the tides by the Outer Banks, the rivers that feed the sounds tend to expand at their mouths into shallow estuaries. Albemarle, the northernmost sound, receives the Pasquo-

3. This is a variation of a technique employed in Graeme Caughley, *The Deer Wars: The Story of Deer in New Zealand* (Auckland: Heinemann, 1983), 15–21.
4. Donald W. Meinig, *The Shaping of America*, vol. 1, *Atlantic America, 1492–1800* (New Haven Conn.: Yale University Press, 1986), 172–3.
5. Arthur Pierce Middleton, *Tobacco Coast: A Maritime History of Chesapeake Bay in the Colonial Era* (1953; reprint Baltimore: Johns Hopkins University Press, 1984), 38–43; Carville V. Earle, *The Evolution of a Tidewater Settlement System: All Hallows Parish, Maryland, 1650–1783* (The University of Chicago Department of Geography Research Paper no. 170, 1975), 19–20.

tank, Chowan, and Roanoke rivers. Farther south, flowing into Pamlico Sound, are the Tar, Neuse, and Trent.[6]

From the southern end of Pamlico Sound, the coast begins a more dramatic swing to the southwest. Although no large bays or sounds command attention, the coast is still irregular, dotted with small inlets and numerous offshore islands. Here we know the primary Atlantic tributaries by Indian, African, and European names. From north to south, we identify the Cape Fear, Waccamaw, Pee Dee, Santee, Edisto, Combahee, Savannah, Ogeechee, Altamaha, and Satilla rivers. Like the streams immediately north, these rivers tend to widen as they approach the sea. Here, too, streams feel the effects of the tides, as water backs up the rivers and then flows out again at regular intervals.[7]

A "camera's eye" view of the region would also reveal another general characteristic of these southeastern rivers and streams. With a few exceptions (notably the tributaries on the eastern shore of Chesapeake Bay) the rivers tend to flow roughly west to east, a trend that provides an important clue to the area's overall topography. Much of the South Atlantic region can be described as a giant slope, rising east to west out of the sea. This general seaward incline results from the combined effects of three smaller natural regions well known to geologists and physiographers.

Easternmost of these geographic provinces is the Atlantic coastal plain, actually a broad, exposed, inland extension of the submerged continental shelf. The width of the coastal plain varies throughout the region, but it is generally narrower toward the north, expanding farther inland to the south. The eastern or "outer" coastal plain is relatively level or slightly rolling, resembling the undulating floor of the sea.[8] Farther west, the "inner" coastal plain is a bit more irregular, characterized by slightly sloping uplands. Elevations across the coastal plain range from zero at sea level to seven hundred feet at its western limits. This generally smooth, even monotonous, topography helps account for the sluggish, meandering nature of the major Atlantic tributaries.[9]

At its western boundary, the inner coastal plain meets the Piedmont Plateau, a belt of rolling hilly uplands which, like the coastal plain, broadens in its

6. H. Roy Merrens, *Colonial North Carolina in the Eighteenth Century* (Chapel Hill: University of North Carolina Press, 1964), 20 (map); Meinig, *Atlantic America*, 147; Isaiah Bowman, *Forest Physiography of the United States and Principles of Soils in Relation to Forestry* (1911; reprint, New York: Arno, 1970), 518.

7. Meinig, *Atlantic America*, 179; Duncan Clinch Heyward, *Seed from Madagascar* (Chapel Hill: University of North Carolina Press, 1937), 41.

8. Bowman, *Forest Physiography*, 516–18.

9. Charles B. Hunt, *Natural Regions of the United States and Canada* (San Francisco: W. H. Freeman, 1974), 5; David Sutton Phelps, "Archaeology of the North Carolina Coast and Coastal Plain: Problems and Hypotheses," in Mark A. Mathis and Jeffrey J. Crow, eds., *The Prehistory of North Carolina* (Raleigh: North Carolina Division of Archives and History, 1983), 4.

southern reaches. These uplands, too, can be subdivided into an eastern or "lower piedmont," where elevations may be as low as two hundred feet and a western or "upper piedmont" where the hills and ridges approach two thousand feet.[10] Some of the larger coastal plain streams are still distinct in the piedmont. The Potomac, Rappahannock, James, and Roanoke drain the narrower northern section of the plateau. Farther south, where the piedmont is broader, important river systems include: the Dan, which joins the Roanoke; the Haw and Deep rivers, which feed the Cape Fear; and the Yadkin and Catawba, which help form the Pee Dee and Santee, respectively. Still farther south, the Savannah, as well as the Oconee and Ocmulgee (headwaters of the Altamaha) dissect the plateau.[11] Due to increased elevations, piedmont streams sometimes move rapidly, finally tumbling onto the Atlantic coastal plain in a series of shoals and rapids along an indistinct boundary known as the fall line.[12]

On the west, the piedmont meets the third important landform of the South Atlantic region: the Appalachian Highlands. At the left of our photograph, this region shows up as a series of mountain ridges where altitudes generally range from a thousand to more than six thousand feet above sea level. Some taller peaks lie in the Blue Ridge province, a narrow band of mountains that stretch north to south along the western edge of the piedmont. West across the Blue Ridge (on the backside of the southeastern slope) lies the Ridge and Valley province typified by lower, more rounded mountains and long stretches of relatively flat valleys.[13] Many of the major river systems of the piedmont and coastal plain head in the eastern Blue Ridge Mountains, fed by groundwater and runoff from rain and snow. From the western slope of the Blue Ridge to the Ridge and Valley province, most of the major streams flow roughly west and south (The New River is an exception) toward the Ohio and Mississippi rivers and the Gulf of Mexico.[14]

What our camera cannot reveal (at least to the untrained eye) is that some of these landforms are incredibly old, even by geologic standards. The origins of the Appalachians can be traced to a point 750 million years ago when a huge, single "megacontinent" split into two large land masses and several smaller

10. Stanley Wayne Trimble, *Man-Induced Soil Erosion on the Southern Piedmont, 1700–1970* (Ankeny, Iowa: The Soil Conservation Society of America, 1974), 8–9.

11. Meinig, *Atlantic America*, 147, 179; Hunt, *Natural Regions*, 257; H. Trawick Ward, "A Review of Archaeology in the North Carolina Piedmont," in Mathis and Crow, *Prehistory of North Carolina*, 54.

12. Bowman, *Forest Physiography*, 623–4.

13. Steven M. Stanley, *Earth and Life Through Time* (New York: W. H. Freeman, 1986), 219–20; Charles M. Hudson, *The Southeastern Indians* (Knoxville: University of Tennessee Press, 1976), 18–19.

14. Burton L. Purrington, "Ancient Mountaineers: An Overview of Prehistoric Archaeology of North Carolina's Western Mountain Region," in Mathis and Crow, *Prehistory of North Carolina*, 89.

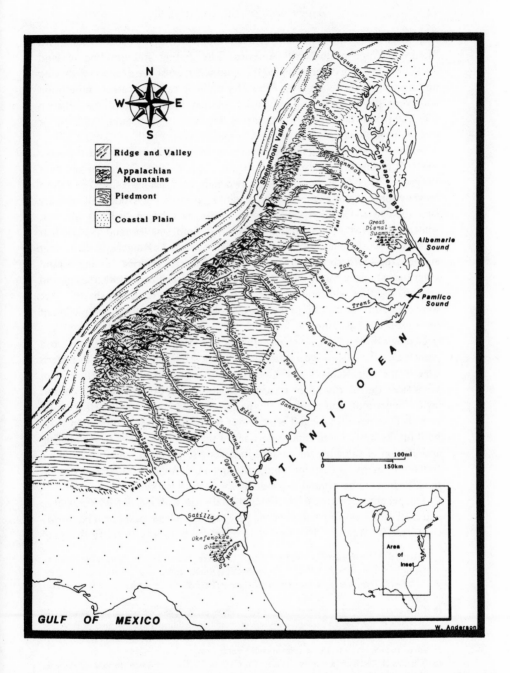

fragments. Roughly 250 million years later, some of the fragments collided with "Laurentia," or proto-North America. The grating and grinding of land masses against each other wrinkled the continental crust like a huge rug, driving up the spine of the mountains. After fifty million years of weather and erosion had worn down those original peaks, another series of collisions between Laurentia and the offshore fragments resulted in a second orogeny, or mountain-building episode, 400 to 350 million years ago.[15]

Following still another fifty-million-year interval, Laurentia and the large western continent, Godwanaland, again merged into the supercontinent Pangaea. The collision between these two giant land masses resulted in a third orogeny some 300 to 250 million years ago. Fifty- to seventy-odd million years later (200 to 180 million years past) Pangaea, too, began to break up, first splitting into two large continents and then into smaller land masses that eventually became the continents recognizable today. As Pangaea divided, what are now the southern uplands became part of North America, leaving behind sister formations in Europe and Africa. The intervening eons of weathering and erosion, together with additional periods of folding and uplift, shaped what were once Alp-like peaks into the low mountains, ridges, valleys, and piedmont the Europeans encountered.[16]

Geologically speaking, the coastal plain is a much younger formation. At a point some 180 million years past, a great sea stretched inland to the eastern edge of the Appalachians or the piedmont. About thirty-five to forty million years later, the interior of the continent began to rise, driving back the sea and laying down mud and sand on the newly exposed continental shelf. Similar periods of ocean advance and retreat over the next hundred-odd million years built up the western and central portions of the plain. The ongoing weathering and erosion of the adjacent western uplands also played a part in the plain's formation, as rivers carrying sand, silt, and clay from the interior deposited those sediments on ground exposed by the retreating ocean.[17]

The peculiar structure of the outer coastal plain with its islands, peninsulas, and tidal estuaries is a product of the very recent geologic past, forming during the Great Ice Age, or Pleistocene epoch, probably twenty to thirty thousand

15. Frederick A. Cook, Larry D. Brown, and Jack E. Oliver, "The Southern Appalachians and the Growth of Continents," *Scientific American* 243 (October 1980), 163–5; Albert E. Cowdrey, *This Land, This South: An Environmental History* (Lexington: University Press of Kentucky, 1983), 1.

16. Cook et al., "Southern Appalachians," 163–5. These paragraphs are intended only as a general overview of the long and complex process of mountain building. I am indebted to Professor Loren Raymond, Department of Geology, Appalachian State University, for providing references and explanations that a layman could comprehend.

17. Thomas H. Clark and Colin W. Stearn, *The Geologic Evolution of North America: A Regional Approach to Historical Geology* (New York: Ronald, 1960), 150–68; Hunt, *Natural Regions*, 122.

years ago. Although the glaciers left southeastern North America untouched, their retreat coincided with an uplift of portions of the outer plain. At this point, the Chesapeake region may have towered a thousand feet above sea level. Rejuvenated by the uplift, the streams of the outer plain cut into softer deposits to form valleys, leaving the more resistant material as watersheds between the various rivers. The valley that Chesapeake Bay now occupies was cut by the Susquehanna River. Sometime after the formation of the various river valleys, the Chesapeake region of the coastal plain began to sink. That process, together with rising sea levels triggered by glacial melting, pushed the Atlantic inland until the ocean engulfed the easternmost valleys and pushed its tides up the lower reaches of the major streams. The land that resisted erosion and "drowning" by the Atlantic remained above the sea level to become the necks and peninsulas visible between the rivers.[18] Farther south, the rising sea also engulfed the rivers, creating less well-defined estuaries. Such ocean flooding might also be partially responsible for the development of the numerous swamps and marshlands along the coast of the Carolinas and Georgia.[19]

Ecological change went hand in hand with geologic evolution. Shortly (geologically speaking) after the breakup of Pangaea, cone-bearing trees (conifers) probably dominated North American forests. Roughly one hundred million years ago, however, flowering plants began their rise to ecological prominence, while diversification among the insects allowed for pollination and the development of highly specialized plants such as deciduous trees. After falling temperatures, the arrival of a comet, or some other still-unexplained phenomenon led to the extinction of dinosaurs, mammals and birds emerged as the dominant land animals.[20] Some twenty-five million years ago, those warm-blooded creatures seem to have inhabited a huge deciduous forest that occupied an almost unbroken belt across the earth's northern continents. Broadleaf trees dominated the vegetation, but the woods also contained numerous conifers. California redwoods and sequoias, as well as the magnolias and sweet gums still present in the American South, may be remnants of this forest, offering some clue to its original range and composition.[21]

As the continent underwent further topographic change, the forests followed suit. The development of the Rocky Mountains and other western mountain ranges – important determinants of temperature and rainfall – augmented continual global cooling that eventually culminated in the glacial advance of the

18. Middleton, *Tobacco Coast*, 42–3.
19. Robert Q. Oaks, Jr. and Donald R. Whitehead, "Geologic Setting and Origin of the Dismal Swamp, Southeastern Virginia and Northeastern North Carolina," in Paul W. Kirk, Jr., ed., *The Great Dismal Swamp* (Charlottesville: University Press of Virginia for the Old Dominion University Research Foundation, 1979), 19–21.
20. Stanley, *Earth and Life*, 495–8, 509–13.
21. Jonathan L. Richardson, *Dimensions of Ecology* (Baltimore: Williams & Wilkins, 1977), 128–30.

Ice Age. Even though the glaciers did not extend into the South Atlantic region, the colder climates associated with the various ice sheets created forests like those now present in northern New England and southern Canada. Before the last major glacier retreated, northern conifers such as spruce and jack pine grew in central North Carolina. Tundra might have been part of the vegetation pattern in the higher Appalachians. Even after the final glacier's retreat (some twelve to fourteen thousand years ago), the ensuing warmer temperatures did not produce something akin to the forests seen by Europeans for another seven to nine thousand years.[22] Although European explorers spoke (and historians still speak) of a "New World," the topography and vegetation of the South Atlantic region, and indeed all of North America, existed only as the products of extensive, long-term, geologic and climatic change.

With the region's basic topography and the long view of its formation in mind, we can take a closer look at precolonial climates, soils, and vegetation patterns. Trees, smaller plants, and dirt, however, are not easily observed from above. For a description of the forests, it will be best to put aside the "satellite overview" in favor of an imaginary "walking tour" of the region. This trek could begin almost anywhere, but the objective is to cover as much ground as possible and to gain an appreciation for change and diversity. A good starting point is the outer coastal plain along the southern shore of Georgia.

Regardless of season, the weather would be relatively comfortable. Average July temperatures range between 80°F and 90°F. Winters are moderate, with average January readings between 50°F and 55°F. On the offshore islands and the outer edge of the mainland, the soil generally looks and feels like grey sand. Its color and consistency result from a number of factors, including marine deposits, silt and gravel left by flooding rivers, and decomposition of vegetation – a process facilitated by the warm climate. Moisture, too, affects the soil. The coastal plain annually receives forty to sixty inches of precipitation, most of which falls as rain. Water moves quickly through the sandy ground, leeching away minerals and leaving behind oxides that sometimes lend a yellow or reddish cast to the ground.[23]

These sandy soils produce many diverse trees and plants that form what ecologists define as the "southern mixed hardwood" or "magnolia-maritime"

22. Ibid. See also W. A. Watts, "Post Glacial and Interglacial Vegetation History of Southern Georgia and Central Florida," *Ecology* 52 (1971), 676–90.
23. Charles O. Paullin, *Atlas of the Historical Geography of the United States*, ed. John K. Wright (Carnegie Institution of Washington and the American Geographical Society of New York, 1932), plates 1, 4, 5; H. B. Vanderford, *Managing Southern Soils* (New York: John Wiley, 1957), 52, 293; Ann Sutton and Myron Sutton, *Eastern Forests*, The Audubon Society Nature Guides (New York: Knopf, 1986), 112. Temperatures might have been slightly cooler during the colonial period, due to a climatic variation in the Western Hemisphere known as "the Little Ice Age." Exactly how much difference this made along the South Atlantic coast remains an open question.

forest. Along the barrier islands and hillier dunelands where dry conditions prevail, two of the most notable species are the cabbage palmetto and a hardy, sand-adapted shrub called "yaupon." The palmetto (as its name implies) resembles a small palm, lending an almost tropical aura to the outer coast. Yaupon frequently grows in thickets that are sometimes dense enough to block the wind and salt spray from the ocean. Inland, on the leeward side of such barriers, larger trees can be found. Among the most prominent are southern magnolias and giant evergreen live oaks that sometimes grow on slightly raised mounds known as hammocks.[24] Other large trees that can be observed in the region include American beech, American holly, red bay, laurel oak, and pignut hickory. Spanish moss, capable of absorbing moisture directly from the air, often hangs from the treetops making the woods appear dark and foreboding.[25] Overall, this forest resembles a sort of "oasis at the edge of the sea," where dense growth seems to spring almost magically from dry sand.[26]

Not all coastal plain habitats are so well drained. A short walk in almost any direction along the south Georgia coast would inevitably bring the traveler to a river or creek and the accompanying wetlands. Fed by plentiful rainfall and various coastal plain streams, marshlands abound along the South Atlantic seaboard. Where the water retains a high salt content, cordgrass, marsh hay, and a variety of small shrubs dominate the vegetation. Farther inland, brackish overflow might produce black rushes and coarse saltgrass. Still farther upstream, other rushes, sedges, grasses, and cattails grow in freshwater marshes along the rivers.[27] From a distance, some of these marshlands resemble grassy meadows and were sometimes misidentified as such by European explorers.[28]

Continuing inland up one of the rivers, a traveler might well encounter one of the numerous swamps that dot the outer coastal plain. Depending on local topography, these wetlands might span a few acres or (as in the case of Georgia's Okefenokee Swamp) hundreds of square miles.[29] Where such areas

24. Victor E. Shelford, *The Ecology of North America* (Urbana: University of Illinois Press, 1963), 67–8; John L. Vankat, *The Natural Vegetation of North America: An Introduction* (New York: Wiley, 1979), 148–9.

25. Vankat, *Vegetation of North America*, 148–9.

26. Sutton and Sutton, *Eastern Forests*, 115.

27. Shelford, *Ecology of North America*, 70; John M. Barry, *The Natural Vegetation of South Carolina* (Columbia: University of South Carolina Press, 1980), 182–90.

28. See, for example, George Percy, "Observations gathered out of A Discourse of the Plantation of the Southerne Colonie in Virginia by the English," in Edward Arber, ed., *Travels and Works of Captain John Smith*, 2 vols. (Edinburgh: John Grant, 1910), vol. 1, lxix; and Robert Horne, "A Briefe Description of the Province of Carolina," in Alexander S. Salley, ed., *Narratives of Early Carolina*, Original Narratives of Early American History, gen. ed. J. Franklin Jameson (New York: Scribner, 1911), 69.

29. Stetson Kennedy, *Palmetto Country*, American Folkways, gen. ed. Erskine Caldwell (New York: Duell, Sloan, & Pearce, 1942), 18.

have been "drowned" by the Atlantic, the water level fluctuates with the tides. Other so-called "inland swamps" result from streams simply flattening out as they meander across the level outer plain. Soils are darker here due to alluvial deposits and formation of peat. Higher hammocks in such swamps can support live oak and magnolia, whereas shrubs, grasses, and vines grow in low-lying regions. Interspersed with the grasses one might find pure stands of the most distinctive tree of the southern swamplands: the bald cypress. Ranging up to 120 feet in height, these large, needle-leafed, deciduous trees with their water-resistant wood are well adapted to the boggy habitat. As in drier regions, Spanish moss frequently hangs from the branches of wetlands trees.[30]

Outer coastal plain forests would look much the same as we made our way up the lower South Carolina shore, but a careful observer could note subtle differences. Traveling north, magnolias might be less prominent. Live oak and red juniper (which colonists mistakenly labeled "red cedar") are dominant in this maritime forest.[31] Approaching the Cape Fear region, other changes would become apparent. In these comparatively higher latitudes, the coast remains somewhat cooler, especially during the winter months. July temperatures averge 75°F to 85°F; January readings between 35°F and 50°F. Such climatic variations work to reduce warm-weather vegetation. Yaupon is still present along much of the North Carolina coast, but palmettos are rare north of Cape Fear. Live oaks also diminish farther north, replaced in the drier regions of Virginia and Maryland by black walnut, white oak, and several types of hickory.[32]

Wetter forests in the north also reflect the cooler climate. Bald cypress, common in the swamps and lowlands of eastern North Carolina, becomes less abundant as the coastal plain narrows into Chesapeake Bay. In contrast, a tree that might become more visible as one walked north is a second type of juniper that Europeans misidentified as "white cedar." Known today as the Atlantic white cedar, this large evergreen can be found from Florida to Maine.[33] Some of the most extensive cedar groves along the south Atlantic, however, were in the Great Dismal Swamp, a twenty-two-hundred square-mile tract of wetlands lying between the lower James River and Albemarle Sound. The extensive peat beds of the Great Dismal proved ideal for white cedar. In such areas, the evergreens formed vast, pure cedar forests, where giant trees towered fifty to eighty feet above the boggy terrain. In other parts of the Great Dismal (and in

30. Shelford, *Ecology of North America*, 75; Sutton and Sutton, *Eastern Forests*, 365.
31. Shelford, *Ecology of North America*, 58; Carl Ortwin Sauer, "The Settlement of the Humid East," in United States Department of Agriculture, *Climate and Man: Yearbook of Agriculture, 1941* (Washington, D.C.: United States Department of Agriculture, 1941), 159.
32. Paullin, *Atlas of Historical Geography*, plate 5; Sutton and Sutton, *Eastern Forests*, 409, 435.
33. Sutton and Sutton, *Eastern Forests*, 367.

smaller northern swamps), white cedar might be interspersed with red maple, black gum, or any number of common wetlands trees.[34]

As we move west away from the outer coastal plain, wetland and the associated trees would become less common. The yellow, sandy soils of the drier regions would gradually give way to a redder clay-sand mixture. Topography is more uneven here. Indeed, in the Carolinas, we might take note of a band of sandhills where the terrain is almost rolling. Well removed from the moderating effects of the ocean breezes, the inner plain is also more susceptible to temperature extremes. Although average readings are similar to those farther east, scorching July days and subfreezing January nights are not uncommon.[35]

No matter where a traveler stands in the inner coastal plain, he would probably be within sight of a tree immortalized by southern writers, poets, and musicians: the pine. Few trees are better adapted to a particular environment than those pines native to the South. With one or two possible exceptions, all southern pines require a mineral seedbed, a trait that makes them ideally suited to the sandy coastal plain.[36] Moreover, the trees grow in a variety of habitats. Slash pine, for instance, flourishes in the swampy, almost tropical lowlands of southeastern Georgia. The loblolly pine, whose name literally means "mud-puddle," also grows in wet ground. But loblollies are also known as "bull pines" due to their prodigious size and remarkable ability to invade dry, flat terrain or even hilly uplands. At the time of colonization, the most predominant coastal plain conifer was probably the longleaf pine. Well adapted to the hot, dry flatlands and undulating sand hills, the trees formed a vast band of pinelands, which stretched from extreme southeastern Virginia, across the Carolinas and the Deep South, and into Texas. For fifteen hundred miles, the scaly-barked trees reigned supreme, interrupted only here and there by an occasional inland swamp and its accompanying hardwoods.[37]

The great stands of pine common to the coastal plain woods resulted from a force many modern Americans still regard as a destroyer of forests: fire. Fires kindled by lightning occurred in the piedmont and mountains but were probably more common in the coastal plain, where generally warmer and drier conditions combined with frequent spring and summer thunderstorms to create

34. Oaks and Whitehead, "Geologic Setting," in Kirk, *Dismal Swamp*, 1–3; Gerald F. Levy, "Atlantic White Cedar in the Great Dismal Swamp and the Carolinas," in Aimlee D. Lederman, ed., *Atlantic White Cedar Wetlands* (Boulder, Colo.: Westview Press, 1987), 58; B.W. Wells, "Ecological Problems of the Southeastern U.S. Coastal Plain," *Botanical Review* 8 (1942), 543–4.

35. Barry, *Vegetation of South Carolina*, 97–114

36. E. V. Komarek, "Effects of Fire on Temperate Forests and Related Ecosystems," in T. T. Kozlowski, ed., *Fire and Ecosystems* (New York: Academic Press, 1974), 257; Vankat, *Vegetation of North America*, 147.

37. Sutton and Sutton, *Eastern Forests*, 107–20, 355–7.

a suitable environment for periodic natural burns. Unlike the wildfires today's foresters fear, most lightning-set fires did not become conflagrations. Often accompanied by light precipitation, which kept the forest floor damp, such localized blazes burned slowly and only at ground level, sometimes smoldering for several days until additional rain extinguished them.[38] Such small fires were well known to European explorers. Indeed, John White's party may have seen just such a creeping surface fire in 1590 while searching for the "lost" Roanoke colony. Investigating smoke they thought might indicate a settlement, White's group went ashore to find only "grass and sundry rotten trees burning about the place."[39]

Pines flourished in such an environment for a number of reasons. Ecologists classify the southern pines as pioneer species, meaning that they are among the first trees to appear after a site has been burned or otherwise cleared. If allowed to grow undisturbed by fire for long periods, pines eventually give way to mixed hardwood or oak-hickory forests. Occasional fires work to destroy these competing trees, allowing the conifers free reign. With their generous supply of resin, the pines themselves might seem especially vulnerable and if a fire burns hot enough, they are. But once they reach the sapling stage, most pines are well equipped to endure moderate ground fires. Protected by thick, porous bark that insulates their heartwood, the trees generally survive light burns with little more than a slightly scorched lower trunk.[40]

Although all the pines owed their existence to fire, the various stands of the trees could differ greatly in appearance. In some wetter parts of the vast longleaf forest, bluestem and other native grasses grew under the lofty pine canopy, creating an open, parklike effect. Where drier conditions prevailed (as in the sandhills), pines stood alone or apart in bare sand with only a few stunted oaks and coarse wire grass growing between them.[41] Pinelands subject to more frequent burning over long periods sometimes became savannas, characterized by even more widely spaced trees, little or no underbrush, and an abundance of grasses. In those parts of the coastal plain where the water table lies close to the

---

38. Stephen H. Spurr and Burton V. Barnes, *Forest Ecology* (New York: Ronald, 1973), 353; Lawrence S. Barden and Frank W. Woods, "Characteristics of Lightning Fires in the Southern Appalachian Forests," *Proceedings of the Tall Timbers Fire Ecology Conference* 13 (1973), 356–7.

39. David B. Quinn, ed., *The Roanoke Voyages*, 2 vols. (London: The Hakluyt Society, 1955), vol. 2, 613. John White arrived in August, prime thunderstorm and lightning fire season in the coastal plain. While in the vicinity of Cape Lookout, his party encountered "very foule weather with much rain, thundering, and great spouts." (Quinn, *Roanoke Voyages* vol. 2, 608.)

40. Spurr and Barnes, *Forest Ecology*, 353; Vankat, *Vegetation of North America*, 147; Komarek, "Effects of Fire," in Kozlowski, *Fire and Ecosystems*, 255–8, 262; Stephen J. Pyne, *Fire in America: A Cultural History of Wildland and Rural Fire* (Princeton N.J.: Princeton University Press, 1982), 143–60.

41. Shelford, *Ecology of North America*, 81.

surface, savannas can become nearly saturated and trees such as cypress or various oaks may spread over the grassland. Under such wet conditions, savannas might also produce showy flowering plants. At the time of the European discoveries, savannas extended sporadically along the coastal plain from southern Virginia through Georgia, creating broad, grassy plains within the pine, oak, and mixed hardwood forests.[42]

Natural fires in the coastal plain helped maintain other plants and trees. Under certain conditions, blackberries or wild strawberries cropped up in the open sunny environments left behind after periodic burns. Atlantic white cedar also needs an open seedbed and exposed peat soil to germinate. Fires occurring in the northern coastal plain wetlands helped burn off accumulated ground litter and opened the forest canopy, allowing those trees to gain a toehold. Sassafras, a tree some Europeans valued as a cure for everything from bubonic plague to venereal disease, also sprouts prolifically after a burn.[43] Descriptions of the trees around the Jamestown settlement suggest that parts of the Chesapeake region may have been subject to occasional fires. Members of Christopher Newport's 1607 expedition reported that the region produced "Saxafroge what store we pleast," and another English visitor to the lower James described cedar and other sorts of "goodly trees" as well as "beautiful strawberries, four times bigger and better than ours in England."[44]

Walking from the inner coastal plain into the piedmont, a traveler might or might not notice an immediate difference in topography and vegetation. Along some of the major rivers, such as the Potomac, James, Neuse, and Savannah, the fall line is well defined, and dramatic waterfalls or cascades would signal the new geographic boundary. In other regions, away from the rivers, the change would be less pronounced. Variations in vegetation might be equally subtle at first. Longleaf pines would become less common, but white oaks, sweet bays, and sassafras could all be found in the lower piedmont.

Gradually, however, differences would become more readily apparent. Due to increased elevation, temperatures (especially at night) would be slightly

42. Barry, *Vegetation of South Carolina*, 158–61; Komarek, "Effects of Fire," in Kozlowski, *Fire and Ecosystems*, 261–2; Wells, "Ecological Problems," 544.
43. Henry J. Oosting, "The Comparative Effect of Surface and Crown Fires on the Composition of a Loblolly Pine Community," *Ecology* 25 (1944), 61–9, *passim*; Murray F. Buell and Robert L. Cain, "The Successional Role of Southern White Cedar, *Chamaecypaius Thyoides*, in Southeastern North Carolina," *Ecology* 24 (1943), 91; Eyvind Thor and Gary M. Nichols, "Some Effects of Fire on Litter, Soil, and Hardwood Regeneration," *Proceedings of the Tall Timbers Fire Ecology Conference* 13 (1973), 320.
44. [Gabriel Archer?] "The Description of the Now-Discovered River and Country of Virginia, with the Likelyhood of Ensuing Ritches by England's Ayd and Industry," *Virginia Magazine of History and Biography* 14:4 (April 1907), 375–6; Percy, "Observations," in Arber, *Captain John Smith*, vol. 1, lxii–lxiii.

Figure 1.1. Sassafras leaves, a welcome sight for European explorers who thought the trees' roots could cure a wide variety of diseases. Illustration by Marion Ruff Sheehan. From Joan Parry Dutton, *Plants of Colonial Williamsburg* (Colonial Williamsburg Foundation, 1979), 49.

cooler. The soil takes on a still redder tone due to the residual clays common to the plateau. In the upper piedmont, it becomes an almost bloodred marl.[45] Deciduous trees are abundant throughout the region. White, red, post, and black oaks; yellow poplars; mockernut and shagbark hickories make up a significant part of piedmont vegetation. Swamps are generally less common than in the coastal plain. Most piedmont wetlands lie along the eastern reaches of creeks and rivers. Subject to periodic flooding and supplied with alluvial soil, these bottomland forests might produce such trees as willow, alder, elm, red maple, and sweetgum.[46] In the hillier regions of the upper piedmont, rolling topography keeps most areas well drained. Precipitation that remains in the ground is quickly soaked up by the larger trees, making it difficult for other, smaller species to germinate. As they mature, the dominant trees form a thick canopy that blocks out the summer sun. The darkness, too, limits the growth of competing underwood so that many sections of the oak and hickory forest remain open and parklike.[47]

As a rule, the broadleaf deciduous trees keep the piedmont forest floor shaded in summer, maintaining cooler moist conditions near the ground and limiting the fire season to short periods in early spring (if the weather is dry) and late fall before the winter rains begin. But some lightning fires do occur, giving rise to the ubiquitous southern pines. As in the coastal plain, different parts of the piedmont are home to different conifers.[48]

Shortleaf pine, one of the most widely distributed southern conifers, grows throughout the piedmont. Loblolly pines are more common in the southern reaches of the plateau from Georgia to the Carolinas. From North Carolina to Maryland, pitch pines grow on steep slopes as well as in lower wetlands. Virginia pine, as its name suggests, is a more northerly tree that grows in the plateau's higher latitudes.[49] Probably because forest fires are less frequent in the piedmont, pines tend to mingle with deciduous vegetation instead of forming pure stands. One estimate suggests that the presettlement forest in the Georgia piedmont consisted of 35 to 40 percent hardwood stands, 45 percent mixed pine and hardwood, with only 15 percent pure pine groves. Indeed, the entire southern piedmont forest might best be characterized as "oak-hickory-pine."[50]

45. Paullin, *Atlas*, plate 2; Vanderford, *Southern Soils*, 57–60.
46. Shelford, *Ecology of North America*, 57–9, 118.
47. E. Lucy Braun, *Deciduous Forests of North America* (Philadelphia: Blackston, 1950), 262–7, 195–220; Michael G. Barbour et al., *Terrestrial Plant Ecology* (Menlo Park, Calif.: Benjamin-Cummings, 1980), 509.
48. Komarek, "Effects of Fire," in Kozlowski, *Fire and Ecosystems*, 269–70; Barden and Woods, "Lightning Fires," 354–5; Merrens, *Colonial North Carolina*, 192.
49. Sutton and Sutton, *Eastern Forests*, 357–9; Elbert L. Little, *The Audubon Society Field Guide to North American Trees* (New York: Knopf, 1980), 298–9.
50. Vankat, *Vegetation of North America*, 147.

Another fire-maintained plant could also be found growing in the piedmont; in fact it sprouted in certain wetlands throughout much of the American South. It shared coastal plain swamps with the cypresses and gums; it grew along piedmont river floodplains with red maples; it even flourished along some of the streams of the lower Appalachians. Explorers and colonists called the plant "cane," and the areas in which it thrived became known as "canebrakes." A type of bamboo, cane produces a heavy underground stem that allows the plant to store food, but remains out of reach of foraging animals and fire. When a canebrake burns, vigorous new shoots spring from the protected roots. During the warm, wet weather of early summer, such sprouts can grow at an incredible rate – sometimes as much as an inch and a half in twenty-four hours – and form dense thickets. At the time of European exploration, the most impressive canebrakes were formed by a species commonly called "giant cane" or "large cane." Patches of giant cane might reach thirty feet in height and individual plants approached two inches in diameter.[51] In the absence of fire, however, canebrakes reach maturity in a relatively short time or, as one eighteenth-century North Carolinian described it, "they grow old [and] bear an Ear like Oats ... soon after which they decay both Root and Branch."[52]

Cane is only one of many forms of vegetation common to both the piedmont and mountains. Like the transition from coastal plain to piedmont, a walk from the plateau into the Appalachians probably would not be marked by a sudden and distinct change in forest patterns. Millions of years of erosion have so weathered the mountains that the climb out of the piedmont is at first gradual. The ancient cycle of weathering has also made the soils stony and thin in many places. Residual clays are still evident, but have a darker color due to the thick mat of humus covering the ground. Average temperatures are cooler. Rain and snow are more abundant, augmented by heavy dewfall and moisture that accumulates from low-hanging clouds. Because the streams here move fast over elevated terrain, wetlands are rare, forming primarily on valley floodplains or where springs or seeps intersect the surface.[53]

On the lower slopes, various oaks, hickories, red maples, and sassafras are interspersed with pitch and Virginia pines. As we move up the slopes, one noticeable change is the forest undergrowth. Mountain laurel and rhododendron now grow underneath the hardwoods in dense shrub thickets. We might also observe another large hardwood on the lower slopes: the American chestnut. It is a majestic tree with dense foliage, producing egg-shaped, edible

51. Shelford, *Ecology of North America*, 102, 118; Ralph H. Hughes, "Fire Ecology of Canebrakes," *Proceedings of the Tall Timbers Fire Ecology Conference* 5 (1966), 149–57.
52. John Brickell, *The Natural History of North Carolina* (1737; reprint, Murfreesboro, N.C.: Johnson, 1968), 84.
53. Paullin, *Atlas*, plate 4; Sutton and Sutton, *Eastern Forests*, 83–6.

nuts in autumn. The preponderance of this species helps give the southern Appalachian forest its ecological definition as an "oak-chestnut" region.[54]

But, as in the coastal plain and piedmont, such general labels tend to obscure the diversity of the woodlands. In small valleys, ravines, and coves, trees remain sheltered from wind and extremes of temperature, conditions that give rise to other large hardwoods. Yellow poplars here may reach thirty feet in circumference. The yellow birch and sugar maple, also common in such habitats, range from thirteen to fourteen feet around. Conifers are also present. One of the most common is the eastern hemlock. It, too, can be immense, ranging from sixty to seventy feet in height. On exposed southern ridges where drier conditions prevail, occasional fires, landslides, or other clearing agents encourage pines. Two of the more visible high-country conifers are the table mountain pine, a species restricted to the southern Appalachians, and the eastern white pine, a tree found in the upper latitudes of eastern North America.[55]

In the highest altitudes of the Appalachians, more specialized conifers dominate. Above four thousand feet, the climate resembles that of southern Canada with cool summer temperatures and many subfreezing winter days. The forest here is actually an extension of the boreal vegetation found between Newfoundland and Alaska. Red spruce and Fraser fir form a thick coniferous canopy that restricts underlying growth. Where wind and erosion have broken down rocky ridges and created new topsoil, the conifers mingle with yellow birch, eastern hemlock, or other hardwoods.[56]

Descending the western slope of the Blue Ridge, a traveler would generally move through the various mountain vegetation zones in reverse order, first noting spruce or birch and then the more numerous oaks and hickories. In northwestern Virginia, such a trek would bring one into the Shenandoah Valley. The unique structure of the Shenandoah resulted from weathering of limestone and shale underlying the valley floor. These softer formations eroded more quickly than the rocks on the mountain slopes, leaving a long narrow trough of lowland between the peaks. Limestone deposited from the weathering enriched the soil, providing early European settlers with "the largest area of fine continuous agricultural land in the Virginia Appalachians."[57] Bordered on the west by the slopes of the Ridge and Valley province, the Shenandoah Valley varies from eight to twenty-six miles in width, narrowing to rolling hills in its

54. Sutton and Sutton, *Eastern Forests*, 396; Vankat, *Vegetation of North America*, 144–5; Shelford, *Ecology of North America*, 42–3.
55. Shelford, *Ecology of North America*, 30; Sutton and Sutton, *Eastern Forests*, 84–5, 364, 359, 355; Purrington, "Ancient Mountaineers," in Mathis and Crow, *Prehistory of North Carolina*, 94–5.
56. Purrington, "Ancient Mountaineers," in Mathis and Crow, *Prehistory of North Carolina*, 85.
57. Vanderford, *Southern Soils*, 65.

southern reaches and flattening out into more gently undulating terrain to the north. The Shenandoah River, its tributaries, and the headwaters of the James drain the slopes and valley floor. At the time of settlement, Shenandoah vegetation probably resembled that of the upper piedmont. White, black, and red oaks, hickories, chestnuts, walnuts, and maples seem to have been most numerous and probably mingled with smaller stands of pine. Periodic fires might also have created small and widely dispersed patches of grassland within valley forests.[58]

From the highest peaks of the Blue Ridge to the floor of the Shenandoah Valley, the forests of the Appalachians are as different from those of the low-lying outer coastal plain as Canada is from Florida. Rather than one thick, unbroken stand of trees, the southern woods can best be characterized as a patchwork of adjacent, but often dissimilar communities. And, as our brief tour suggests, clear-cut boundaries between the vegetation types were usually the exception instead of the rule. Pines mingled with oaks and hickories; live oaks grew alongside magnolias; grassy savannas seemed to crop up almost at random. Walking only a few miles in any direction could bring a traveler into contact with myriad types of vegetation. Yet despite this hodgepodge appearance, all the various forests are linked by complex patterns of topography and long geologic history to form a region that is at once both diverse and distinct.

The various forests, fields, rivers, streams, and wetlands of the South Atlantic region furnished habitats for an equally infinite variety of wildlife. One of the most numerous and therefore easily observable mammals was the white-tailed deer. In the coastal plain deer might be visible browsing the new growth of savannas or foraging for acorns, berries, and mushrooms among the live oaks. In older pine forests, deer fed on the tender shoots of sprouting oaks and other hardwoods. The most suitable habitats for deer, however, lay in oak-hickory forests, especially in the bottomlands along river floodplains. In those regions, whitetails found acorns in abundance as well as newly sprouting growth from such trees as maple and sassafras. Canebrakes, with their nutritious forage and thick growth, provided both food and dense cover that aided deer in avoiding predators.[59] Before the arrival of Europeans, deer may have roamed through

58. Robert D. Mitchell, *Commercialism and Frontier: Perspectives on the Early Shenandoah Valley* (Charlottesville: University Press of Virginia, 1977), 19, 21–4.
59. John D. Newsom, "History of Deer and Their Habitat in the South," in *White-tailed Deer in the Southern Forest Habitat: Proceedings of a Symposium at Nacagdoches, Texas, March 25–6, 1969*, Forest Service, United States Department of Agriculture (Nacagdoches, Tex.: Southern Forest Experiment Station, 1969), 1; J. J. Stransky, "Deer Habitat: Quality of Major Forest Types in the South," ibid., 42–3; Richard White, *The Roots of Dependency: Subsistence, Environment, and Social Change Among the Choctaws, Pawnees, and Navajos* (Lincoln: University of Nebraska Press, 1983), 10; Leonard Lee Rue, *The Deer of North America* (New York: Crown, 1978), 7, 438–41; Shelford, *Ecology of North America*, 23, 68, 82.

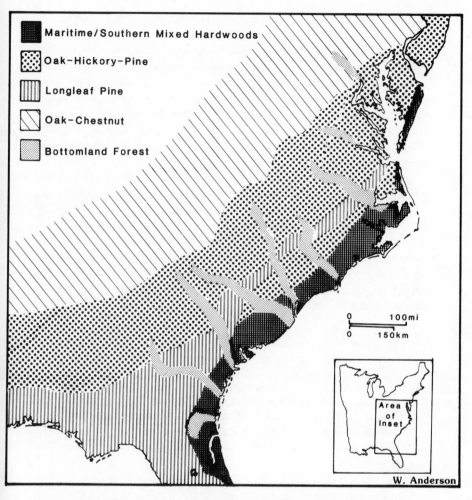

Approximate Range of Dominant Forest Types. Sources: John L. Vankat, *The Natural Vegetation of North America: An Introduction*, p 136; Victor E. Shelford, *The Ecology of North America*, pp 19, 56–88.

southern forests in large herds; some explorers reported more than two hundred whitetails feeding in the savannas and woods along coastal plain rivers.[60]

Canebrakes, savannas, and grassy pinelands also provided habitats for other animals that a modern observer would recognize, but be surprised to find in the region. Bison, more commonly called buffalo, probably ranged as far south as Georgia. Wapiti or American elk, too, might have inhabited parts of the South (although this remains a matter of some debate among ecologists and historians). Healthy adult buffaloes and elks could often outrun predators or fend them off with horns and hooves and consequently they favored open terrain more than deer.[61]

Among the predators deer and buffaloes sought to avoid were panthers and bobcats. Both were relatively common from the swamps of Georgia to the uplands of Maryland. Wolves were also prominent throughout the region.[62] These "dogs of the woods" traveled in packs at night, stalking the deer herds and frequently raising their voices in a bone-chilling cacophony. Anyone traveling through the coastal plain and piedmont lowlands might well have an experience similar to that of John Lawson, an Englishman who journeyed through the Carolinas shortly after 1700. While camped along a Santee River swamp, Lawson reported that

> When we were all asleep, in the Beginning of the Night, we were awaken'd with the dismall'st and most hideous Noise that ever pierc'd my Ears: This sudden Surprizal incapacitated us of guessing what this threatening Noise might proceed from; but our Indian Pilot [guide] (who knew these parts very well) acquainted us, that it was customary to hear such Musick along that Swamp-Side, there being endless Numbers of Panthers, Tygers [bobcats?], Wolves and other Beasts of Prey, which take this Swamp for their Abode in the Day, coming in whole Droves to hunt the Deer in the Night, making this frightful Ditty 'till Day appears, then all is still as in other Places.[63]

Another large beast that could be found in a wide variety of forest habitats was the black bear. In spring, bears might be observed along rivers of the

60. See, for example, William Strachey, *The Historie of Travell into Virginia Britannia*, ed. Louis B. Wright and Virginia Freund (London: Hakluyt Society, 1953), 126; and Thomas Ashe, "A Compleat Discovery of the State of Carolina," in Bartholomew R. Carroll, ed., *Historical Collections of South Carolina*, 2 vols. (New York: Harper Bros., 1836), vol. 2, 72.

61. Erhard Rostlund, "The Geographic Range of the Historic Bison in the Southeast," *Annals of the Association of American Geographers* 50 (1960), 395–407; Peter Mathiessen, *Wildlife in America* (New York: Viking, 1959), 62–3; William S. Powell, "Creatures of Carolina from Roanoke Island to Purgatory Mountain," *North Carolina Historical Review* 50 (1973), 159.

62. Neil W. Hosley, "Management of the White-tailed Deer in its Environment," in Walter P. Taylor, ed., *The Deer of North America* (Harrisburg, Pa.: Stackpole, 1956), 219–21.

63. John Lawson, *A New Voyage to Carolina*, ed. Hugh Talmage Lefler (Chapel Hill: University of North Carolina Press, 1967), 32–3.

Figure 2.1. A somewhat sinister representation of the opossum, a mammal Europeans had not seen before they came to the Americas. From *Encyclopedia Britannica* (Edinburg, 1771), Vol. 2, Pl. LXVIII. Reproduced by courtesy of Colonial Williamsburg Foundation Library, Special Collections.

coastal plain and piedmont feeding on fish. As the weather warmed, the animals moved to forest edges, savannas, and other open terrain to find the berries and fruits that made up much of their summer diet. In fall, bears roamed the live oak woods of the coastal plain and hardwood forests farther inland. There the giant beasts gorged themselves on acorns, nuts, and wild grapes in preparation for the winter ahead.[64]

Smaller mammals, including raccoons, squirrels, and skunks, also favored hardwood forests, where darkness and tall trees provided refuge from predators. One of the most common small mammals throughout the region was the opossum. Representing one of the oldest forms of mammalian life, these "living fossils" were not native to Europe and consequently excited much curiosity among explorers. A number of wetlands mammals also inhabited the swamps, marshes, and river floodplains. Otters, muskrats, and southeastern minks all might attract the attention of any traveler. Beavers, too, thrived in such habitats.[65] Because they are most active at night, these industrious rodents might not be glimpsed during a daylight trek. But dams and lodges fashioned of poplar and ash cuttings would be unmistakable signs of a beaver colony. The Great Dismal Swamp was one region that probably supported a large beaver population. Indeed, beaver dams on the Northwest and Pasquotank rivers might have been responsible for some of the ponding and peat formation in the Great Dismal.[66]

Reptiles, too, could be found in the wetlands. From southern Virginia to Georgia, the nighttime symphony of swamp-dwelling wolves might be interrupted by the raucous bellow of an alligator. Early travelers and writers also spilt much ink trying to assess the habits of that most feared North American reptile, the rattlesnake. (One popular myth held that the snake could charm squirrels and other small game from trees simply by staring at them.) The eastern cottonmouth and southern copperhead, which were at least as common and perhaps equally dangerous, drew comparatively little notice.[67]

64. William Byrd II, *Histories of the Dividing Line Betwixt Virginia and North Carolina*, ed. William K. Boyd (1929; reprint, Mineola, N.Y.: Dover, 1967), 196–8; Shelford, *Ecology of North America*, 29, 59, 69, 82.

65. Eleanor C.J. Horwitz, ed., *Clearcutting: A View From the Top* (Washington, D.C.: Acropolis, 1974), 29; Roger A. Caras, *North American Mammals: Fur-Bearing Animals of the United States and Canada* (New York: Gallahad Books, 1967), 274–5.

66. John O. Whittaker, Jr., *The Audubon Society Field Guide to North American Mammals* (New York: Knopf, 1980), 459; Leonard Lee Rue, *The World of the Beaver*, (Philadelphia: Lippincott, 1964), 31–2; Oaks and Whitehead, "Geologic Setting," in Kirk, *Dismal Swamp*, 21; Charles O. Handley, Jr., "Mammals of the Dismal Swamp: A Historical Account," in ibid., 319.

67. Shelford, *Ecology of North America*, 74, 75, 81, 85; Joseph Ewan and Nesta Ewan, eds., *John Banister and his Natural History of Virginia, 1678–1692* (Urbana: University of Illinois Press, 1970), 374.

Figure 2.2. An eighteenth-century print of an alligator. Those who camped or settled along coastal plain rivers could expect to hear the bellow of this curious American reptile. From *Encyclopedia or Dictionary of Arts, Sciences, and Miscellaneous Literature* (Philadelphia, 1798), Vol. 9, Pl. CCLXI. Reproduced by courtesy of Colonial Williamsburg Foundation Library, Special Collections.

At certain seasons, a traveler might also observe some of the many varieties of fish common to the South Atlantic region. Many of these would look familiar. Spanish mackerel, bonitos, red drums, and sea bass swam in the ocean waters immediately offshore. In fall, migrating bluefish became so obsessed with their pursuit of smaller fish that they sometimes chased their prey into small tidal pools. When the tides receded, bluefish frequently remained trapped in the shallow water. Crabs, clams, scallops, and oysters might also be left behind by the outgoing tides.[68]

Farther inland, every creek, brook, and river abounded with various fresh-water fish: bream, bass, catfish, and freshwater eels in the lowlands; perch and trout in the faster flowing streams to the west. In spring, the streams of the coastal plain came alive with ocean fish going up the rivers to spawn. Herrings and alewives appeared in March, accompanied later by striped bass, sea trout, shad, smelt, and a few flounder. One of the largest migratory species was the sturgeon. These bottom-dwelling fish ranged in size from three to six feet and came up the tidewater rivers in droves. Smaller, younger sturgeon arrived in March to be followed by their older and larger relatives who sometimes remained in the rivers until September.[69]

Like the waters, South Atlantic skies teemed with life. During the warm months, cranes, herons, eagles, hawks, ospreys, and other smaller birds could be seen along the coast feeding on the abundance of fish. As the weather cooled and the ocean fish moved out of the streams, migratory wildfowl moved in. In fall, coastal waters seemed covered with a wide variety of ducks, geese, and swans.[70] Other birds also made a seasonal appearance in the region. As spring berries and wild fruits ripened, swarms of small, brightly colored Carolina parakeets moved into the woods to feed. One Englishman who saw the parakeets thought they resembled East Indian parrots. The presence and numbers of the tropical birds, he reasoned, might mean that Virginia lay near a "South Sea" that would afford the much-coveted quick passage to the Orient.[71]

As plentiful as they were, however, parakeets could not rival the hordes of passenger pigeons that passed through the South Atlantic region each year on their way to the warmer climes farther south. At times the birds clustered together in clouds of wings and feathers that blotted out the sun. When they

68. Lawson, *New Voyage*, 159; Erhard Rostlund, *Freshwater Fish and Fishing in Native North America* (Berkeley: University of California Publications in Geography, 1952), 73–4.
69. For contemporary accounts of fish in inland waters, see [Archer?], "Now Discovered River," 374; and Ralph Hamor, *A True Discourse of the Present Estate of Virginia, and the success of the affaires there til the 18 of June 1614* (London, 1615), 21. Powell, "Creatures of Carolina," 156–7. Rostlund, *Freshwater Fish and Fishing*, 73–4.
70. Ewan and Ewan, *John Banister*, 43, 355.
71. Strachey, *Historie of Travell*, 128. See also Matthiessen, *Wildlife in America*, 114–5.

roosted, pigeons broke limbs from trees and covered the ground with so much dung that underlying vegetation perished. Passing through oak lands, the birds might consume every acorn and leave a bare forest floor in their wake. Because they returned to their spring breeding grounds in the north via a more westerly route, pigeons could only be seen in late fall or early winter. Yet few sights would be more impressive to the modern observer than the annual flights south.[72]

Another bird whose size and numbers might amaze a traveler was the wild turkey. Unlike the coastal water birds and passenger pigeons, turkeys observed no special seasons or territorial boundaries. Throughout the region, flocks of two hundred or more birds could be found in a variety of forest habitats. In the central and western uplands, the birds fed on acorns and other nuts available in the hardwood forests. Farther east, turkeys inhabited the pinelands and maritime woods where they ate pine mast and acorns from live oaks. Fattened on the bounty of southern forests, the birds obtained prodigious size, perhaps weighing more than thirty pounds.[73]

As useful as it might be for observing forests and wildlife, a walking tour could not reveal one crucial force at work in the presettlement woods. All ecosystems, forested or otherwise, depend on a continuous flow of energy to sustain them. That energy passes through the system by way of various food chains or, more properly, food webs. Sunlight provides the initial energy, which green plants capture and either use for growth or store in starches, protein, or other nutrients. Mature plants return seeds and dead matter to the soil, providing organic material, which in turn renews the plants. Herbivores, such as bison, deer, and smaller mammals, obtain their energy indirectly from the plants they consume. Carnivores, such as wolves, acquire their energy thirdhand from the plant-eaters they kill and pass it along to decay bacteria and the soil through bodily wastes or flesh left behind after they feed. In each transfer, some energy is lost, so that no food chain is one hundred percent efficient; "a pound of deer meat cannot produce a pound of mountain lion."[74] Due to this inefficient flow of energy, the amount of new growth within a given area of the southern forest determined the number of deer and the number of wolves or other predators – a fundamental relationship that made the forest a dynamic living system.

72. Ewan and Ewan, *John Banister*, 43; Strachey, *Historie of Travell*, 127; Lawson, *New Voyage*, 50–1, 145–6; A. W. Schorger, *The Passenger Pigeon: Its Natural History and Extinction* (Madison: University of Wisconsin Press, 1955), 268–9.

73. Bourne, *Narratives of de Soto*, vol. 1, 71; Lawson, *New Voyage*, 153; A. W. Schorger, *The Wild Turkey: Its History and Domestication* (Norman: University of Oklahoma Press, 1966), 224–5.

74. Raymond F. Dassman, *Wildlife Biology* (New York: Wiley, 1964), 29. There are many food chains within a forested ecosystem. This is intended only as an example of the processes relating to energy flow.

The continuous movement of energy within the various forest systems meant that, like most living things, the woods underwent constant change. When beavers dammed creeks to create ponds, they reduced the flow rate, causing silt to accumulate in the streambed. If the dams held for long periods or leaked only slightly, the silt might reach the water's surface, creating a marshy stand of grass and eventually a meadow. If deer became too plentiful in a certain region, they might reduce the number of sprouting hardwoods, perhaps allowing pines to maintain dominance longer. In contrast, too many wild turkeys feeding on longleaf pine mast might enable the hardwoods to gain a toehold sooner. A migrating flock of passenger pigeons could clear an oak forest of acorns or deposit so much dung that the existing ground cover perished, to be replaced by plants more suited to the nitrogen-laden waste.[75]

Other, perhaps less obvious, forces also engendered change in the early woods. Insects and fungi attacked trees causing them to decay and die. Hurricanes, tornadoes, thunderstorms, and ice toppled such deadwood or broke and uprooted living trees, creating open areas that gave life to vegetation generally kept out by the lack of light. Constant action by wind and salt spray from the ocean worked to stunt live oaks growing along the South Atlantic coast so that, in some locales, those normally tall, straight trees instead formed small, twisted, dense thickets. Even farther west, the forests probably underwent constant change. Recent studies indicate that such seemingly stable woods are not completely self-perpetuating and permanent, even if the climate remains unchanged. Young trees may not quite replace old ones as they die, or as wildlife moves into more open areas, the energy flow may slow down, limiting the organic matter available to the soil.[76] Thus, there is a danger in describing any past landscape. It might appear static from a satellite photograph or even during a walking tour. In fact, the basic landforms and vegetation patterns would look similar on succeeding days, in succeeding years, or even succeeding centuries. But, in reality, any past landscape remains an elusive entity, one that changed from day to day, hour to hour, or (in the case of storms) minute to minute.

Our adopted perspectives on the South Atlantic landscape are flawed in one other way. As dispassionate observers, interested in nature for its own sake, we

75. Caras, North American Mammals, 264; Spurr and Barnes, Forest Ecology, 373–4; Robert S. Campbell, "Manipulating Biotic Factors in the Southern Forest," in Norman E. Linnartz, ed., The Ecology of Southern Forests, 17th Forestry Symposium (Baton Rouge: Louisiana State University Press, 1968), 64–5; William D. Boyer, "Longleaf Pine Seed Predators in Southwest Alabama," Journal of Forestry 62 (1964), 481–2.
76. Spurr and Barnes, Forest Ecology, 476. Charles Moehring, "Climatic Elements in the Southern Forest," in Linnartz, Ecology of Southern Forests, 13–14; Barbour, Terrestrial Plant Ecology, 577; Eugene P. Odum, Ecology, (New York: Holt Rinehart & Winston, 1963), 88.

have remained apart (perhaps even aloof) from the geologic formations, forests, and animals we described. No human who actually lived in the region could remain so detached. Once they took up residence in the fields and forests, they, like other animals, became dependent on the environment for food, water, and day-to-day necessities. But whereas humans have the same basic biological needs as all organisms, their relationship to the natural world differs "qualitatively" from that of other animals. In short, people think. They remember the past, experience the present, and imagine the future. Consequently, their actions are not solely the result of "biological urges." Upon hearing a howling wolf, a deer might instinctively flee the predator. A person who chooses to run or reaches for a weapon in a similar situation does so because of the ways he thinks about wolves – how he remembers them from the past and imagines them in the future.[77]

Humans are also social animals. Their thoughts and actions are inevitably shaped by the habits and practices of the societies in which they live, a complex web of group experience commonly known as culture. Simply defined, culture means "a way of life, the framework within which any group of people – a society – comprehends the world around it and acts in it."[78] The weapon a human takes up when hearing a howling wolf is one of the tools produced within his society and therefore is an integral part of his culture. But other, more abstract facets of social experience can be equally important to people and their environment. Religion, economics, and political organization often help determine how humans perceive nature and the ways in which food sources and other essentials are to be used. People, then, actually inhabit two environments at once. They not only live on the physical landscape, but also dwell within a second cultural environment composed of material goods, beliefs, and patterns of behavior.[79]

Within any human society, the cultural and physical environments interact, a process that affords man a measure of control over the natural world. Black bears, for instance, survive the southern winter by putting on an extra layer of fat and going into a sort of semihibernation, two distinctly biological responses developed over eons of evolution. Any bear, or bearlike animal, that failed to develop those traits has long since vanished. Humans have no such evolutionary advantages. Yet they can adapt to the same winter conditions by using tools (elements of material culture) to cut trees for housing and firewood.[80]

77. Rene Dubos, *Man Adapting* (New Haven, Conn.: Yale University Press, 1965), 2–7.
78. Ibid., 8–10; Gary B. Nash, *Red, White, and Black: The Peoples of Early America* (Englewood Cliffs, N.J.: Prentice-Hall, 1974), 4.
79. Jesse D. Jennings, *Prehistory of North America* (New York: McGraw-Hill, 1968), 47–8.
80. Brian M. Fagan, *The Great Journey: The Peopling of Ancient America* (London: Thames & Hudson, 1987), 62.

In adapting to their surroundings, the tool-wielding, thinking humans who inhabited North America added new dynamics to the landscape. And the changes they wrought generally proved more sweeping and systematic than alterations created by beavers, browsing deer, or black bears. The story of human alterations along the South Atlantic begins with the physical and cultural environments of the area's first human inhabitants: Indians and their Paleolithic ancestors.

3

Perspectives on the people, 1500

The same glaciers that influenced the prehistoric woodlands also allowed the first humans to move into North America. As the ice sheets advanced and retreated, sea levels fell and rose accordingly, periodically exposing and then reflooding various islands and shorelines. The ancestors of the southern Indians probably walked into America from Asia some forty thousand years ago. They came through central Beringia, a recently exposed, dry, and almost treeless bridge of Arctic lowland between Siberia and Alaska. Human beings might have made it to the South Atlantic region as early as thirty-eight thousand years ago. Archaeologists are reasonably certain that man had become a permanent fixture in the southern woods twelve to fourteen thousand years ago when the last of the glaciers began to retreat.[1]

The frigid climate into which these ice-age adventurers migrated offered them an important ecological advantage over the peoples they left behind. As these first Americans moved across Beringia and the upper reaches of the continent, the prolonged and bitter cold restricted the growth of many disease-causing organisms transported from Eurasia. Over time, such deadly contagions as smallpox, measles, and influenza disappeared from the human population of North America. Until contacted by Europeans, Indians would face comparatively few diseases that could check population growth.[2]

Prehistoric North America was also home to large, cold-adapted mammals, such as the mammoth and the straight-horned bison. Those animals provided the human residents with much of their meat supply. Across the continent, humans hunted the beasts with sharp spears that could be thrown short distances or thrust into the animals at close range. In addition, they sometimes stampeded an entire herd over a precipice or into a gully. Those beasts not immediately killed by the fall could be quickly dispatched with boulders or spears, and the entire kill could be butchered on the spot.

Assessing the ecological impact of such prehistoric hunting is even more risky and uncertain than dating man's exact time of arrival in the Americas. But

---

1. Brian M. Fagan, *The Great Journey: The Peopling of Ancient America* (London: Thames Hudson, 1987), 106–11; Charles M. Hudson, *The Southeastern Indians* (Knoxville: University of Tennessee Press, 1976), 36–8; Albert E. Cowdrey, *This Land, This South: An Environmental History* (Lexington: University Press of Kentucky, 1983), 11–12.
2. Calvin Martin, *Keepers of the Game: Indian-Animal Relationships and the Fur Trade* (Berkeley: University of California Press, 1978), 48–9.

existing archaeological and ecological evidence does provide grounds for some interesting speculation. If the cold climate filtered out disease-causing microbes, these first humans would have faced few natural checks on their population. They also must have enjoyed a virtually unlimited food supply. When man first enters an ecosystem, the animals he hunts have no knowledge of the defensive measures necessary to avoid his weapons. Such early association between human and animal populations usually produces a predator – prey relationship ecologists describe as "strongly limiting," meaning that the prey (in this case, mammoth and bison) might be completely exterminated, precisely what happened in North America.

Archaeologists date the mammoth's extinction at about eleven to nine thousand years ago and believe the ancient bison vanished about one thousand years later. Because both disappeared at a time when glaciers were retreating and the continent was growing warmer, climate might have played a role in their disappearance. But highly efficient hunting by humans could also have contributed to it. More important, the availability of game and lack of disease might have fostered a population explosion, during which the hunters spread across all of North America. Such a boom, however, must have been short lived. Unbalanced predator–prey relationships usually have a limited life span, for as the prey declines, so, too, do the predators. As the hunters killed off the large, land animals, the human population must have dwindled from lack of food. Thousands of years before Columbus or even the Norse voyages, all of North America had probably experienced a dramatic ecological upheaval.[3]

The end of glaciation forced those Indians who survived in the South Atlantic region to adapt to warmer temperatures and the changing forest pattern. Oaks, hickories, and other deciduous trees now furnished nuts and fruits that could be gathered at certain seasons. Hunting remained an important facet of Indian subsistence, but deer, bear, elk, turkey, and other smaller animals replaced mammoth and bison as basic sources of meat. Indians near the coast also made use of mussels, oysters, and the many varieties of fish that inhabited the rivers and streams. Instead of following roaming herds of

3. Paleo-Indian hunting techniques have been detailed in many works. Originally the descriptions included here appeared in C. Vance Haynes, Jr., "Elephant-Hunting in North America," *Scientific American* 214 (July 1966), 104–12; and Joe Ben Wheat, "A Paleo-Indian Bison Kill," *Scientific American* 216 (January 1967), 44–52. Theories about the extinction of large herbivores and human populations are based on the work of paleontologist Paul S. Martin, most accessible in his essay, "The Discovery of America," *Science* 179 (1973), 969–74. For a description of strongly limiting predator-prey relationships, see Eugene P. Odum, *Ecology* (New York: Holt, Rinehart & Winston, 1963), 101–3. This sequence of events and the debate over Martin's theories are summarized in Hudson, *Southeastern Indians*, 41–2; Cowdrey, *This Land, This South*, 12–13; and Alfred W. Crosby, *Ecological Imperialism: The Biological Expansion of Europe, 900–1900* (New York: Cambridge University Press, 1986), 16–17, 276–80.

mammoth and bison, Indians began to confine their subsistence activities to a definite territory. Although they moved from site to site fishing, hunting, or gathering wild foods, they depended on locally available resources and became more sedentary than their ancestors.[4]

Indian subsistence patterns became further circumscribed as the natives began to grow some of their food. In its early stages, Indian agriculture relied on indigenous plants, such as sunflower, sumpweed, knotweed, and maygrass, all of which produced edible seeds that might be stored for future consumption. Little more than selectively cultivated weeds, these first domesticated species flourished best in open ground that featured bare soil and limited competition from other plants. Such environments could readily be found along river floodplains, where receding waters annually deposited darker alluvial soils. Indians soon showed a preference for settling such sites, a trait that further tied particular groups to certain regions.

Near the end of the second millennium B.C., the natives began to add tropical crops to their agricultural repertoire. Bottle-nosed gourds and squash, two plants originally domesticated in Mexico, arrived first. These crops served a dual purpose because, in addition to their edible seeds, both produced hard rinds that could be dried and cut to form handy containers. Around 200 B.C., a variety of Central American corn, known as "tropical flint," also found its way to the South. Tropical flint added important vegetable protein to the Indians' diet, but probably did not adapt well to the cooler North American climate. By A.D. 1,200 southern Indians had begun to cultivate a second type of corn. This species, eastern flint, probably originated in the Guatemala highlands, where it adapted to moist soils and cooler weather, characteristics that made it ideally suited for cultivation in the South Atlantic region. At about the same time, the natives also acquired several common beans, including kidney, snap, and pole varieties. As Indians began to grow and harvest the introduced tropical plants, indigenous crops such as sunflowers declined in importance, and by the time of European contact, corn, beans, and squash dominated native agriculture.[5]

Agriculture did not reach every part of the region at the same time nor have an equal impact in all areas. Depending on latitude, the growing season along the Atlantic coastal plain could be as long as 240 days, allowing Indians to

---

4. Hudson, *Southeastern Indians*, 54–6; Daniel H. Usner, "A Cycle of Lowland Forest Efficiency: The Late Archaic-Woodland Economy of the Lower Mississippi Valley," *Journal of Anthropological Research* 39 (Winter 1983), 433–44.

5. Both weeds and crops share a "weedy tendency" or an ecological adaptation to open or disturbed habitats. The only difference between weeds and crops is that the crops are desired; the weeds are not. See J. G. Hawkes, "The Ecological Background of Plant Domestication," in Peter J. Ucko and G. W. Dimbley, ed., *The Domestication and Exploitation of Plants and Animals* (London: Gerald Duckworth and Company, 1969), 18–19. On the origins of Indian agriculture, see Hudson, *Southeastern Indians*, 62–3, 80.

cultivate two or more crops per year. In the mountains, though, that period might be limited to 180 days, forcing the natives to rely more on hunting and gathering. A longer growing season in the east did not always mean more farming. Some more northerly coastal plain natives probably farmed less intensively than their southwestern neighbors because their settlements along tidal rivers gave them easy access to other nutritious foods such as oysters and migratory ocean fish.[6] Throughout the region, Indians tended to use farming in conjunction with hunting and gathering, demonstrating a remarkable ability to blend agricultural innovation with traditional means of acquiring food.[7] Although he might have overstated the importance of corn to the coastal natives, Virginia colonist Robert Beverley seems to have understood the complementary relationship between agriculture, hunting, and gathering. Writing in 1705, Beverley noted that

> Indian corn was the Staff of Food upon which the Indians did ever depend; for when Sickness, bad Weather, War, or any other ill Accident kept them from Hunting, Fishing, and Fowling; this with the addition of some Peas, Beans, and other such Fruits of the Earth as were then in Season; was the Families Dependence, and the Support of their Women and Children.[8]

By providing corn and beans when wild foods were scarce, Indian farming probably allowed for population growth in the centuries before contact. Because the earliest European explorers introduced epidemic diseases that quickly decreased Indian numbers, native populations are difficult to gauge.[9] Rough estimates, however, suggest that South Atlantic Indian populations were large. Perhaps thirty-three thousand (and possibly many more) natives inhabited coastal Virginia and Maryland.[10] The numerous fires and

6. Hudson, *Southeastern Indians*, 20–1.
7. Neil Salisbury, "American Indians and American History," in Calvin Martin, ed., *The American Indian and the Problem of History* (New York: Oxford University Press, 1987), 50.
8. Robert Beverley, *The History and Present State of Virginia* (1705), ed. Louis B. Wright (Chapel Hill: University of North Carolina Press for the Institute of Early American History and Culture, 1947), 143.
9. On the role of agriculture in Indian population growth, see William Cronon, *Changes in the Land: Indians, Colonists, and the Ecology of New England* (New York: Hill Wang, 1983), 42. In the last twenty years, historians and anthropologists have drastically altered their estimates of precolonial Indian populations. For summaries of the literature, see Francis Jennings, *The Invasion of America: Indians, Colonists, and the Cant of Conquest* (New York: Norton, 1975), 15–31; and Henry F. Dobyns, "Brief Perspective on a Scholarly Transformation: Widowing the 'Virgin' Land," *Ethnohistory* 23/2 (1976), 95–104.
10. Christian F. Feest, "Virginia Algonquians," in Bruce G, Trigger, ed., *Northeast*, Handbook of North American Indians, gen. ed. William C. Sturtevant, 20 vols. (Washington, D.C.: Smithsonian Institution, 1978), vol. 15, 256; idem, "Nanticoke and Neighboring Tribes," ibid., vol. 15, 242. That Indian populations in the Chesapeake might have been larger is

settlements Verrazzano saw along the North Carolina coast suggest that it, too, was home to a sizeable Indian population; seven thousand or more natives probably lived there. Farther south, some 1,750 natives occupied a hundred mile-long strip of coast between the Santee and Savannah rivers.[11] In the uplands and mountains where the natives farmed intensively, Indians were also numerous. The Cherokees, for example, may have numbered thirty thousand or more before contact with Europeans.[12]

As the varying populations suggest, southern Indian cultures were hardly identical. In some ways, the natives exhibited as much diversity as the early landscape. Anthropologists have identified at least four language families with the region: Algonquian, typified by the coastal natives of Virginia, Maryland, and North Carolina; Iroquoian, among the Cherokees and Tuscaroras; Siouan, among the Catawbas; and farther south, Muskogean, among the Creeks, Chickasaws, and Choctaws. As anthropologist Charles M. Hudson has described it, "the languages which belonged to these families were as different from each other as English is from Chinese."[13]

But if several millennia of human experience bred variety among Indians, the natives' long-term adaptation to the South Atlantic environment also created a certain amount of uniformity. By the time Europeans arrived at the dawn of the sixteenth century, all Indians in the region practiced four basic types of subsistence. They hunted game animals, fished the streams and rivers, planted and harvested crops, and gathered available wild foods. James Adair, an English trader with the Indians, was one writer who recognized such

suggested by Powhatan's comment that he had "seene the death of all my people thrice and not one living of those 3 generations, but my selfe." W[illiam] S[ymonds], *The Proceedings of the English Colonies in Virginia since their first beginning from England in the year of our Lord 1606, till this present 1612, with all the accidents that befell them in their Journies and Discoveries* (Oxford, 1612), 60–1, Pennsylvania State Libraries Microforms, Reel 628. See also J. Leitch Wright, Jr., *The Only Land They Knew: The Tragic Story of the American Indians in the Old South* (New York: Free Press, 1981), 25.

11. Lawrence C. Wroth, ed., *The Voyages of Giovanni da Verrazzano, 1524–1528* (New Haven, Conn.: Yale University Press, 1970), 134; Theda Perdue, *Native Carolinians: The Indians of North Carolina* (Raleigh: Division of Archives and History, 1985), 25; Christian F. Feest, "North Carolina Algonquians," in Trigger, *Northeast*, vol. 15, 272; Gene Waddell, *Indians of the South Carolina Lowcountry 1562–1751* (Spartanburg, S.C.: Reprint, 1980), 14–15.

12. Peter H. Wood, "The Changing Population of the Eighteenth-Century South: An Overview, By Race and Subregion, From 1685 to 1790," in Peter H. Wood, G. Waselkov, and M. Thomas Hatley, eds., *Powhatan's Mantle* (Lincoln: University of Nebraska Press, forthcoming). Wood estimates the Cherokee population at 30–35,000 in 1685. Wood also suggests that, by that point, the Cherokees had at least partially recovered from diseases and accompanying depopulation triggered by de Soto's expedition. If so, a precontact estimate might well be similar. I am indebted to Professor Wood for permission to read and use his essay in advance of publication.

13. Charles M. Hudson, *Four Centuries of Southern Indians* (Athens: University of Georgia Press, 1975), 3.

similarities. As Adair told his readers in 1775, the natives' "rites and customs are in several respects different. But they agree in essentials throughout the whole extent of the American world." What Adair and many other Europeans failed to realize, however, was that those essentials emerged only after thousands of years of social development. Some of the first Europeans to visit the South Atlantic coast may have thought they had discovered a "plain wilderness" inhabited only by "savages," but they really encountered a people and a land with a history as diverse and dynamic as their own.[14]

One key part of that history was the development of an elaborate belief system that the natives used to explain the human role in the natural world. The way in which Indians perceived their relationship to plants and animals is probably best illustrated by the Cherokee oral tradition that tells of the origins of disease and medicine. The Cherokees, the story goes, once lived in peace with nature, but as their population grew and their settlements spread, they began to crowd out the animals. Moreover, humans invented bows, knives, blowguns, and other weapons with which to hunt the larger beasts and carelessly trampled smaller creatures under their feet. In an effort to remedy the problem, the animals met in council and, after discussing several possible solutions (including using the natives' own weapons against them and engendering dreams of decaying fish that would destroy Indian appetites), decided to invent and name many new diseases that could kill off their human anatagonists. Upon learning of the animals' plans, the plants, who remained friendly toward people, agreed to furnish cures for some of the new ailments so that Indians might defeat the animals' designs. A number of trees, shrubs, and herbs then took on medicinal qualities and when native conjurers failed to recognize a given illness and its remedy, they could consult the spirits of certain plants for help.[15]

Historians and anthropologists still have much to learn about the native belief system. But many scholars would agree that men and other living things "were not as sharply separated" as they were in the cosmology of western Europeans. The Cherokees seem to have realized that humans can become too populous and thereby damage or destroy their surroundings. In such cases, Indian cosmology allowed animals or the elements to strike back if people became too callous in their dealings with them.[16]

14. Quotations from: James Adair, *A History of the North-American Indians, Their Customs, &c.* (1775), ed. Samuel Cole Williams (Johnson City, Tenn.: Watauga Press, 1930), 405; and William Strachey, *The Historie of Travell into Virginia Britannia*, ed. Louis B. Wright and Virginia Freund (London: Hakluyt Society, 1953), 39. Salisbury, "American Indians and American History," 54; Hudson, *Four Centuries*, 3.

15. James Mooney, *Myths of the Cherokee and Sacred Formulas of the Cherokee* (Nashville: Cherokee Heritage Books, 1982), 250–2.

16. Charles M. Hudson, "The Cherokee Concept of Natural Balance," *The Indian Historian* 3 (1970), 51–4.

To avoid retaliation, the natives had to observe certain guidelines in their hunting. Cherokee hunters prayed to the wind to cover their scent and, when taking deer, they prayed for the animals' forgiveness. When the hunters brought meat to their villages, Cherokee conjurers first offered some of it to the "keepers of the 4 winds" so they would not send bad weather to destroy crops. Other natives engaged in these or similar ceremonies. John Lawson reported that young Indian men never ate the first bear, deer, or fish they killed for fear the animals would become angry and never again allow themselves to be taken. William Byrd II, who surveyed the boundary between Virginia and North Carolina in 1728, marveled at an Indian's reluctance to prepare deer and turkey together, because cooking beasts of the field and birds of the air in the same pot might offend "The Guardian of the Forest."[17]

Other rituals surrounded the plant world. Perhaps the most significant of these was the Green Corn Ceremony, an elaborate ritual of purification and celebration associated with the ripening of maize. Although the exact nature of the ceremony differed from group to group, the festival generally involved dancing, fasting, cleaning of houses and gathering places, building new fires, and forgiving transgressions of the previous year – all as part of an effort to thank the providers of corn and start the new year with a clean body and spirit.[18] William Bartram, a Quaker naturalist who traveled in the South during the mid 1770s, also discovered something of the Indian reverence for corn when a Cherokee chieftain offered him some for his horse. Bartram interpreted this gesture as an indication of "the highest esteem" since Indians believed "corn was given by the Great Spirit only for food for man." Wild plants inspired similar admiration. When gathering ginseng, an aromatic medicinal herb, the Cherokees spoke of it as a "sentient being . . . able to make itself invisible to those unworthy to gather it." In searching for the fragrant roots, Indian collectors passed over the first three plants they encountered and took the fourth only after offering a prayer and the gift of a small bead as compensation to the plant's spirit. After this gesture, other plants could be taken at will.[19]

Their belief in the spirituality and human volition of plants and animals probably helps explain why the natives did not keep livestock. Because Indians believed wild animals capable of retaliation if wronged, the natives might have

17. Alexander Longe, "A Small Postscript on the Ways and Manners of the Nashon of Indians called Charikees," ed. David H. Corkran, *Southern Indian Studies* 21 (October 1969), 12; John Lawson, *A New Voyage to Carolina*, ed. Hugh Talmage Lefler (Chapel Hill: University of North Carolina Press, 1967), 219; William Byrd II, *Histories of the Dividing Line Betwixt Virginia and North Carolina*, ed. William K. Boyd (1929; reprint Mineola, N.Y.: Dover, 1967), 194.

18. John Witthoft, *Green Corn Ceremonialism in the Eastern Woodlands* (Ann Arbor: University of Michigan Press, 1949), 17–19, 82–5.

19. William Bartram, *Travels of William Bartram*, ed. Mark Van Doren (New York: Dover, 1955), 285; Mooney, *Myths and Sacred Formulas of the Cherokees*, 425.

been unwilling to capture the beasts and force them to the yoke.[20] Indians did have dogs, but as William Strachey, secretary of the Jamestown colony, noted, they bred no "Cattell nor bring up tame poultry, albeit they have great store of Turkeys, nor keepe byrds, Squirrels, nor tame Partridges, swan, duck, nor Geese." Although Europeans marveled at the lack of livestock, the Indians' reluctance to tame the beasts of the field probably served the natives well. Some of the same diseases the Indians left behind in Asia, including pox viruses and influenza, can be passed back and forth between domesticated animals and humans. Where people and beasts live together, such contact constantly produces new and more virulent strains of the various disease organisms so that neither humans nor animals ever develop complete immunity. By refusing to surround themselves with domesticated animals, Indians never created such a disease environment. Consequently, they continued to avoid many of the afflictions that plagued Europeans and might otherwise have become established in native villages.[21]

But even if the natives did not have to use domestic beasts, they did have to rely on other plants and animals whom they regarded as their spiritual kin; indeed they had to destroy them in order to survive. Their belief system probably played a key role in allowing the natives to work out this fundamental tension between themselves and nature. By asking a dead deer's forgiveness, celebrating the maturity of corn, or appeasing the spirit of ginseng, Indians could take what they needed from the forest without violating or compromising that basic spiritual relationship between people, plants, and animals. In using the resources available to them Indians were only human. For human beings, whether Indian, European, African, or Asian, always exert a certain amount of control over their environment. In so doing, they inevitably change the face of the land on which they live. In the South Atlantic region, as in other areas of North America, the pattern and extent of those alterations reflected both native culture and the peculiarities of the environment itself.[22]

If their belief system permitted Indians to take what they needed from the land, the forests dictated when and how they could take it. One of the most striking features of any temperate forest is seasonal variation. In the pine forests

20. Clara Sue Kidwell, "Science and Ethnoscience: Native American World Views as a Factor in the Development of Native Technologies," in Kendall E. Bailes, ed., *Environment and History: Critical Issues in Comparative Perspective* (Lanham, Md.: University Press of America, 1985), 281.
21. Quotation from: Strachey, *Historie of Travell*, 79–80. Martin, *Keepers of the Game*, 49; Crosby, *Ecological Imperialism*, 31.
22. Christopher Vecsey, "American Indian Environmental Religions," in Vecsey and Robert W. Venables, eds., *American Indian Environments: Ecological Issues in Native American History* (Syracuse, N.Y.: Syracuse University Press, 1980), 22–3; "Indians in the Land: A Conversation between William Cronon and Richard White," *American Heritage* 37/5 (August/September 1986), 20; Cronon, *Changes in the Land*, 13.

and among the evergreen live oaks of the outer coastal plain, seasonal differences might have been difficult to discern. But in the inland deciduous forests, the changes were striking. Sap rose and fell in the deciduous heartwood, turning the dark summer forest into open, leafless winter woods.[23] Like Indians elsewhere, those of the South Atlantic region paid particular attention to these changes. Among some natives, the various months took on names that described the weather or the foods available at that time. In the coastal plain, March might be known as "herring month." Indians might refer to April or May as the time "when Turkey-Cocks gobble" and describe June as "strawberry month." Other natives employed simpler methods of marking the seasons. In the western mountains and foothills, an area subject to great seasonal variation, the Cherokees distinguished between *gogi*, the warm season between April and October, and *gola*, or the cold time that spanned the rest of the year. Regardless of the complexity of their calendars, Indians understood that the variable climate determined their subsistence patterns. Food and other necessities had to be taken where and in what quantity they could be found, and that meant moving or altering their diet as the forest about them changed.[24]

At the time of contact, Indians set up their villages along rivers among the oaks, hickories, and other hardwoods common to such sites. Such towns became base camps from which to explore and use the resources of the surrounding territory. William Bartram discovered that inland natives frequently placed their villages in an area "convenient for procuring game," with "a large district of arable land adjoining or in its vicinity." Or the Indians might choose "a convenient fertile spot at some distance from their town" to which they journeyed in spring to plant their crops. Coastal natives probably planted in the mixed hardwood forests ten to twenty miles inland, thereby avoiding the sandy soils and foul weather common to the shoreline, as well as the infertile pine barrens and sandhills farther west. Indian travels and knowledge of these various woodlands often amazed European observers. John Lawson thought it remarkable that even though Indians knew nothing of the English compass, they could "draw Maps very exactly, of all the Rivers, Towns, Mountains, and Roads" several days' journey away. Their willingness to sleep outside in warm weather and a disdain for what Europeans considered basic household

23. Scholars are now well aware of the importance of changing seasons in North American Indian subsistence. Two works that explain the relationship in some detail are Cronon, *Changes in the Land*, 37–9; and Hudson, *Southeastern Indians*, 269–72. Like Cronon and Hudson, I have organized the following paragraphs on Indian subsistence according to the four seasons. To do otherwise would present a distorted picture of native subsistence. On seasonal variation in the southern deciduous forest, see John L. Vankat, *The Natural Vegetation of North America: An Introduction* (New York: Wiley, 1979), 132.

24. Quotations from John Lawson, *A New Voyage to Carolina*, ed. Hugh Talmage Lefler (Chapel Hill: University of North Carolina Press, 1967), 240. Hudson, *Southeastern Indians*, 270; Cronon, *Changes in the Land*, 43.

amenities further aided extended forays into the forest. According to Robert Beverley, "a Grass-plat under the covert of shady Tree, is all the lodging they require, and is as pleasant and refreshing to them, as a Down Bed and fine Holland sheets are to us."[25]

Europeans found the division of labor within Indian society even more difficult to comprehend. William Byrd described it this way. "The little work that is done among the Indians is done by the poor Women, while the men are quite idle, or at most employed only in the Gentlemanly Diversions of Hunting and Fishing." Women ran the households, cooked, made pottery, gathered firewood, and most striking in English eyes, tended the fields. But Byrd's assessment is only generally correct. Men usually took sole responsibility for the ritually important tobacco crop, and women sometimes aided in procuring fish. Byrd and other colonists also failed to recognize the benefits of such a system. Hunting and fishing required men to be away from the villages for long periods, and by attending to the village duties, Indian women helped facilitate the forest travels.[26]

At the onset of the warm season, March in the coastal plain and April or May further west, able-bodied men left the villages to fish. Along coastal rivers, the natives used weirs to capture the migrating ocean species. The traps usually consisted of two parallel lines of small poles woven together with marsh reeds or oak strips to form a hedge. Indians then placed the hedges across the streambed at high tide, leaving openings that allowed fish to enter but not escape. When the tides receded, sturgeon, herring, shad, and alewives remained confined in shallower water, where they could be clubbed with sticks, dipped out with nets attached to long poles, or speared with shafts of green cane tipped with spiked deer horns or turkey claws. Farther inland, where swifter currents and a lack of tidal activity made wooden weirs less effective, the Indians erected small stone corrals, built in a "V" shape with the small end of the enclosure pointing downstream. The natives then waded into the river above the trap and scared the fish into the larger opening, driving them toward the narrow end where they could be easily killed.[27]

If deep water made trapping fish difficult, Indians sometimes stretched a

25. Quotations from Bartram, *Travels*, 400; Lawson, *New Voyage*, 214; Beverley, *History and Present State of Virginia*, 177. Waddell, *Indians of the South Carolina Lowcountry*, 47–8.
26. Quotation from Byrd, *Dividing Line*, 116. Hudson, *Southeastern Indians*, 264–9. A good discussion of sex roles as they pertained to forest travels (though not specifically about the South) is Anthony F. C. Wallace, *The Death and Rebirth of the Seneca* (New York: Random House, 1972), 28–30.
27. Lawson, *New Voyage*, 217–18; Samuel Cole Williams, ed., *Lieut. Henry Timberlake's Memoirs, 1756–1765* (Johnson City, Tenn.: Watauga Press, 1927), 69; Erhard Rostlund, *Freshwater Fish and Fishing in Native North America* (Berkeley: University of California Publications in Geography, 1952), 88–101; Hudson, *Southeastern Indians*, 284.

single line across the stream and attached several shorter strands to it. At the end of these lines, they fixed hooks made from deer or turkey bones and baited them with shellfish or other cut bait. Paddling dugout canoes, the natives inspected their lines several times a day, removing fish and rebaiting the hooks. In larger streams and when fishing offshore, Indians sometimes took their boats out at night, using torches made from longleaf pine to attract their quarry and killing the fish with bows and arrows. While men pursued fish in the streams and ocean, women and children made short trips from the villages to gather oysters and other shellfish.[28] Children also enjoyed taking crayfish, which they lured with pieces of venison skewered on a stick of cane. When the small crustaceans clutched the meat with their claws, Indians quickly pulled up the sticks and flung the crayfish far up on the bank. According to John Lawson, this method could produce "several bushels" of crayfish in a short time.[29]

Judging from European accounts, most springtime fishing expeditions enjoyed similar success. John Smith reported that coastal Virginia Indians lived almost exclusively upon fish during March and April and Lawson noted that inland natives relied heavily on "Trout and other species of Fish which these parts afford." In spite of the vast numbers taken by Indians, fish populations seem to have suffered few ill effects. High water during early spring probably allowed many spawning fish to escape the weirs, ensuring the survival of enough fry to replace those taken. Moreover, most natives made no attempt to lay in a large surplus of fish. Smith found that "Powhatan their great king and some others that are provident, rost their fish and flesh upon hurdles ... and keepe it till scarce times," but for most South Atlantic Indians, spring fishing provided only a great seasonal feast that lasted for the duration of the spawning runs.[30]

As the weather continued to warm and spawning activity decreased, Indian fishing became more sporadic, but one summertime technique could be highly effective. As James Adair explained it,

> In a dry summer season they gather horse chestnut and different sorts of roots, which having pounded pretty fine and steeped a while in a trough they scatter this mixture over the surface of a middle sized pond and stir it about with poles till the water is sufficiently impregnated with intoxicating bittern; the fish are soon inebriated and make to the surface with their bellies uppermost.

28. Hudson, *Southeastern Indians*, 284.
29. Lawson, *New Voyage*, 218.
30. John Smith, "A Map of Virginia. With a Description of the Countrey, the Commodities, People, Government and Religion," in Philip L. Barbour, ed., *The Complete Works of Captain John Smith (1580–1631)*, 3 vols. (Chapel Hill: University of North Carolina Press for the Institute of Early American History and Culture, 1986), vol. 1, 162; Lawson, *New Voyage*, 218.

The modern horse chestnut is a tree introduced from southeastern Europe. The nuts to which Adair referred must have been those of the red buckeye, a common southern tree whose fruit contains active ingredients like those of retenone, an organic poison. When applied in sufficient quantity, the toxin attacked the fish's central nervous system and produced the stupefying effect.[31]

Adair's reference to horse chestnut also suggests that he understood similar methods employed in Europe, where poachers used the nuts to tap private ponds. Black slaves also knew much about fish poisoning and since Adair wrote in 1775, the techniques he mentions might have been introduced to the natives after contact. However, several groups, including the Powhatans, report a long tradition of catching fish with poison and the Cherokees apparently used pounded walnut bark to produce the same effect as the buckeye. Agricultural Indians, who understood and often seemed preoccupied with the resources of the plant world, might easily have learned to poison fish on their own.[32]

The paralyzing effects of the buckeye are only temporary and as Adair noted, those fish "speedily removed to good water . . . revived in a few minutes." But most never got that chance. Indians gathered them up by the basketful and feasted for several days. These excursions became great social gatherings, organized and directed by local chieftains or shamans. Although they might appear quite destructive, such poisoning parties had few detrimental effects on fish habitat. The need to saturate a small area of a pond or stream with herbal poisons precluded their use on large rivers or during the periods of high water associated with spawning runs. Poisoning remained only an occasional exercise and seems to have been mainly a tactic of inland natives who used it to supplement staple foods such as corn and wild game.[33]

Just as women contributed to the haul of fish by gathering oysters and mussels, men helped out with the heavier agricultural duties. Clearing new ground began with the first hint of warm weather, perhaps as early as late February or the first of March, before the fish began to run. As the sap rose in the larger trees, the men used stone axes to remove the bark to a point three or four feet above the ground, a technique that drained off sap and kept the trees from sprouting new leaves. After piling smaller wood and kindling around the base of the trees, Indians set fire to the scarred lower trunks. According to John Smith, this practice quickly "scortch[ed] the roots" so that, deprived of further

---

31. Quotation from: Adair, *North-American Indians*, 232. Hudson, *Southeastern Indians*, 284; Rostlund, *Freshwater Fish and Fishing*, 127–8; Elbert L. Little, *The Audubon Society Field Guide to North American Trees, Eastern Region* (New York: Knopf, 1980), 585, 587.
32. Rostlund, *Freshwater Fish and Fishing*, 127–8; Peter H. Wood, *Black Majority: Negroes in Colonial South Carolina from 1670 through the Stono Rebellion* (New York: Norton, 1975), 122–3.
33. Quotation from Adair, *North American Indians*, 232. Rostlund, *Freshwater Fish and Fishing*, 128.

Figure 3.1. Indians roasting fish. Engraving by Simon Gribelin, based on the work of English artist John White. From Robert Beverley, *The History and Present State of Virginia* (London, 1705), 14. Reproduced by courtesy of Colonial Williamsburg Foundation Library, Special Collections.

nutrients, the trees would "grow no more." To remove the undergrowth, the natives first hacked out a broad strip across the outer edge of the land they intended to cultivate and then fired the brush and underwood, using the cleared path as a fire break "in order to prevent the whole forest from burning." Once the smaller growth burned, the ground could be planted with the larger trees left standing until decay allowed them to be pushed over and removed.[34]

Men occasionally took time out from fishing to help prepare the ground for planting, but that task usually fell to women. Using hoes made of wood, bone, or shell, Indian women broke up the ground to a depth of four to five inches. They then worked the soil into small hills about three feet apart. Several grains of corn and beans could be planted in each hill with squash and pumpkins sown in shallow trenches between the mounds. Among those groups heavily involved in agriculture, planting took place in several stages. Women seeded the smaller garden plots near the habitations as soon as weather permitted, planting corn that would bear ears by the beginning of summer and could be eaten green. The natives held off planting the larger communal fields until wild fruits and berries ripened, a ploy that served "to draw off the birds from picking up the grain." In the southern coastal plain where the first frosts might not appear until mid- or late November, Indians could continue to plant well into June and still anticipate harvesting their crops before the cold season began.[35]

As the plants began to sprout, the land turned into an agricultural jungle. Beans, squash, and corn grew together in a tangled mass of leaves and stalks. Pumpkins or gourds popped up at irregular intervals within the dense foliage. Because the larger fields served an entire village, no fences delineated individual shares. Yet, as John Lawson observed, "every man knows his own, and it scarce ever happens, that they rob one another of as much as an Ear of Corn."[36]

Although Indian agriculture seemed fit to "choak up the fields," Europeans had to admit that native farming techniques generally produced bumper crops.

34. Smith, "Map of Virginia," in Barbour, *Complete Works of Smith*, vol. 1, 157; William Byrd II, *The Natural History of Virginia or the Newly Discovered Eden*, ed. Richard Croom Beatty and William J. Mulloy (Richmond: Dietz, 1940), 92–3.

35. Quotation from: Adair, *North-American Indians*, 436. For other contemporary accounts of Indian planting, see Smith, "Map of Virginia," in Barbour, *Complete Works of Smith*, vol. 1, 157; and Thomas Harriot, "A Briefe and True Report of the Newfound Land of Virginia," in David B. Quinn, ed., *The Roanoke Voyages*, 2 vols. (London: Hakluyt Society, 1955), vol. 1, 341–2. These techniques have been detailed in many secondary works, including Lewis Cecil Gray, *History of Agriculture in the Southern United States to 1860*, 2 vols. (1932; reprint, Gloucester, Mass.: Peter Smith, 1958), vol. 1, 3–9; G. Melvin Herndon, "Indian Agriculture in the Southern Colonies," *North Carolina Historical Review* 44 (1967), 283–97; and Hudson, *Southeastern Indians*, 289–99.

36. Quotation from Lawson, *New Voyage*, 184; Richard White, *The Roots of Dependency: Subsistence, Environment, and Social Change among the Choctaws, Pawnees, and Navajos* (Lincoln: University of Nebraska Press, 1983), 22; Cronon, *Changes in the Land*, 44.

Most observers attributed such production solely to the soil's natural fertility, but other, more subtle environmental factors contributed to the high yields. Beans helped replace nitrogen taken out of the soil by the other crops, while the competition between various plants for sunlight and moisture gradually forced them to develop larger hardier seeds that, in turn, increased the harvest. Planting corn in hills also encouraged the stalks to send out buttress or bracer roots from the lower part of the stem, which functioned like tiny guy wires to keep the plants from falling over during periods of hard rain and high winds. In addition, the thick cover provided by beans and squash reduced weed growth in and around the hills.[37]

During the growing season, the standing trees and tangle of cultivated crops worked to keep rain from washing away the soil around the hills. In the more level coastal plain, erosion was practically nonexistent in Indian fields. In the piedmont and mountains, however, stream valleys were comparatively narrow and subject to more frequent flooding than those farther east. Although Indians generally located their towns so as to avoid the rising rivers, some of their adjacent fields might have been subject to scouring and erosion when rivers overflowed their banks. Sheet erosion from rainfall might also have been a problem in fields farther inland. For the most part, however, soils remained in place. Many of the first Europeans to see the interior were amazed at the clarity of the various streams and rivers, which seemed to carry little sediment even during high water.[38]

Even if it did not erode, no soil could support such intensive farming forever. No matter where or how it is practiced, agriculture always disrupts the already inefficient flow of energy within the ecosystem. Man consumes the fruits and seeds of the species he cultivates so that the soil never recovers the energy stored in those parts of the plants and gradually becomes depleted.[39] European farmers eventually learned to delay soil exhaustion by treating the ground with manure or turning under the dead stalks and vines to return other organic matter to the ground. Because Indians kept no livestock, either for food or draft animals, they had no such fertilizer. Instead, they employed the same method originally used to clear their lands, burning off dead plants to make way for a new crop. Such fires helped release nitrogen from the leftover vegetable matter

37. Quotation from Adair, *North-American Indians*, 237. Lawrence Kaplan, "Archaeology and Domestication of American *Phaseolus* (Beans)," *Economic Botany*, 19 (1965), 365–7; Paul Weatherwax, *Indian Corn in Old America* (New York: Macmillan, 1954), 70.
38. Herndon, "Indian Agriculture," 287; Stafford C. Happ, "Sedimentation in South Carolina Piedmont Valleys," *American Journal of Science* 243 (1945), 116–17; Arthur R. Hall, "Soil Erosion and Agriculture in the Southern Piedmont: A History" (Ph.D. Thesis, Duke University, 1948), 32–3; Stanley Wayne Trimble, *Man-Induced Soil Erosion on the Southern Piedmont, 1700–1970* (Ankeny, Iowa: Soil Conservation Society of America, 1974), 32, 22–5.
39. Raymond F. Dassman, *Wildlife Biology*, (New York: Wiley, 1964), 35–7.

and although most of the critical element escaped in gases produced by the flames, the ash residue also contained "mineralized nitrogen," which proved highly beneficial to new plants. Explorers and colonists had less technical explanations, but clearly understood the results of the process. John Brickell, who published the *Natural History of North Carolina* in 1737, observed that Carolina Indians "never Dung their Land, but set fire to the Weeds, which makes very good Manure."[40]

Even periodic burning could not maintain Indian fields forever. When land no longer produced, the natives simply moved on, deadening trees in another area and planting again. Eventually, the old plots might be returned to cultivation, but in the meantime, the forest slowly went about its work of reclaiming the land. In the coastal plain, where more frequent fires kept the forest in a state of flux, such openings in the woods occurred naturally, but in the piedmont old Indian fields added a new dynamic to the landscape. Showy, flowering, indigenous weeds such as horseweed and white aster appeared during the first two years after the fields lay fallow. By the third summer, broomsedge, a tall blue-green or reddish-brown bunch grass, grew on the deserted sites, creating weedy meadows in the midst of the forest. Under the right conditions, wild strawberries or blackberries might crop up in the sunny clearings. If the fields remained untended for more than three years, "pioneer" trees such as loblolly and Virginia pines invaded the plots, eventually growing in thick, pure stands and replacing the weeds and grasses. As the pines reached maturity 80 to 140 years after abandonment, dogwoods, sourwoods, and red maples moved in, to be followed later by oaks and hickories.[41]

Europeans occasionally noted the presence of other plants in and around old Indian fields. A number of explorers and travelers described various wild legumes, which they usually called "vetch," "ground nuts," or "wild pea vines." Such terminology makes it difficult to identify such ground cover, but the plants might have been cultivated beans that "escaped" from Indian fields and took up residence in the nearby forests and fields. Christian Gottlieb Reuter, surveyor for the Moravians who settled in piedmont North Carolina in the eighteenth century, noted that "Indian beans resemble garden Beans,

40. John Brickell, *The Natural History of North Carolina* (1737; reprint, Murfreesboro, N.C.: Johnson, 1968), 273; P. J. Viro, "The Effects of Forest Fire on Soil," T. T. Kozlowski, ed., *Fire and Ecosystems* (New York: Academic Press, 1974), 39.
41. W. D. Billings, *Plants and the Ecosystem*, 3d ed. (Belmont, Calif.: Wadsworth Pub., 1978), 105–6; Stephen H. Spurr and Burton V. Barnes, *Forest Ecology* (New York: Ronald, 1973), 491; R. E. Wilkinson and H. E. Jaques, *How to Know the Weeds*, 2d ed. (Dubuque, Iowa: William C. Brown, 1972), 190–1, 164, 21; United States Department of Agriculture, Agricultural Research Service, *Common Weeds of the United States* (Mineola, N.Y.: Dover, 1971), 36, 400.

though they are small. They grow abundantly in the woods, especially on good soil."[42]

Indian crops that escaped into the wild and the pattern of "old field succession" associated with abandoned fields enhanced the diversity of the piedmont woods, but large tracts of forest remained untouched because the Indians' stone tools could not remove or deaden the largest trees. Lawson reported that "the Indians are not inclinable to settle the richest land, because the Timbers are too large for them to cut down, and too much burthened with Wood for their Laborers to make Plantations of." Indeed, Lawson continued, much of the Carolina upcountry had "no inhabitants but the Beastes of the Wilderness."[43]

Although Lawson did not know it, one of the largest of those beasts, the buffalo, might not have found its way to Carolina had Indians not cleared small patches of woods. The dense oak-hickory and oak-chestnut forests of the piedmont and mountains kept the animals out of the upper Southeast until after 1500. By the mid sixteenth century, however, the farming Indians had probably created enough openings in the upland forests to allow bison to migrate through them. Bison never became as common east of the mountains as they did farther west, and Indians had no intention of attracting the animals when they abandoned their fields, but the migrations illustrate one way in which Indian agriculture might influence both plant and animal populations.[44]

Planting and fishing kept the natives busy during much of the spring, but in the summer they had time for other activities, such as religious festivals, warfare, and various sports. Green corn, small and large game animals, roots, and wild vegetables became the dietary staples of inland natives whereas those along the coast continued to rely on fish. Indians living along the tidal rivers of the coastal plain often left the villages, moving upstream to hunt and gather the available wild foods. Such summer migrations played a key role in helping Indians maintain their health. The unrelenting heat common to the outer coastal plain made the rivers run low and brackish, and as colonists at Jamestown discovered, drinking the tainted water could bring on a fatal case of salt poisoning. Farther up the rivers, the water ran swifter and clearer, and the summer abundance of squirrels, turkeys, berries, and other wild produce helped accommodate the seasonal travels. As autumn approached, Indians moved back to the villages in order to protect their maturing crops from crows,

42. Adelaide L. Fries, et al., eds., *Records of the Moravians in North Carolina*, 11 vols. (Raleigh: North Carolina Historical Commission, 1922–69), vol. 2, 568; Hall, "Soil Erosion and Agriculture," 54–5.
43. Lawson, *New Voyage*, 89.
44. Erhard Rostlund, "The Geographic Range of Historic Bison in the Southeast," *Annals of the Association of American Geographers* 50 (1960), 395–407.

raccoons, bears, and other varmints. Harvesting late corn, beans, squash, and pumpkins continued well into fall, making the final weeks of the warm season a time of feasting and plenty.[45]

With their crops stored and their bellies full, Indian men prepared for the annual hunt. Throughout the warm season, the natives took game whenever they could, and many explorers who traveled the coastal rivers in spring received gifts of deer, bear, and turkey from Indians. At the beginning of the cold season, however, a number of environmental factors combined to make it the best time for hunting. The great quantity of nuts and acorns available then not only provided food for the hunters, but also attracted large flocks of turkeys and numerous bears and deer to the oak-hickory forests. After foraging on the mast in preparation for winter, the animals reached their heaviest weights and furnished more meat and fat than at any other time. In preparation for the cold months ahead, the animals acquired their heaviest coats of the year, making fall or early winter the best season to procure skins for clothing and bedding.[46]

Other peculiarities of animal behavior aided cold-weather hunters. In the milder climes along the South Atlantic coast, black bears do not den up for the entire winter like their counterparts in the mountains. Instead, the animals usually nap for several days at a time, venturing out frequently on warm days. But even in the coastal plain, bears became somewhat sluggish and easier to hunt with the onset of cold weather. In contrast, bucks, made bold by the rutting season, became more active, abandoned some of their usual caution, and were more easily approached and killed. Migrations of waterfowl into the southern coastal plain and the southerly movements of passenger pigeons meant that more birds were in the area than at any other time. With wildlife on the move, most of the able-bodied men, women, children, and adolescents moved to set up temporary lodging in their hunting grounds.[47]

Like their use of weirs to trap spawning fish, Indian hunting techniques took advantage of changes in animal behavior. Using a bow made of hickory or southern witch hazel and arrows tipped with stone, turkey claws, or deer antlers, a single Indian hunting alone often disguised himself in a deerskin and crept through the woods imitating the habits of his prey. When a whitetail

---

45. Smith, "Map of Virginia," in Barbour, *Complete Works of Smith*, vol. 1, 162; Carville V. Earle, "Environment, Disease, and Mortality in Early Virginia," in Thad W. Tate and David L. Ammerman, eds., *The Chesapeake in the Seventeenth Century: Essays on Anglo-American Society* (Chapel Hill: University of North Carolina Press for the Institute of Early American History and Culture, 1979), 106–7; Adair, *North-American Indians*, 438.

46. For archaeological evidence concerning the seasonal exploitation of game, see Bruce D. Smith, "Middle Mississippian Exploitation of Animal Populations: A Predictive Model," *American Antiquity* 39 (1974), 274–91. See also Hudson, *Southeastern Indians*, 272; and White, *Roots of Dependency*, 26–7.

47. Roger A. Caras, *North-American Mammals: Fur-Bearing Animals of the United States and Canada* (New York: Gallahad Books, 1967), 57, 437–8; Hudson, *Southeastern Indians*, 274–5.

allowed him to get close enough, the hunter shot the animal and tracked it through the forest using bloodstained foliage as a trail. This "deer decoy" method proved especially effective against rutting bucks that sometimes charged the hunters looking to lock horns in a fight.[48]

For taking several deer or other game animals at one time, however, Indians employed a technique known as fire hunting. John Smith's description suggests just how efficient the tactic could be. "Having found the Deare," Smith explained, "they environ them with many fires and betwixt the fires they placed themselves . . . The Deare being thus feared [frightened], by the fires and their voices, they chace them so long within that circle, that many times they kill 6, 8, 10, or 15 at a hunting." Where topography permitted, Indians used fire to drive game onto a narrow peninsula or into a river where, as Smith noted, "with their boats they have Ambuscadoes to kill them."[49]

The exact impact of such intensive hunting is difficult to measure. Venison was the meat Indians consumed most frequently, yet the vast numbers of deer seen by explorers and early colonists would seem to indicate that native depredations had little effect on the herds. Moreover, modern wildlife researchers know that, if allowed to reproduce unchecked, deer can overpopulate, overbrowse their habitat, and become susceptible to famine and disease.[50] But, as Lawson's tales of howling beasts demonstrate, deer did have other natural enemies, including wolves, bobcats, and panthers. Those predators often took young, aged, or diseased animals, thereby providing a natural check on the herds. Indian hunters were less selective in the types of animals they killed. Ralph Hamor, a Virginia colonist, believed that God must have provided some natural grass or herb that allowed the deer to increase. Without such divine intervention, Hamor believed "the Naturalls [Indians] would assuredly starve: for the Deare (they kill as doe wee Beefes in England) all the year long, neither sparing yong nor olde, no not the Does readie to fawn, nor the yong fawnes, if but two daies old."[51]

Hamor's argument for providence notwithstanding, the survival of both deer and Indians probably can be attributed to other factors. Although Indians did take some deer year round, they acquired most of their venison in late fall and

48. Hudson, *Southeastern Indians*, 275–6.
49. Quotation from Smith, "Map of Virginia," in Barbour, *Complete Works of Smith*, vol. 1, 164. Hudson, *Southeastern Indians*, 276.
50. Leonard Lee Rue III, *The Deer of North America* (New York: Crown, 1978), 330–40; Hudson, *Southeastern Indians*, 275.
51. Quotation from Ralph Hamor, *A True Discourse of the Present Estate of Virginia, and the successe of the affaires there till the 18 of June 1614* (London, 1615), 20. Paul Errington, *Of Predation and Life* (Ames: Iowa State University Press, 1967), 223–4; Frank B. Barrick, "Deer Predation in North Carolina and Other Southeastern States," in *White-Tailed Deer in the Southern Forest Habitat: Proceedings of a Symposium at Nacagdoches. Texas, March 25–26, 1969* (Nacagdoches, Tex.: Southern Forest Experiment Station, 1969), 28–9.

winter. By then a new generation of fawns had already been born and the young deer were rapidly growing strong enough to survive on their own if their mothers should fall to an Indian arrow. Deer might also have benefited from other facets of Indian subsistence. Forest succession on abandoned Indian farmland provided areas where whitetails could browse new growth and still escape into the woods to avoid both natives and four-footed enemies. Moreover, Indians hunting deer were limited in the territory they could cover. Stalking whitetails on land hunted by other natives could easily provoke a war.[52]

But this complementary relationship does not mean that Indians made a conscious effort to maintain the deer or that the natives never pressured the herds. Many of the first Europeans to explore the South Atlantic coast reported that the largest herds resided far up the rivers, away from the Indian villages of the coastal plain. Such comments could reflect the animals' natural preference for oak and hickory forests farther inland, but they might also indicate local shortages of venison. In areas where topography made it difficult for deer to escape native hunters, the effects might have been more dramatic. Noting that Indians along Chesapeake Bay used that region's peninsulas and necks of land as natural corrals for game, John Smith observed that "little commeth there which they [the Indians] devoure not."[53]

Smith extended his analysis of Indian hunting to include "Hares, partridges, Turkies or Egges, fat or leane, young or old" of which the natives "devoure all they can catch in their power." However, these and other animals probably suffered less than deer. Black bears have a low reproductive rate and might have decreased had Indians hunted them as staple food. But although they enjoyed the taste of bear's flesh, the natives valued the animals primarily for fat from which Indians produced oil for cooking and grease to repel bothersome summer insects. Taken in winter, a single fat bear could produce a great quantity of oil, making it unnecessary to kill more than a few. Besides, bear hunting could be dangerous. As the giant beasts retired to hollow trees for their brief winter naps, the natives sometimes set the dens on fire, smoking out the sleepy animals and shooting at them as they fled. Once wounded, a bear became a vicious adversary

52. White, *Roots of Dependency*, 9–10, 27; John Philip Reid, *A Law of Blood: The Primitive Law of the Cherokee Nation* (New York: New York University Press, 1970), 134–5. Reid recounts an incident during which Catawbas and Cherokees quarreled over hunting territories. This specific incident took place after European contact, but still suggests that Indians ranging too far in search of game could provoke war.

53. Quotation from Smith, "Map of Virginia," in Barbour, *Complete Works of Smith*, vol. 1, 164. For accounts of larger deer herds to the west, see Strachey, *Historie of Travell*, 124; and Harriot, "Briefe and True Report," in Quinn, *Roanoke Voyages*, vol. 1, 355.

and, to avoid being mauled, native hunters sometimes had to scramble up slender saplings too small for the animals to climb.[54]

Like bears, passenger pigeons provided an important source of oil and grease. Roosting in the lower limbs of trees, the birds became easy prey for Indians who invaded the roosts at night with torches fashioned from split pine limbs. The bright lights blinded the pigeons and native hunters knocked them from their perches with long poles, a technique that allowed them to "bring away some thousands" of the birds. Like fish-poisoning expeditions, roost raids were occasional outings that could take place only during fall migrations and only when the birds chose to roost nearby. In addition, the natives preferred to kill squabs, which produced the best meat and most oil. Large numbers of pigeons could escape and breed again, assuring the survival of the species.[55]

Whenever they could, Indians killed and ate wild turkeys, but those prodigious birds preferred loftier roosts than passenger pigeons and could not be taken in quantity. Instead, the natives often had to stalk turkeys on foot, scatter the flocks, and hope that three or four would take refuge in a neighboring tree, where they could be shot down with bows and arrows. Migratory waterfowl probably required similar tactics and although they might be hunted well into winter, their populations suffered few ill effects. Likewise, rabbits, squirrels, and other small game depended on their high reproductive rates to ensure survival against Indian hunting, in much the same way as they endure the depredations of modern man and his sophisticated weapons.[56]

While Indian men pursued the various game animals, women maintained the temporary households and gathered nuts from the winter forest. Nuts had myriad uses in Indian kitchens. Hickory nuts might be pounded between two stones to produce a powdery nutritious meal that tasted "as well as any Almond." The meal could then be thrown into a pot of boiling water and the entire mixture strained to create an oily "hickory milk . . . as sweet and rich as fresh cream" that supplied a liquid base for corn cakes. Boiling live oak and other acorns helped extract natural oil from the nuts, which the natives used for cooking. Roasted over a fire, chestnuts and chinquapins became tasty complements to venison and other game. The Indians' fondness for nuts also created

54. Quotation from Smith, "Map of Virginia," in Barbour, *Complete Works of Smith*, vol. 1, 165. H. B. Battle, "The Domestic Use of Oil Among Southern Aborigines," *American Anthropologist* 24 (1922), 173; Adair, *North-American Indians*, 331; Hudson, *Southeastern Indians*, 279–80.
55. Quotation from Lawson, *New Voyage*, 50. Hudson, *Southeastern Indians*, 280; A. W. Schorger, *The Passenger Pigeon: Its Natural History and Extinction* (Madison: University of Wisconsin Press, 1955), 137–8.
56. Smith, "Predictive Model," 289; Hudson, *Southeastern Indians*, 280; A. W. Schorger, *The Wild Turkey: Its History and Domestication* (Norman: University of Oklahoma Press, 1966), 380–1.

subtle variations in the forest pattern. Nuts discarded or lost soon sprouted, and mast-bearing trees sometimes grew in profusion around the Indian villages. Thomas Harriot probably saw accidentally transplanted hickories, black walnuts, and chinquapins when he reported chestnuts in "great store" along the North Carolina coast.[57]

A number of other trees and plants common to South Atlantic forests also furnished useful products. In the western piedmont and mountains, Indians found it worthwhile to tap the silver and sugar maples that grew in the higher elevations. After collecting the sap in gourds, they boiled it to create a sugary syrup that could be used to sweeten a variety of dishes. Indians living farther west also had access to many leaves and roots that produced natural dyes. Both western and eastern natives especially valued a plant Europeans knew as "vermilion," the roots of which produced a red powder the natives mixed with bear grease to make body paint. They not only applied the mixture for decoration (when, as Lawson noted, "they intend to be fine"), but also used it on their hair to repel lice. Eastern natives who craved the root were more than willing to travel west for it. But in summer, marauding Iroquois, enemies of several southern tribes, made their way into the western forests. South Atlantic Indians in search of vermilion often found such expeditions costly in terms of lives and captives. The red root eventually became so valuable that some coastal plain Indians tried to transplant it near their villages, an experiment that failed when the plants did not adapt to the hotter, drier conditions.[58]

Most forest products were easier to come by. When the natives could not get witch hazel or hickory for their bows, they substituted mulberry or locust, both of which provided the necessary strength and flexibility. Some Indians also needed tough, pliable wood for their wigwams. The Algonquian peoples, who lived in the vicinity of Chesapeake Bay and in eastern North Carolina, usually selected long, narrow, saplings of hickory, pine, or cedar. They implanted the larger ends of the poles in the ground and tied the tops together with oak strips to form a circular or Quonset-shaped framework. The natives then covered the scaffolding with other readily available forest products, such as cane, reeds, or bark from white cedar, pine, or other suitable trees. In the South Carolina low country, Indians constructed houses of wattle and daub with roofs of thatched palmetto leaves. The Creeks probably erected similar shelters in their towns, but as one European observer noted in the 1730s, "When they camp during travelling or the hunt, they peel a pine tree and make a hut of bark or else of

57. Quotations from Lawson, *New Voyage*, 105; Bartram, *Travels*, 57; and Harriot, "Briefe and True Report," in Quinn, *Roanoke Voyages*, vol. 1, 350. Battle, "Use of Oil," 173–4; Hudson, *Southeastern Indians*, 301; Quinn, *Roanoke Voyages*, vol. 1, 351, n. 1.
58. Lawson, *New Voyage*, 174, 28.

skins and a few poles." Farther west in the mountains, the Cherokees built houses of white clay and cane.[59]

For their canoes, Indians preferred large pines or yellow poplars. They used fire both to fell the giant trees and to hollow out the canoes, producing dugouts thirty to forty feet long and two or more feet across. The boats could carry up to twenty passengers and although bulkier than the birch bark canoes used farther north, they were easily maneuvered and with proper handling could "be forced up a very strong current." Removing a few saplings or isolated larger trees to make houses or canoes left openings in the forest canopy, which allowed more light to reach the forest floor, but probably engendered no more change in vegetation patterns than similar gaps created by wind and ice storms. It was Indian demand for another seemingly abundant product that had the greatest impact on the appearance of the standing forest.[60]

Even in the more temperate South Atlantic forests, Indians needed much firewood. In the uplands, nighttime winter temperatures often dropped below freezing. Indeed, John Lawson (much like Europeans who observed New England Indians) found Carolina wigwams "as hot as Stoves" and believed anyone sleeping there would surely "sweat all night." In addition, Indians required wood for cooking, for preserving meat and nuts, and for boiling bark to tan animal skins. According to several European observers, natives with access to pine preferred that wood for all their fires. Because it burns so rapidly, pine is a much less efficient fuel than oak or hickory. John Brickell believed the natives liked pine because "the Smoak never offends the Eyes," a characteristic he attributed to the "Volatile parts of the Turpentine," which were naturally "friendly and Balsamic."[61]

Because they slept in such confined, smoky quarters, Indians frequently contracted conjunctivitis, and the medicinal pine vapors might indeed have soothed their eyes. (Europeans would later use turpentine and resin for a wide variety of medicinal purposes.) But the natives probably had other reasons for burning pine. With their light, brittle wood, pine limbs or smaller trees could

59. Quotation from Kristian Hvidt, ed., *Von Reck's Voyage: Drawings and Journal of Philip Georg Frederich von Reck* (Savannah: Beehive Press, 1980), 50. Lawson, *New Voyage*, 109, 180–2; Waddell, *Indians of the South Carolina Lowcountry*, 45; David C. Corkran, *The Cherokee Frontier: Conflict and Survival, 1740–1762* (Norman: University of Oklahoma Press, 1962), 4.

60. Quotation from Williams, *Timberlake's Memoirs*, 85. Arthur Barlowe, "Discourse of the First Voyage," in Quinn, *Roanoke Voyages*, vol. 1, 104–5.

61. Quotations from Lawson, *New Voyage*, 180; and Brickell, *Natural History*, 287. Virginia naturalist John Banister also observed Indians burning pine, noting that "tho it blacks the face, [it] offends not the eyes, & is used by Indians far & near." Joseph and Nesta Ewan, eds., *John Banister and His Natural History of Virginia, 1678–1692* (Urbana: University of Illinois Press, 1970), 372. For similar reactions to the heat inside Indian dwellings farther north, see Cronon, *Changes in the Land*, 48–9.

Figure 3.2. Indians burning trees for canoes. Engraving by Simon Gribelin, based on the work of English artist John White. From Robert Beverley, *The History and Present State of Virginia* (London, 1705), 62. Reproduced by courtesy of Colonial Williamsburg Foundation Library, Special Collections.

be blown down by even moderate winds or broken in winter by freezing rain. Under the right conditions, pine or mixed pine-hardwood forests could become quite littered with such debris, which Indian women could easily gather and carry to the villages. Because their lack of metal tools made it difficult for Indians to cut down large oaks and hickories and split them into usable cordwood, pine deadfalls must have been a primary source of fuel. Removing fallen wood created open forests in areas that otherwise would have appeared darker and more foreboding to early colonists. Commenting on what he regarded as the happy result of such wood-gathering in Virginia, John Smith wrote, "Neare their habitations is but little small wood, or old trees on the ground, by reason of their burning of them for fire. So that a man may gallop a horse amongst these woods any waie, but where the creekes or Rivers shall hinder."[62]

Across North America, Indians not only burned dead wood, they also set the living forest on fire. Off the Carolina coast in 1524, Verrazzano saw Indians intentionally burning the woods and smelled "the sweet fragrance [of the smoke] a hundred leagues away." While exploring Chesapeake Bay in 1607, George Percy spotted smoke in the woods and found that "the savages had been burning down the grass," a fire he thought might be a signal to other Indians "to bring their forces together and so give us battell." Near Chickahominy River, Smith encountered "aboundance of fires all over the woods" and William Byrd reported that other Virginia Indians regularly fired the forest. By the mid eighteenth century, so many colonists had observed Indians kindling woods fires that William De Brahm's report on conditions in South Carolina listed "The Burning of the Grass and Underwoods in the Forests" as "an ancient Custom of the Indians."[63]

As much as it intrigued Europeans, the natives' use of fire has proved to be of even more interest to modern scholars. Writing in 1910, Hu Maxwell of the United Stages Forest Service described Virginia Indians as "wasteful and destructive savages," who were "by nature incendiary" and squandered the

62. Smith, "Map of Virginia," in Barbour, *Complete Works of Smith*, vol. 1, 162.
63. Wroth, *Voyages of Verrazzano*, 134; George Percy, "Observations Gathered Out of a Discourse of the Plantation of the Southerne Colonie in Virginia," in Edward Arber, ed., *Travels and Works of Captain John Smith*, 2 vols. (Edinburg: John Grant, 1910), vol. 1, lxii; John Smith, "A True Relation of Such Occurrences and Accidents of Noate as Hath Hapned in Virginia . . . ," in Barbour, *Complete Works of Smith*, vol.1, 49; Byrd, *Dividing Line*, 223; John Gerar William De Brahm, *Report of the General Survey in the Southern District of North America*, ed. Louis De Vorsey, Jr. (Columbia: University of South Carolina Press, 1971), 80. Among the many secondary works that describe Indian burning are: Stephen J. Pyne, *Fire in America: A Cultural History of Wildland and Rural Fire* (Princeton, N.J.: Princeton University Press, 1982), 66–122; White, *Roots of Dependency*, 10–11; and Cronon, *Changes in the Land*, 49–51.

region's resources like pirates plundering a treasure ship. More recently, scholars have looked for and emphasized other effects of Indian fires. They argue that the natives kindled light ground fires that, although they altered the forests, ultimately proved beneficial to both Indians and the woodlands. Both views oversimplify a number of complex ecological and historical problems. Few forces in nature are as unpredictable as fire. In any given area, its effects depend on a wide range of geographical and environmental factors, important considerations in a topographically and climatically diverse region.[64]

One important variable governing the effects of woodland fire is the amount of heat generated by the blaze. Heat depends on the fire's intensity, and intensity on the fuel supply. The initial fuel for such fires is usually ground litter made up of twigs, leaves, broken limbs, and bark that accumulate on the forest floor. The amount of litter varies according to forest type. In pinelands, where the trees depend on fire, litter accumulates rapidly; in oak woods, where trees are less prone to break from wind or ice, it piles up slowly. Seasonal change also affects litter accumulation. In deciduous forests, leaf fall greatly increases the amount of potential fuel, making autumn and early winter a time of intense fires. The volume of available fuel can be further affected by the time elapsed since the last burn. One fire can consume much of the forest litter, and woods fired every year are less susceptible to an intense fire than those burned sporadically and at long intervals.[65]

The varying amounts of fuel in South Atlantic forests helped determine when and how often Indians could burn. Those who inhabited inland oak woods probably fired the forest annually and did their burning in early winter when enough dry leaves and twigs had collected to facilitate a fire. In the drier, mixed hardwood and pine-hardwood forests of the coastal plain, Indians could burn at other seasons and might have fired the woods twice a year: in fall and again in spring, as an extension of agricultural clearing. Such frequent fires kept litter accumulation to a minimum so that seasonal blazes burned slowly and at ground level. In this respect, they did resemble lightning fires, but without the additional moisture common to thunderstorms, Indian-set blazes could burn longer and cover a larger area. However, the natives rarely allowed that to happen. Along the South Atlantic, as over most of North America, intentional burning remained largely a local practice, limited to forests around the villages

64. Hu Maxwell, "The Use and Abuse of the Forests by the Virginia Indians," *William and Mary Quarterly College Magazine*, 2d ser. 19 (October 1910), 73–103; Gordon M. Day, "The Indian as an Ecological Factor in the Northeastern Forest," *Ecology* 34 (1953), 329–46; Calvin Martin, "Fire and Forest Structure in the Aboriginal Eastern Forests," *The Indian Historian*, 6 (1973), 38–42; Pyne, *Fire in America*, 20–33, 78, 84–99; Vankat, *Natural Vegetation*, 45–56.
65. Pyne, *Fire in America*, 35, 145–6.

and nearby woods. Large sections of woodlands remained untouched by the fires.[66]

In the burned areas, older standing trees suffered only slight damage. As De Brahm felt compelled to point out, "Persons who are not acquainted with the Nature of burning the Woods in America . . . might suppose that the trees are liable to be set a burning." If that were the case, De Brahm continued, "all the Trees in America would have been burnt down, before any European came there." The trees survived because Indian-set fires rarely burned hot enough to do them any harm. The thick bark on the larger pines kept them well protected and the lack of fuel prevented the fires from igniting the mature oaks and hickories. As De Brahm noted, "a full grown Tree never catches Fire, unless at the Bottom, with no more effect than to have his Bark a little sindged."[67]

Along with accumulated litter, the real victims of such fires were small saplings, grasses, and plants that grew on the forest floor. Consequently, seasonal burning established open woodlands and widely spaced trees around the Indian villages, a phenomenon that helps account for some of the parklike pine and oak forests noted by colonists. Other ecological effects were less obvious. As Indians discovered when they burned their old fields, a light fire on relatively level land can deposit a layer of nitrogen-rich ash. In the coastal plain, periodic burns probably increased soil fertility. But in other regions, soil may have suffered. In rocky, upland areas, such as the upper piedmont and mountains, seasonal burning may cut into the accumulated humus, thereby destroying some of the minerals available to trees. Repeated burning of sloping terrain can also increase erosion. The remaining large trees help break up and scatter moisture, but without forest litter to absorb and hold them, winter rains can remove a portion of the topsoil, making it difficult for plants and trees to regenerate.[68]

Where fire enriched the soil, undergrowth came back quickly. Bluestem and other native grasses soon grew under the tall trees to be followed by various shrubs and newly sprouting hardwood trees. Such new growth often attracted

66. It is difficult to determine exactly when and how often Indians burned the southern woods. As the cited accounts indicate, explorers spotted fires all over and at different times of year. However, settlers who learned woods burning from the Indians practiced it annually, perhaps indicating that yearly fires were the rule among the natives. For an example, see Byrd, *Dividing Line*, 228. On the role of available fuel in determining the frequency of Indian fires, see Emily W. B. Russell, "Indian-set Fires in the Forests of the Northeastern United States," *Ecology* 64 (1983), 80–3. On burning as a local phenomenon, see Day, "Indian as an Ecological Factor," 342. As Russell notes ("Indian-set Fires," 85), the many oak forests discovered by colonists along the Atlantic coast also indicate that Indians did not burn vast territories.

67. De Brahm, *General Survey*, 80, 81. De Brahm's account describes both Indian fires and those set by settlers.

68. Spurr and Barnes, *Forest Ecology*, 239–40; Cronon, *Changes in the Land*, 50; Hall, "Soil Erosion and Agriculture," 28.

birds and browsing game animals, a trend De Brahm recognized when he noted that Indians burned "in order to allure the Deers upon the new grass."[69] Under the right conditions, predators such as wolves and foxes might move in to feed on the herbivores, speeding up the energy flow and increasing the entire animal population. But like the edge habitats created by Indian agriculture, such forage grounds appeared at random and were inefficiently maintained. Although whitetail deer graze bluestem and other grasses, they favor woody plants, shrubs, and sprouting hardwoods. Periodic burning of bottomland and hardwood forests can help promote such growth. But in pine forests, regular burning of the woods helps eliminate competing hardwoods that otherwise offer suitable browsing. Indeed, periodic fires create a grassy habitat more suited to quail and other upland birds than to the larger game animals. In those areas, deer may have responded to the grass, but they probably sought their favorite foods elsewhere.[70]

Regular burning created other difficulties for Indians. Firing oak woods in late fall or early winter eliminated some of the mast available to both Indians and the animals they hunted at that season. Moreover, in consuming the forest litter, ground fires also destroyed a great deal of potential firewood and could have contributed to local shortages of that precious resource. Other useful products, such as saplings and bark for wigwams, pine needles and reeds for weaving baskets, and materials for bows, arrows, and axes might also have been in short supply in areas frequently burned.[71]

If seasonal burning created as many problems as it solved, why did Indians continue the practice? The answers lie not in the intricacies of fire ecology, but in the more practical and larger context of native subsistence patterns. As people of the forest, Indians enjoyed its bounty, but also had to put up with its pests. A host of insects plagued them at various seasons, including ticks, chiggers, lice, biting flies and mosquitoes, spiders, and most commonly, fleas. Stopping at an Indian dwelling along Santee River, Lawson found it teeming with "Millions of Fleas," adding that most native wigwams were usually "fuller of such Vermin, than any Dog-Kennel." Fleas were also abundant around places where Indians dressed deerskins because the tiny insects could hide in

---

69. Quotation from De Brahm, *General Survey*, 80; Cronon (*Changes in the Land*, 49–51) notes similar observations in New England.
70. Paul A. Schrauder and Howard Miller, "The Effects of Seasonal Burning on Deerfood and Cover," in *White-tailed Deer in the Southern Forest Habitat*, 83; White, *Roots of Dependency*, 10–11; D. R. Klein, "Food Selection by North American Deer and Their Response to the Over-utilization of Preferred Plant Species," in *Animal Populations in Relation to their Forest Resources, British Ecological Symposium* 10 (Oxford: Blackwell Scientific Publications, 1970), 25–46; E. V. Komarek, "Effects of Fire on Temperate Forests and Related Ecosystems," in Kozlowski, *Fire and Ecosystems*, 268–9.
71. Russell, "Indian-set Fires," 85–6.

the thick deerhair. Southern farmers still burn fallow fields and woodlands near their homes to keep down such flea infestations, and Indians found it equally effective. Commenting on these and other benefits, De Brahm wrote: "The fire of the burning old Grass, Leaves, and Underwoods consumes a Number of Serpents, Lizards, Scorpions, Spiders and their Eggs, as also Bucks [bugs], Ticks, Petiles [reptiles], and Muskitoes, with other Vermins, and Insects in General very offensive, and some very poisonous, whose Increase would, without this Expedient, cover the Land, and make America disinhabitable."[72]

Thick, overgrown forests not only harbored fleas and ticks, they might also shelter marauding Iroquois or local enemies. Open woodlands near the villages provided an effective security zone where intruders or their tracks might be easily identified. Forests choked with undergrowth also stood in the way of Indian travels. The natives needed quick access to their hunting and fishing grounds as well as an easy route over which to transport seeds and produce to and from outlying fields. John Smith realized the important role open woods played in Indian travel when he captured a Manahoac Indian in the Virginia piedmont and asked him what lay beyond the mountains. The Indian replied simply, "the Sunne," telling Smith that he knew nothing else "because the woods were not burnt." Adding an explanatory note, Smith told his readers, "They cannot travell but where the woods are burnt."[73]

If fire aided woodland travel, such journeys also facilitated the spread of fire. During their extended trips away from the villages, Indians occasionally set those woods on fire, either by accident or on purpose. George Percy identified one potential source of accidental fire while exploring coastal Virginia when he discovered "a place where they [the natives] had made a great fire, and had been newly rosting oysters." Upon seeing the Englishmen, the Indians fled, leaving both the fire and shellfish still burning. Although that fire apparently never got out of hand, similar abandoned camps could present a serious fire hazard. William Byrd reported that Iroquois war parties, venturing south to attack their enemies, often left their campfires burning, which "soon put the adjacent Woods into a flame." Considering the extent of Indian travels, that scene must have been repeated many times in South Atlantic forests, especially because Indians hunted in the oak woods in fall, when they were dry and most susceptible to a spark.[74]

72. Quotations from Lawson, *New Voyage*, 30; and De Brahm, *General Survey*, 81. Cronon, *Changes in the Land*, 51; Hilliard Henson, "Why Incendiary Fires in the Southern Appalachians?" *American Forests* 48 (1942), 419; H. L. Stoddard, Sr., "The Use of Fire in Pine Forests of the Deep Southeast," *Proceedings of the Tall Timbers Fire Ecology Conference* 1 (1962), 31–42; Pyne, *Fire in America*, 145–52.

73. Quotation from Barbour, *Complete Works of Smith*, vol. 2, 176. De Brahm, *General Survey*, 81; Cronon, *Changes in the Land*, 50.

74. Percy, "Observations," in Arber, *Travels and Works*, vol. 1, lxii; Byrd, *Dividing Line*, 218.

The hunt itself might be another source of an accidental blaze. The circular fires used to hunt deer sometimes kindled the surrounding forests. At times such fires could be a welcome sight to tired and hungry Englishmen. Once, while low on provisions, Lawson's party found "the Woods newly burnt, and on fire in many places," a sign that gave them "great Hopes that Indians were not far off." The next day the expedition came upon a group of Santee hunters who relieved their plight with barbecued turkeys, bear's oil, and venison.[75]

Fires accidentally set by Indians while hunting or traveling varied in intensity, but most were more destructive than the controlled seasonal ground fires. In areas not frequently burned, litter and brush piled up on the forest floor, providing enough fuel for a devastating wildfire that might blacken vast expanses of forest and kill or displace wildlife. While surveying the dividing line, Byrd came upon a patch of ground so desolate that he "could not see a Tree of any Bigness standing within our Prospect." Byrd noted that the destruction could have been due to caterpillars, but thought fire a more likely cause, adding that, "The Woods are not there burnt every year, as they generally are amongst the Inhabitants. But the Dead Leaves and Trash of many years are heapt up together, which being at length kindled by the Indians that happen to pass that way, furnish fewel for a conflagration that carries all before it."[76]

Whether accidental or intentional, fires set by Indians enhanced the hodgepodge quality of the various forests. In some instances, Indian burning might have helped maintain pinelands, savannas, and canebrakes and may have briefly increased wildlife populations. At other times, in other areas, it might rob the soil of minerals, increase erosion, or destroy available animal forage and cover. Occasionally, Indians were responsible for destructive wildfires like those feared by modern foresters. Like humans throughout history, Indians became important "fire agent[s]" in South Atlantic forests, augmenting the comparatively low number of blazes kindled by lightning and increasing the odds for both beneficial and destructive woods fires.[77]

This view of Indians as somewhat haphazard burners is also consistent with their overall patterns of subsistence and use of the forests. When they had food, Indians consumed it quickly, sometimes gorging themselves with five or six meals in one day. As Hugh Jones, an early eighteenth-century mathematics professor at the College of William and Mary noted, "They have no notion of providing for futurity; for they eat night and day while their provision lasts, falling to as soon as they awake, and falling asleep again as soon as they are well

75. Lawson, *New Voyage*, 31.
76. Byrd, *Dividing Line*, 228.
77. E. V. Komarek, "Effects of Fire," 253; Spurr and Barnes, *Forest Ecology*, 487–8; Roy Komarek, "Comments on Fire and the Natural Landscape," *Proceedings of the Tall Timbers Fire Ecology Conference* 13 (1973), 3; Pyne, *Fire in America*, 66–70.

crammed." Indians were equally cavalier about food shortages. During their summer migrations, when they depended largely upon berries and other wild produce, they sometimes went for days without food. Late winter, too, could bring periods of sporadic hunger as game animals moved out of the oak forests and supplies of corn began to dwindle. In keeping with their stoic nature, the natives accepted such lean times as inevitable and rode them out without complaint. Their seemingly imprudent eating habits and willingness to go hungry in a land of apparent plenty never ceased to amaze Europeans. John Smith spoke for many Englishmen when he remarked about the "strange" manner in which the Indians' "bodies alter[ed] with their diet." Like "deare and wilde beastes they seem[ed] fat and leane, strong and weak."[78]

Just as they failed to understand the complementary nature of sex roles in Indian society, Europeans saw few advantages in a way of life that seemed to squander so many resources. In part, they were blinded by their inability to recognize the shortcomings of their own subsistence patterns. In Europe, farmers enclosed small, private plots and produced all they could, hoping to market the surplus. They relied on domestic animals, such as cattle, hogs, and sheep for their meat, thereby eliminating the need to hunt. Yet, like Indians, colonists sometimes suffered periodic shortages of food and other necessities. Droughts, floods, insects, birds, disease, or a host of other natural disasters could quickly destroy enclosed crops and livestock. Warfare or political turmoil might sever international commercial ties and cut off needed raw materials. Indians usually avoided such problems. If floods or drought destroyed their crops, they turned to fish, venison, nuts, or hundreds of other wild foods so that temporary shortages became less threatening and could be accepted as a matter of course. Within seasonal limits, the natives enjoyed as much or perhaps even more security than their English counterparts, a lesson the Jamestown colonists learned when they turned to the Indians for food to see them through the winter.[79]

To achieve that security, Indians depended on the forests. The South Atlantic landscape reflected that dependence in the form of open woodlands, weedy old fields, pines growing in pure stands on former agricultural sites, or occasionally blackened forests destroyed by wildfire. For several millennia before European contact, Indians took whatever the land offered. Sometimes they took it efficiently; on other occasions they reduced animal populations, depleted soil, and demolished plant life. In some cases, seasonal variation

78. Hugh Jones, *The Present State of Virginia* (1724), ed. Richard L. Morton (Chapel Hill: University of North Carolina Press, 1956), 55; Smith, "Map of Virginia," in Barbour, *Complete Works of Smith*, vol. 1, 162–3.

79. Calvin Martin, "Ethnohistory: A Better Way to Write Indian History," *Western Historical Quarterly* 9 (January 1978), 46–7; Cronon, *Changes in the Land*, 51–2; White, *Roots of Dependency*, 29–32.

decided what they could take; at other times, their technology helped dictate how the land would be used. Even the very nature of the security they sought determined the ways in which they utilized the land. Always confident that they could obtain whatever they required in sufficient quantities, the natives saw no need to overuse a single resource or to take more than enough to meet their immediate needs. Scholars now know that it is misleading to classify Indians as either despoilers or preservers of nature. "Conservation" and "waste" are modern concepts that Indians would not have understood. But, like all human beings, the natives did understand that they had to acquire enough food and other necessities to live from season to season. And within the context of their culture, belief system, and the forests they inhabited, Indians simply did what was necessary to ensure their survival.[80]

80. "Indians in the Land, A Conversation Between Richard White and William Cronon," 20–1.

4

Europeans going thither

In comparing Indian subsistence to that of animals, John Smith and other colonists gave vent to an idea that had long been part of the European conscience. Conquistadores used it to justify their depredations in Mexico and South America, claiming that cruel, barbaric, and bestial Indians deserved no less than total subjugation to the cultured and peaceful Spanish. Native resistance to the intended conquest only enhanced the image, and a number of translated Spanish treatises warned Europeans journeying to America that they could expect to confront unruly savages governed only by animal passions. English and French explorers who followed the conquistadores added their own embellishments. Those who read Verrazzano's accounts of Indians found out that the natives wore only animal skins, ran and maneuvered through the woods with great agility, and possessed "sharp cunning" – characteristics that did little to dispel the man–beast image initially created by the Spanish.[1]

At the same time, however, another vision of the Indian vied for a place in the European imagination. Not all reports from the New World suggested bestial inhabitants. Some explorers wrote of generous Indians, innocent and childlike in their dealings with Europeans. Other writers told of friendly natives who welcomed visitors and gladly shared provisions.[2] Occasionally, this more favorable view surfaced alongside derogatory comments. Even while warning of their cunning nature, Verrazzano had to admit that the natives showed "great delight at seeing us," explained "where we could most easily secure the boat," and "offered us some of their food."[3]

Although it seems to defy logic, this seemingly schizoid view of Indians and their subsistence patterns held special appeal for Elizabethan explorers. Most Englishmen initially envisioned neither widespread settlement nor large-scale agricultural production in America. Instead they planned on searching for gold and silver, discovering the Northwest Passage, and in the meantime, trading with Indians. To ensure its success, such a commercial venture not only required natives who were technologically and culturally inferior and therefore

---

1. Quotation from Lawrence C. Wroth, ed., *The Voyages of Giovanni da Verrazzano, 1524–1528* (New Haven, Conn.: Yale University Press, 1970), 134. Gary B. Nash, "The Image of the Indian in the Southern Colonial Mind," *William and Mary Quarterly*, 3d ser. 29 (1972), 199–201.
2. Nash, "Image," 210.
3. Wroth, *Voyages of Verrazzano*, 134.

in need of English goods, but also Indians intelligent enough to recognize the advantages of such commodities and amicable enough to swap their resources for items offered by European traders.[4]

Their first contact with the natives on Roanoke Island in 1584 seemed to confirm both the validity of the scheme and English beliefs about New World inhabitants. Within three days of arrival, Englishmen sighted Indians in dugout canoes coming to meet them. The visitors offered one of the natives a hat, shirt, and taste of wine, receiving in return a load of fish. After this initial contact, more Indians came to greet the Englishmen and a wide variety of goods began to change hands. Describing the casual manner in which the trade developed, Arthur Barlowe, a captain on the 1584 expedition, wrote, "A daye or two after this, we fell to trading with them, exchanging some things we had for Chammoys, Buffe, and Deere skinnes." Soon, Barlowe continued, "there came downe from all parts great store of people, bringing with them leather, corrall [shells], divers kindes of dies very excellent, and exchanged with us."[5]

To Barlowe and his companions it seemed as if the natives paid outrageous prices for English goods. The natives offered twenty deerskins for a single metal dish, fifty hides for one copper kettle, and "very good exchange" for hatchets and knives.[6] Indian traders, however, thought the rate of barter more than fair. Animal skins were common items, readily procured in the nearby forests, whereas knives, hatchets, and utensils were looked upon as exotic luxury goods. Moreover, coastal Carolina natives probably already knew something of the value of such items thanks to two European ships that had foundered off the treacherous Outer Banks some twenty-five years earlier. The first vessel, probably Spanish, seems to have gone down in 1558. After nursing the survivors back to health, Indians helped the Europeans construct two dugout canoes in which they might journey south to New Spain. But the tiny vessels proved no match for the tricky tides and currents, and the natives eventually found the empty boats washed ashore on a nearby island. Early contact with Spanish sailors must have introduced the natives to European technology, for when part of a second vessel turned up on the beach six or seven years later, they pulled out the nails and spikes and fashioned them into crude metal instruments.[7]

Even without these fortuitous encounters, Englishmen would have found the natives eager to obtain metal goods. As the explorers soon realized, Indians did not necessarily have to understand the function of European products in

4. Nash, "Image," 205.
5. "Arthur Barlowe's Discourse of the First Voyage," in David B. Quinn, ed., *The Roanoke Voyages*, 2 vols. (London: Hakluyt Society, 1955), vol. 1, 100, 103, 98. Nash, "Image," 207.
6. "Barlowe's Discourse," in Quinn, *Roanoke Voyages*, vol. 1, 101.
7. James Axtell, *The European and the Indian: Essays in the Ethnohistory of Colonial North America* (New York: Oxford University Press, 1981), 253; "Barlowe's Discourse," in Quinn, *Roanoke Voyages*, vol. 1, 111 n. 4, 104 n. 3.

order to want them. Instead, the natives often employed such goods within the context of their own culture, frequently assigning them a new value or significance. Barlowe reported that one of the local werowances immediately took a fancy to a "bright tinne dishe," but instead of eating from it, the chieftain "clapt it before his breast, & after[wards] made a hole in the brimme thereof, & hung it about his necke, making signes, that it would defende him against his enemies arrowes."[8]

Indians had other reasons for greeting Englishmen enthusiastically. Long before Elizabethan adventurers arrived at Roanoke or Spanish ships sank offshore, the natives had swapped goods with their western neighbors. The inland tribes offered products from the oak and hickory forests, including flint, a harder species of cane, turkey and grouse feathers, animal skins, and the treasured red roots. In exchange, they received salt, dried fish, deerskins, shells, and medicinal plants from the coastal woods. Such trade probably developed as a sideline to Indian travels. Natives passing through friendly villages were usually greeted with hospitality and treated to tobacco, food, and other refreshment. In return, the traveler might offer his host shells, red roots, or other items as a gesture of friendship. Those Indians who presented the English adventurers with fish and skins did so out of a long tradition of gift giving and intended them as tokens of their desire for peaceful relations with their visitors.[9]

Having encountered a people already well versed in the rudiments of trade and having received such a warm welcome, Englishmen waxed eloquent about the prospects for long-term commerce with the natives. In his 1588 treatise, Thomas Harriot confidently wrote that although "In respect of us they [the Indians] are a people poore," they seemed "very ingenious" and showed "excellencie of wit" in the use of English goods. Furthermore, Harriot predicted, "they upon due consideration shall finde our manners of knowledges and craftes to exceed theirs" and continue to "desire our friendships & love." Although the Indians apparently possessed little precious metal, English traders could look forward to a profitable haul of furs from otters, minks, beavers, and muskrats. In addition, deerskins could be acquired "from the naturall inhabitants, thousands yeerely by way of trafficke for trifles." Adding a final and distinctly ecological note, Harriot reported that so many whitetails roamed the coastal forests that even an extensive trade would result in "no more wast or spoyle of Deare then is and hath beene ordinarily in time before."[10]

8. Quotation from "Barlowe's Discourse," in Quinn, Roanoke Voyages, vol. 1, 100–1. Axtell, European and Indian, 254–6.
9. Charles M. Hudson, The Southeastern Indians (Knoxville: University of Tennessee Press, 1976), 316; Axtell, European and Indian, 258.
10. Thomas Harriot, "A Briefe and True Report of the Newfound Land of Virginia," in Quinn, Roanoke Voyages, vol. 1, 371, 372, 330–1; Nash, "Image," 208.

Harriot wrote his "Briefe and True report" in an effort to discourage adverse rumors about the Roanoke expeditions and to encourage Englishmen to go to the New World, intentions that help account for the tract's upbeat tone. But for all his optimism, Harriot had to admit that even the casual exchange of goods had caused Indian-English relations to deteriorate. As he explained in concluding his treatise, "some of our companie towardes the ende of the yeare, shewed themselves too fierce in slaying some of the people, in some towns, upon causes that on our part, might easily enough have bene borne with all." In spite of the Indians' good will, Englishmen seemed destined to find the bestial savages about whom they had heard and read so much.[11]

Indians, however, probably cared less about the sporadic violence than about the immediate ecological consequences of commerce. Along the Carolina coast, Harriot and the other Roanoke adventurers witnessed one of the earliest and most significant changes in the natural environment of the South Atlantic colonies: the introduction of disease-causing microbes from Europe. At Roanoke, as in other parts of the Americas, the new microorganisms quickly invaded Indian bodies, which lacked the capacity to repel them. The natives' susceptibility resulted primarily from their long isolation from such diseases. For several millennia Indians had lived in a land free of Old World pathogens. Consequently, the natives had never developed the antibodies that might have helped ward off infection. Contact with explorers and colonists who carried the organisms set off devastating epidemics that swept through Indian villages like fire in a dry forest.[12] Describing the devastation in coastal Carolina, Harriot wrote, "within a few dayes after our departure from every such towne, the people began to die very fast, and many in short space; in some townes about twentie, in some fourtie, in some sixtie, & in one six score, which in trueth was very manie in respect of their numbers." Harriot went on to note that "The disease also was so strange, that they neither knew what it was," and even the "oldest men in the country" could not remember a similar episode.[13]

Had the Roanoke explorers talked with natives who lived farther inland, the Englishmen might possibly have found Indians who did remember such trying times. Almost a half century earlier, Spanish explorers had carried infectious

11. Harriot, "Briefe and True Report," in Quinn, *Roanoke Voyages*, vol. 1, 381; Nash, "Image," 208.

12. Alfred W. Crosby, "Virgin Soil Epidemics as a Factor in the Aboriginal Depopulation of America," *William and Mary Quarterly*, 3d ser. 33 (1976), 284–93. Historians have long been aware that Indian isolation from Old World diseases made the natives highly susceptible to European pathogens. But scholars are now realizing the many ways in which both isolation and culture affected native resistance or the lack thereof. See, for example, Calvin Martin, "The Immunological Status of the American Indian in 1492 and Thereafter: Abstract," in Kendall E. Bailes, ed., *Environmental History: Critical Issues in Comparative Perspective* (Lanham, Md.: University Press of America, 1985), 586.

13. Harriot, "Briefe and True Report," in Quinn, *Roanoke Voyages*, vol. 1, 378.

diseases to the interior, leaving empty villages and a few grieving survivors in their wake. Exploring the Indian chiefdom of Cofitachequi in 1540, Hernando de Soto and his band of explorers found that two years earlier an epidemic had left several large towns virtually devoid of people.[14] In one deserted village where the disease had been particularly severe, the expedition found only "four large houses ... filled with the bodies of people who had died of the pestilence." During their stay in the country, de Soto's party also found items of Spanish manufacture stored in Indian graves. The Spanish believed the goods might have come from Lucas Vásquez de Ayllon's ill-fated 1526 expedition, an indication that in the interior, as on the coast, alien goods and alien microbes arrived simultaneously. It was a deadly scenario that would be acted out again and again as colonists gained a foothold along the coast.[15]

For the moment, however, the fate of the "lost" Roanoke colony signaled a twenty-year commercial hiatus between English settlers and South Atlantic Indians. Even after the founding of Jamestown, extensive trade was still slow to develop. The first settlers in Virginia swapped goods with local natives and ships carrying trade goods regularly sailed the rivers of Chesapeake Bay, seeking animal skins from Indians who lived along the estuaries. But with the early success of tobacco agriculture, the Indian trade Harriot had found so promising seemed to lose much of its economic appeal. Worsening relations between Virginia natives and English settlers compounded the problem, prompting the colony to outlaw trade with the natives in 1631. At the same time, officials moved to prohibit the export of deerskins, either hoping to focus colonists' energies on agriculture or perhaps to encourage development of a local tanning industry.[16]

Still, some surreptitious traders successfully circumvented such restrictions, acquiring not only animal skins, but also meat for their families and servants. Other Virginians were even more ambitious, casting an acquisitive eye toward the west and south where both Indians and fur-bearing animals abounded. Beginning in 1644, after Indian attacks on outlying settlements, the Virginia government established forts along major rivers near the fall line. When it proved too costly to keep soldiers stationed there, officials leased the posts to individual colonists who were to staff the forts in return for land and goods

14. A Fidalgo of Elvas, "True Relation of the Vicissitudes that Attended the Governor Don Hernando De Soto," in Edward Gaylord Bourne, ed., *Narratives of the Career of Hernando De Soto*, 2 vols. (New York: Barnes, 1904), vol. 1, 66.

15. Quotation from Garsilasco de la Vega, *The Florida of the Inca*, trans. John Grier Varner and Jeanette Johnson Varner (Austin: University of Texas Press, 1951), 325. George R. Milner, "Epidemic Disease in the Postcontact Southeast: A Reappraisal," *Mid-Continental Journals of Anthropology* 5 (1980), 43–4.

16. W. Neil Franklin, "Virginia and the Cherokee Indian Trade," *East Tennessee Historical Society's Publications* 4 (January 1932), 3; Paul Chrisler Phillips, *The Fur Trade*, 2 vols. (Norman: University of Oklahoma Press, 1961), vol. 1, 165–7.

from the interior. Chief among those selected as caretakers were such prominent planters as Abraham Wood, Edward Bland, William Byrd I, and Cadwallader Jones.[17]

Under the care of such wealthy benefactors, the fall-line forts soon became headquarters for the Indian trade and for exploring the west. During the next quarter century, explorers such as John Lederer, Thomas Batts, Robert Fallam, and James Needham charted the interior, establishing commercial contacts with the Indians they encountered. Thanks to such efforts, Wood, Bland, the elder Byrd, and Jones became successful frontier merchants. They not only acquired pelts from natives who visited their outposts, but also commissioned others to act on their behalf, providing trade goods on credit in exchange for skins to be delivered later. In 1659 the English government lifted the previous restrictions on commerce with the natives, and it was largely through the Indian trade that the Virginia colony expanded its frontiers.[18]

Among the Indians Virginia planter-merchants sought to contact were the Tuscaroras of eastern North Carolina. From the time of the initial expedition to Roanoke Island, the Tuscaroras had been trying to extend their influence over the Algonquian groups who lived in the coastal plain. The Powhatans aided those Indians and for a time apparently kept the Tuscaroras out of the Virginia fur trade. After 1644, when the English defeated and subjugated the Powhatans, the coastal Carolina tribes lost their allies and the Tuscaroras expanded into the outer coastal plain. With more hunting territory available, the Tuscaroras soon became important participants in the Virginia trade. By the late seventeenth century, the Tuscaroras were trading European goods to Indians as far away as the Mississippi Valley and the Great Lakes. They were also supplying the James River traders whith pelts and deerskins.[19]

One of those who dealt with the Tuscaroras was William Byrd I. He and his son William Byrd II became two of the most successful merchants in Virginia. In part, the Byrds prospered because their plantations near the falls of the James River lay nearest the great trading path that stretched across North Carolina to the lands of the Catawbas and Cherokees. After the founding of South Carolina in 1670, however, Byrd and the other Virginians soon found themselves competing with equally ambitious planters and merchants who enjoyed an even more advantageous geographic position. Like their Virginian counterparts, Carolinians employed agents to take goods to the interior and bring back skins. But their packhorse route to the Indians of the piedmont and mountains proved shorter and easier, allowing the Carolina traders to "travel

17. Phillips, *Fur Trade*, vol. 1, 166–7.
18. Ibid., vol. 1, 167–74; Franklin, "Virginia and the Cherokee Trade," 5–8.
19. Thomas C. Parramore, "The Tuscarora Ascendancy," *North Carolina Historical Review* 59 (1982), 307–12.

and abide amongst the Indians for a long space of time; sometimes for a Year, two, or three."[20]

Their keen interest in the Indian trade led the planters and merchants of South Carolina to extend their contacts deep into the southern interior. Southwest of the coastal plain and piedmont lay bottomland forests and canebrakes, which seemed to promise unlimited supplies of game. The region was also home to some of the more populous Indian groups in southeastern North America, notably the Creeks, Chickasaws, and Choctaws. By the end of the seventeenth century, South Carolina traders had ranged as far as the Mississippi River. But Carolinians were not the only Europeans in that region. The Spanish mission system, which sought to convert Indians to Christianity and turn them into sedentary laborers, extended into south Georgia. The French established an outpost at Mobile on the Gulf Coast in 1701 and began trading with the Choctaws and other natives along the lower Mississippi. Over the next six decades, as the strength of the various European powers waxed and waned, a complex pattern of interaction between Spanish, French, English, and Indians would be the hallmark of this "southern frontier."[21]

English traders from Virginia and Carolina sought more than animal skins in the southern woods. Planters in both colonies also made use of Indian slaves. Although at first reluctant to acquire native labor, Virginians began to make more use of Indian slaves when tobacco took over as the colony's primary export crop. Indians captured in war or purchased from backcountry traders "worked for white masters throughout the colony, from the James to the Potomac and from the Eastern Shore to the fall line."[22]

Carolinians, too, engaged in the Indian slave trade. Like Virginians, South Carolina colonists at first used captives taken in war with the coastal Indians. But as demand for labor escalated, planter-merchants in the colony began to encourage Indians to fight each other and to swap captives from these intertribal battles for trade goods. With the outbreak of the War of the Spanish Succession in 1701, South Carolina encouraged her native allies to raid the

---

20. Quotation from John Lawson, *A New Voyage to Carolina*, ed. Hugh Talmadge Lefler (Chapel Hill: University of North Carolina Press, 1967), 190–2. Verner W. Crane, *The Southern Frontier. 1670–1732*, (Ann Arbor: University of Michigan Press, Ann Arbor Paperbacks, 1964), 110.

21. Crane, *Southern Frontier*, 38–46; David H. Corkran, *The Carolina Indian Frontier* (Columbia: University of South Carolina Press, 1970), 7–19; Daniel H. Usner, Jr., "The Deerskin Trade in French Louisiana," *Proceedings of the Tenth Meeting of the French Colonial Historical Society, April 12–14, 1984*, ed. Philip P. Boucher (Washington, D.C.: University Press of America, 1985), 76–81; Richard White, *The Roots of Dependency: Subsistence, Environment, and Social Change among the Choctaws, Pawnees, and Navajos* (Lincoln: University of Nebraska Press, 1983), 34–5.

22. J. Leitch Wright, Jr., *The Only Land They Knew: The Tragic Story of the American Indians in the Old South* (New York: Free Press, 1981), 132–5, quotation from 135.

Spanish mission Indians and those natives who traded with the French in the interior. Some colonists put Indian slaves to work locally, but because the natives sometimes fled to the forests or staged rebellions, Carolina slave merchants shipped numerous Indians to New England, the West Indies, and Virginia. By 1710, perhaps as many as twelve thousand Indians had been sent from South Carolina to the northern colonies and the Caribbean.[23]

As the search for skins and slaves expanded and imperial rivalries flared, most southern Indians discovered what the natives of Cofitachequi and Roanoke Island had found out earlier: contact with traders and settlers usually brought pestilence. Those earliest epidemics that followed de Soto and the Roanoke colonists might have been triggered by typhus or some other common shipboard ailment.[24] By the mid seventeenth century, however, traders and colonists had no trouble identifying the chief killer of Indians along the South Atlantic and throughout North America: smallpox. Among peoples previously unexposed to the contagion, smallpox takes a heavy toll. The disease rarely leaves more than 50 percent of such a population alive, and the death rate can range as high as 90 percent. Introduced into Hispaniola by Spanish sailors in 1519, the deadly virus wreaked havoc across Puerto Rico, Cuba, and on the Mexican coast, eventually findng its way to mainland North America. Although the exact extent of this early epidemic remains unclear, smallpox might have been transmitted to the southern interior and could have contributed to the desolation de Soto witnessed. The disease made one of its first documented appearances along the South Atlantic coast in 1667, when an infected sailor brought the virus into Northampton County, Virginia. Local natives there "died by the hundred."[25]

By the 1690s smallpox was following white traders and Indian middlemen inland, striking the interior with fearsome regularity. Traders and colonists recorded at least five more major epidemics, which typically lasted three to five years: 1696–9, 1729–33, 1738–9, 1755–60, and 1779–83. Natives fortunate

23. Ibid., 142–3; Richard L. Hahn, "The 'Trade Do's Not Flourish as Formerly': The Ecological Origins of the Yamasee War of 1715," *Ethnohistory*, 23 (1982), 344–5; Russell R. Menard, "The Africanization of the Lowcountry Labor Force, 1670–1730," in Winthrop D. Jordan and Sheila L. Skemp, eds., *Race and Family in the Colonial South* (Jackson: University Press of Mississippi, 1987), 98–101.

24. Henry F. Dobyns, *Their Number Become Thinned: Native American Population Dynamics in Eastern North America* (Knoxville: University of Tennessee Press, 1983), 21. Dobyns also argues for the presence of typhus among Sir Francis Drake's crew in 1585–6. See Dobyns, "An Outline of Andean Epidemic History to 1720," *Bulletin of the History of Medicine* 37 (1963), 504–5.

25. Quotation from Thomas B. Robertson, "An Indian King's Will," *Virginia Magazine of History and Biography* 36 (1928), 193. Crosby, "Virgin Soil Epidemics," 292–4; Dobyns, *Number*, 11–16; Peter H. Wood, "The Impact of Smallpox on the Native Population of the 18th Century South," *New York State Journal of Medicine* 87 (1987), 30–1.

Figure 4.1. The earliest known illustration of Indians working in New World tobacco fields. Indian slaves might have performed similar duties for Virginia planters. From Johann Neadner, *Tobacologia Medico-Cheirvrgico-Pharmacevtica* (Leyden, 1622). Earl Gregg Swem Library, College of William and Mary.

enough to survive an initial onslaught of smallpox gained resistance to the contagion, but such acquired immunity could not be passed on to Indian babies; with smallpox striking every twenty to thirty years, each generation faced the specter of wholesale deaths. Moreover, even those with resistance to smallpox remained susceptible to other pathogens. As Lawson succinctly put it, "where the Europeans come, the Indians ... [are] very apt to catch any Distemper they are afflicted withal."[26]

Among people so prone to infection, other diseases, generally considered less virulent than smallpox, proved almost as lethal. After its introduction into Mesoamerica in 1531, measles became the second greatest killer of Indians. Because measles produces a purplish red rash, colonists often confused it with other eruptive diseases such as smallpox and scarlet fever. Judging from outbreaks reported in the late seventeenth and eighteenth centuries, however, measles may have reached epidemic proportions nearly as often as smallpox. In 1693 the Virginia Council proclaimed a day of prayer in hopes of driving the contagion from the colony. Settlers farther south witnessed additional measles epidemics in 1717, 1747, 1759, and 1772. Like smallpox, measles remains incurable even today. Modern doctors keep the disease at bay by treating the symptoms and warding off other infections until the body's defenses destroy the disease. For Indians, however, measles proved doubly dangerous. They not only lacked the necessary antibodies to beat back the contagion, but as their bodies weakened, they became vulnerable to secondary infections.[27]

Partially because it struck in conjunction with measles and smallpox, influenza ranked only slightly behind those diseases as a threat to Indian health. Influenza broke out in Europe in 1556 and plagued the Continent until 1560. Passed on to the Aztecs by Spanish adventurers, the disease seems to have swept through the southern interior in 1559, bringing another wave of death to native societies already reeling from the effects of typhus or other contagions. Influenza produces few unique or distinguishing symptoms, and English colonists often referred to it as an "epidemical cold," "general catarrh," or "Winter Distemper" – terms also applied to an infinite variety of fevers, agues, and respiratory ailments. Such descriptions make later epidemics difficult to identify, but the disease probably ravaged the coastal colonies and the interior at least three more times after English settlement. Between 1696 and 1698 influenza apparently broke out simultaneously with smallpox. In 1761 it struck on the heels of a measles epidemic, possibly spreading across all of North America during a "flu season" that lasted well into July. Between 1778 and

26. Quotation from Lawson, *New Voyage*, 17. Crosby, "Virgin Soil Epidemics," 292–4; Wood, "Impact of Smallpox," 34–5; Dobyns, *Number*, 15; James H. Merrell, "The Indians' New World: The Catawba Experience," *William and Mary Quarterly*, 3d ser., 41 (1984), 542.
27. John Duffy, *Epidemics in Colonial America* (Baton Rouge: Louisiana State University Press, 1953), 164–77; Dobyns, *Number*, 16–17; Crosby, "Virgin Soil Epidemics," 293.

1783, the disease again seems to have surfaced alongside smallpox in a continent-wide epidemic.[28]

If typhus, smallpox, measles, and influenza accounted for the majority of Indian deaths, several other Old World pathogens played smaller roles in the macabre drama. Whooping cough became a serious problem for Indian children. Chicken pox and scarlet fever, two ailments not clearly distinguished until the late eighteenth century, probably cropped up often in native villages, to be mistaken for measles and smallpox. Bubonic plague and diphtheria struck New Spain in the sixteenth and early seventeenth centuries, and typhoid appeared along the Gulf Coast as early as 1528. All these maladies might have found their way into the South Atlantic region in the decades preceding English colonization.[29]

When English colonists did begin to settle along the South Atlantic coast they, too, faced grave threats to their health. During the early years of settlement, the Europeans died from typhoid, dysentery, and a host of other ailments. In later years, colonists suffered alongside Indians during every smallpox, measles, and flu epidemic.[30]

Even so, the settlers eventually won the war of attrition (at least along the coast), a victory that helped guarantee them possession of the land and its resources. Their triumph owed much to the armor of immunity. Antibodies built up through generations of exposure ensured that any epidemic would leave a portion of the population healthy enough to provide food, water, and care for the sick. In Indian villages, however, all the residents frequently fell ill at the same time, leaving no one to hunt, gather food, or nurse the victims. At certain seasons, the absence of such support services could be lethal. Due to cool, dry winds, which might have helped spread the virus, smallpox could leave villages incapacitated in late winter or early spring when food supplies were dwindling and fields needed planting. Under such conditions, what had once been an accepted period of sporadic hunger rapidly escalated into a critical food shortage. Moreover, undernourished natives who survived one epidemic might become even more susceptible to the next contagion.[31]

European colonists not only enjoyed immunity and support services, they also benefited from years of experience with the invisible enemies. Although

28. Duffy, *Epidemics*, 186–8, 197–200; Dobyns, *Number*, 269–70.

29. Dobyns, *Number*, 18–24.

30. Edmund S. Morgan, *American Slavery – American Freedom: The Ordeal of Colonial Virginia* (New York: Norton, 1975), 158–60; Peter H. Wood, *Black Majority: Negroes in Colonial South Carolina from 1670 through the Stono Rebellion* (New York: Norton, 1974), ch. 3; Albert E. Cowdrey, *This Land, This South: An Environmental History* (Lexington: University Press of Kentucky, 1983), 25–6. I shall consider these diseases in more detail in Chapter 5.

31. Shepard Krech, "Disease, Starvation, and North Athapaskan Social Organization," *American Ethnologist* 5 (1978), 710–32; J.M. May, *Studies in Disease Ecology* (New York: Macmillan, 1961), 12.

such infamous techniques as bleeding, leeching, and purging make modern Americans wonder about the proficiency of colonial doctors, the latter understood many of the basic treatments for infectious diseases. Most important, they knew that the maladies spread through contact and often quarantined sickly towns or ships to prevent further infection. They also realized that continued exposure to cold and dampness could bring quick death to victims already debilitated by smallpox, measles, and influenza. By the early eighteenth century, colonial doctors used more sophisticated techniques. During the 1720s English physicians began to practice variolation, a process by which they placed pus from smallpox pustules into an incision in the skin of a healthy person. The resulting infection generally proved mild, and although the effect was temporary, those subjected to variolation had a better chance of surviving an ensuing epidemic.[32]

While colonists had learned to combat the diseases of Europe, Indians had grappled with other health problems. In keeping with their belief in the curative powers of the plant kingdom, Indian shamans used a wide variety of herbs and roots to treat common disorders. To counter the venom of snakes, insects, and spiders, native healers employed numerous snakeroots, including "fern," or seneca, root, an herb belonging to the chicory family. Among the most highly regarded of American medicinal plants, fernroot produced a milky juice that could be taken internally, while its leaves were steeped and applied directly to the bite. Unfamiliar with, and almost in awe of, the American rattlesnake, some Englishmen ascribed great curative powers to the roots; John Lawson believed Indians "the best Physicians for the Bite of these and all other venomous Creatures of the Country."[33] The plants, however, primarily aided in reducing the pain and inflammation of the bite. Medicine men used other tactics to keep their patients alive, such as sucking out poison or applying tourniquets to prevent the spread of venom. The natives used similar practices to treat arrow wounds, burns, assorted inflammations, and rashes. Poultices made from poplar, sassafras, or dogwood bark proved so effective that some of those who traded regularly among the Indians preferred such native remedies to those offered by white physicians.[34]

Much like Europeans, Indians also believed that one way to alleviate or reduce the likelihood of sickness was to rid the body of impurities. One method

32. Duffy, *Epidemics*, 27–30. Wood ("Impact of Smallpox," 32–4) suggests that some colonists might have learned of variolation from slaves who had seen it practiced in Africa.
33. Quotation from Lawson, *New Voyage*, 134. For a contemporary description of seneca root, see William Byrd II, *Histories of the Dividing Line Betwixt Virginia and North Carolina*, ed. William K. Boyd (1929; reprint, Mineola, N.Y.: Dover, 1967), 158–60.
34. Virgil J. Vogel, *American Indian Medicine* (Norman: University of Oklahoma Press, 1970), 223; James Adair, *A History of the North American Indians, Their Customs, &c.*, ed. Samuel Cole Williams (Johnson City, Tenn.: Watauga Press, 1930), 246.

widely used along the South Atlantic coast and in the interior was the consumption of tea, or "black drink," brewed from the leaves of the coastal shrub yaupon. Indians drank yaupon tea at a variety of rituals, and village leaders frequently consumed it when important decisions had to be made. In addition, the natives sometimes employed black drink to induce vomiting in an attempt to cleanse body and spirit. Long before the arrival of Europeans, inland natives journeyed to the coast to secure the leaves and even transplanted yaupon around their villages.[35]

Another purgative technique involved use of the "sweat lodge," a small enclosure covered with skins or bark with a pot of steaming water or red-hot stones in the center. John Smith, who saw Virginia natives using the sweat lodge, reported that so many Indians crowded into the miniature saunas that they soon began to "sweate extreamely." Afterward, the natives might plunge themselves into a nearby creek or river. Such treatments probably did help certain ailments (particularly arthritis and rheumatism, two disorders that afflicted middle-aged and elderly natives). Indeed, Smith noted that the practice provided great relief from "dropsies, swellings, aches, and such like diseases."[36]

Exactly how Indians first perceived the introduced diseases remains somewhat of a mystery. Calvin Martin, a modern historian, has suggested that North American Indians blamed animals for the death and destruction wrought by European pathogens. Or, as another scholar has observed, the natives might have considered smallpox, measles, and other contagions so devastating that they could only be the work of a highly placed deity, one who intervened in everyday affairs to correct a major transgression.[37] While among the Cherokees during the 1738 smallpox epidemic, James Adair noted that the natives considered the epidemic punishment for "the adulterous intercourses of their

35. William L. Merrill, "The Beloved Tree: *Ilex vomitoria* among the Indians of the Southeast and Adjacent Regions," in Charles M. Hudson, ed., *Black Drink: A Native American Tea* (Athens: University of Georgia Press, 1979), 40–82. See also Hudson's "Introduction" in ibid., 1–9.
36. John Smith, "A Map of Virginia. With a Description of the Country, the Commodities, People, Government and Religion," in Philip L. Barbour, ed., *The Complete Works of Captain John Smith (1580–1631)*, 3 vols. (Chapel Hill: University of North Carolina Press for the Institute of Early American History and Culture, 1986), vol. 1, 168.
37. Calvin Martin, *Keepers of the Game: Indian-Animal Relationships and the Fur Trade* (Berkeley: University of California Press, 1978), 113–49. Martin argues that the natives' pursuit of furbearing animals for trade can be partially ascribed to the Indians' belief that the animals were responsible for the new diseases. Evidence to contradict Martin's thesis, as it applies to the southeastern Indians, is presented by Charles M. Hudson, "Why the Southeastern Indians Slaughtered Deer," in Shepard Krech, ed., *Indians, Animals, and the Fur Trade: A Critique of Keepers of the Game* (Athens: University of Georgia Press, 1978), 161–72. Even if one rejects Martin's argument for an Indian "war" against animals, it is still possible that, during the early phases of contact, Indians did indeed interpret the new diseases within the context of their own well-defined world view. See Wood, "Impact of Smallpox," 31.

young married" people, whose sexual sins had polluted certain agricultural fields. But whether they blamed animals or some other agent, one thing seems clear: Indians sought to make the new diseases comprehensible within their belief system and reacted to the epidemics in ways that made sense within the context of their own culture.[38]

Indians also called on familiar cures to combat Old World pathogens. Often, though, the natives succeeded only in hastening their own demise. The black drink could not rid Indian bodies of alien microbes (although some European physicians believed the tea a viable treatment). Effective as poultices might be against wounds and burns, they did little to check virulent eruptive diseases. Medicine men attempting to suck the "poison" from smallpox pustules often infected themselves or carried the contagion to other households. The sweat lodge, too, proved no place for victims of contagious disease. The steamy, cramped conditions helped propagate and spread the deadly microbes, and the ensuing cold bath invited respiratory infections or other complications. Europeans still struggling to comprehend the nature of infectious disorders sometimes concocted elaborate technical explanations for the fatal therapy, but clearly understood its results. "No sooner than they are attack'd with the violent Fevers," wrote Lawson, the Indians "fling Themselves over Head in the Water, in the very Extremity of the Disease; which, shutting up the Pores, hinders a kindly Evacuation of the pestilential Matter, and drives it back; by which Means Death most commonly ensues."[39]

Indians not only tried to counter the unfamiliar diseases with treatment, but also relied on an array of rituals designed to console the mind and spirit. Native healers used dances, chants, and songs to convince their patients that various spirits and divine beings had joined in the battle against disease. Relatives and friends of the victim often aided the shamans, providing important emotional support for both patient and physician. As one Englishman noted while among the Cherokees, "the fathers, mothers, brothers, or nearest relations are always with them; and they will never show anyways cast down before the sick person for fear of discouraging them." Modern physicians now recognize the value of such psychological therapy, realizing that the patient who thinks he will recover often does. However, such techniques are most effective when mind and body work together; the natives' lack of biological defenses usually muted the power

38. Quotation from Adair, *North-American Indians*, 244–5. Hudson uses this passage to support his argument in "Why Indians Slaughtered Deer," 161. Wood, however, ("Impact of Smallpox," 34) suggests that by this time the Cherokees might have been influenced by Christianity, which could account for this interpretation. For a general statement about Indians blending European innovations, including disease, into the native worldview, see Calvin Martin, "Epilogue: Time and the American Indian," in Martin, ed., *The American Indian and the Problem of History* (New York: Oxford University Press, 1987), 197.

39. Quotation from Lawson, *New Voyage*, 17. Wood, "Impact of Smallpox," 31–2.

of positive thinking. Visiting relatives not only saw their loved ones die, but also contracted the infectious ailments themselves, circumstances that made them question the reliability of their physicians and deities.[40]

The hideous symptoms of the various diseases proved as demoralizing as their invincibility. Like all North American Indians, those contacted by South Atlantic colonists and traders took great pride in their appearance. Christopher Newport's expedition found the natives along the James River to be "lusty streight men, very strong" who delighted in "dying and paynting themselves" to call attention to their perfectly formed bodies. Confronted with the toxic red rash of measles and the draining pustules, callous scabs, and horrible scars of smallpox, many Indians elected to take their own lives. While among the Cherokees, James Adair saw Indians cutting their own throats, shooting themselves, or jumping into raging fires to escape the indignity and humiliation of disfigurement. In one instance, even the collective efforts of friends and family could not discourage one great warrior bent on putting an end to his misery. After discovering that his relatives had removed all sharp objects from his abode, he implanted one end of a hoe handle in the ground and repeatedly threw himself upon the "fatal instrument" until he forced it down his throat and "immediately expired."[41]

The various Old World diseases and the complex ways in which natives responded to the epidemics triggered a dramatic decline in Indian populations. But not all groups suffered equally. As English colonists gradually gained a foothold on the South Atlantic coast, those Indians closest to white settlement bore the brunt of the microbial invasion. In addition, the natives had to contend with European encroachment on their hunting and fishing grounds, which periodically led to open war. Indians who survived the dual onslaught of alien pathogens and people either had to relocate and join other natives or be absorbed into the white population.[42]

The earliest and sharpest decline in Indian numbers occurred along the Chesapeake. Early outbreaks of typhus, influenza, and other unidentified diseases might have dropped Virginia's Indian population to about sixteen thousand by the time of English settlement. European immigration and the land requirements of tobacco agriculture combined with sporadic outbreaks of disease to perpetuate the downward spiral. By 1685, after two major Indian

---

40. Quotation from Alexander Longe, "A Small Postscript on the Ways and Manners of the Nashon of Indians called Charikees," ed. David H. Corkran, *Southern Indian Studies* 21 (October 1969), 26. Vogel, *Indian Medicine*, 31–4; Axtell, *European and Indian*, 250.

41. Quotations from [Gabriel Archer?] "The Description of the Now-Discovered River and Country of Virginia, with the Liklyhood of Ensuing Ritches, by Englands Ayd and Industry," *Virginia Magazine of History and Biography* 14:4 (April 1907), 377; and Adair, *North-American Indians*, 246. Wood, "Impact of Smallpox," 34.

42. Merrell, "Indians' New World," 544–7; Wright, *Only Land They Knew*, 24.

wars and at least one devastating smallpox epidemic, the colony's Indian population stood at less than three thousand. By 1730, when Virginia colonists were settling the piedmont and trickling into the Shenandoah Valley, roughly nine hundred natives remained; at the end of the century, that number had fallen to about two hundred.[43]

English settlement came later to the Carolina coastal plain and piedmont. Indians in those two colonies endured longer, but in the end the decline in their numbers was no less severe. In 1685 the native population of each colony's piedmont and coastal plain numbered about ten thousand. Fifteen years later those numbers had been reduced by about a fourth: to seventy-two hundred in North Carolina, seventy-five hundred in South Carolina. Over the next three decades, continuing slave raids, the bloody Tuscarora and Yamasee wars, and encroaching settlement left some four thousand natives in the Carolinas east of the mountains. By century's end, only a tattered remnant of the original coastal plain and piedmont peoples survived: perhaps as few as three hundred in each colony.[44]

For the Cherokees in the mountains, the pattern was somewhat different. After the initial incursions of the Spanish and (presumably) accompanying epidemics, the Cherokees' relative isolation from European settlement allowed their populaions to recover; the Indians probably numbered around thirty-two thousand in 1685. The smallpox epidemic of the 1690s cut that number in half, leaving perhaps sixteen thousand at the turn of the century. After more smallpox and a war with English settlers between 1759 and 1761, Cherokee numbers stood at seven thousand in the 1760s. During the last quarter of the century, the Cherokee population hovered between seventy-five hundred and eight thousand – a quarter of their seventeenth-century total, but a sizable number compared to their counterparts in the coastal plain and piedmont.

West and south of the mountains, the natives were well within range of English traders and their native slave raiders, but "one step removed" from the South Atlantic settlements. Like the Cherokees, the more populous interior groups were partly able to recover from diseases introduced by the early explorers. The Creeks may have numbered about 15,000 in 1685; farther west in the lands of the Choctaws and Chickasaws, the total native population was probably around 35,000. Disease and slave raids reduced those numbers to 11,000 and 14,300 respectively by 1730. Over the latter half of the eighteenth century, however, their distance from English settlements, willingness (particularly on the part of the Creeks) to absorb Indians displaced from other areas,

43. Peter H. Wood, "The Changing Population of the Eighteenth-Century South: An Overview by Race and Subregion, From 1685 to 1790" in Wood, G. Waselkov, and M. Thomas Hatley, eds., Powhatan's Mantle (Lincoln: University of Nebraska Press, forthcoming).
44. Ibid.

and tenacity as warriors and diplomats allowed the larger interior groups to increase their numbers. By 1790 the Creeks had again reached the 15,000 mark. Together, the Choctaws and Chickasaws numbered about 17,800.[45]

In part, the Indians of the interior endured because they gradually learned better techniques for coping with the physical and psychological trauma of Old World epidemics. The Cherokees' experience with smallpox eventually convinced them to abandon sweating and bathing as ineffective treatments. The natives also learned from watching and listening to Europeans. Allegedly acting on the advice of James Adair and other English traders, the Creeks began to invoke strict quarantines in the eighteenth century, posting sentinels outside healthy villages with orders to treat infected Indians and Europeans "as the most dangerous of all enemies."[46]

A closer look at the South Atlantic Indian trade makes it easier to understand Adair's concern for the natives' well-being. Although hides and slaves were the most valuable items traded in the Carolinas and Virginia, Indians also supplied other goods. Horses, so necessary for the lengthy forays into Indian country, seem to have been scarce in South Carolina during the early years of settlement. The Creeks, however, obtained the animals by raiding natives to the south (particularly the Apalachees) and subsequently traded those horses to the English.[47] In the coastal plain and piedmont, colonists continued to trade with nearby natives for food. Joel Gascoyne, author of a tract promoting colonization in South Carolina, informed prospective settlers that the natives readily offered their "services to fish, [and] hunt their Game for a Trifle."[48]

Colonists also traded for a wide variety of medicinal plants both for their own use and to ship abroad. English settlers not only touted seneca root as an antidote for snakebite, but also as a treatment for "gout, dropsy, poison, and other grievous distempers." As Christian Gottlieb Reuter, the Moravian surveyor, noted "It is the best Snakeroot, and the most used by the apothecary, and therefore many hundred pounds are shipped away."[49]

Valuable as it might be, however, seneca ranked well behind that most treasured medicinal plant: ginseng. For centuries tea or powder made from ginseng roots had been used in the Orient as an aphrodisiac and general tonic.

45. Ibid.
46. Quotation from Adair, *North-American Indians*, 364. John Gerar William De Brahm, *De Brahm's Report of the General Survey of the Southern District of North America*, ed. Louis de Vorsey, Jr. (Columbia: University of South Carolina Press, 1971), 107.
47. David C. Corkran, *The Creek Frontier, 1540–1783*, (Norman: University of Oklahoma Press, 1967), 52.
48. Joel Gascoyne, *A True Description of Carolina* (London, 1682), 4.
49. Marion Tinling, ed., *The Correspondence of the Three William Byrds of Westover, Virginia, 1684–1776*, 2 vols. (Charlottesville: University Press of Virginia, 1977), vol. 2, 519; Adelaide L. Fries et al., ed., *The Records of the Moravians in North Carolina*, 11 vols. (Raleigh: North Carolina Historical Commission, 1922–1969), vol. 2, 571.

But by 1700 extensive demand and overharvesting of the root in China had seriously reduced the supply of wild plants. Ginseng flourished in eastern North America, particularly in upland, deciduous forests like those of the southern Appalachians. English merchants were soon shipping ginseng acquired from the Cherokees halfway around the world to meet the demand for the roots in China.[50]

Ginseng roots develop slowly and form peculiar shapes that sometimes resemble parts of the human body. The particular shape of a given root helped determine its value. If shaped like a human arm, it could be used for arm wounds and ailments; if like a leg, it might be applied against problems of the lower extremities. The most valuable ginseng roots were those that looked like miniature humans; they could be employed anywhere on or in the body. The oldest roots also brought good prices because the plant's longevity allegedly could be passed on to humans. As William Byrd II explained in 1735, the root "is highly cordial, it recrutes the wasted spirits, and repairs a decayed constitution. In one word, it makes those who take it frequently live to great age, and in very good health whilst they do live." The plant's "vertues are so great," Byrd wrote on another occasion, "that mankind is not worthy to have it in plenty."[51]

Although most colonists were interested in the medicinal properties of American plants, a few Europeans explored the possibilities of exporting the very dirt itself. Andrew Duché, a Quaker potter who labored in Charles Town and Savannah in the 1730s, was the first Englishman to manufacture porcelain. Crucial to his art was white clay acquired from the Cherokees. By the 1760s Josiah Wedgwood, the famous English potter, had been introduced to Cherokee clay. Wedgwood sent Thomas Griffiths, who owned land in the Carolina piedmont, to treat with the Cherokees and bring back a supply of clay. Griffiths returned to England with more than five tons of the valuable substance, which Wedgwood used well into the 1780s. However, the expense of transporting the clay to England and the difficulty of negotiating with the Indians eventually led Wedgwood to use other clay sources closer to home.[52]

Hides, slaves, horses, game, snakeroots, Cherokee clay – none of these could be acquired in quantity without Indian cooperation. Some Englishmen thought Indian prowess in the forests a natural outgrowth of the natives' supposedly "bestial" character. Noting that native hunters always took more beaver than

50. Alvar W. Carlson, "America's Botanical Drug Connection to the Orient," *Economic Botany* 40 (1986), 233–5. I am indebted to M. Thomas Hatley, Ph.D. candidate at Duke University, for this reference.
51. Quotations from Tinling, *Correspondence of Three William Byrds*, vol. 1, 431, vol. 2, 453–54. Carlson, "Botanical Drug Connection," 235.
52. William L. Anderson, "Cherokee Clay, from Duche to Wedgwood: The Journal of Thomas Griffiths, 1767–1768," *North Carolina Historical Review* 63 (1986), 478–9, 497.

Figure 4.2. Mark Catesby's drawing of a ginseng plant and its miraculous medicinal root. The bird is a whippoorwill. Reproduced by permission from Colonial Williamsburg Foundation Library, Special Collections.

their English counterparts, Mark Catesby explained that Indians "have a sharper sight, hear better, and are endowed with an instinct approaching that of the Beasts," qualities that enabled them "to circumvent the Subtleties of these Wary Creatures." But the Indians' ability to acquire the items Englishmen thought valuable owed more to native culture than to "animal" sensibilities. Generations of experience and travel in the South Atlantic forests made Indians experts at locating game and medicinal plants. As John Smith had observed during the early phases of contact along the Chesapeake, "by their continual ranging, and travel, they [the natives] know all the advantages and places most frequented with Deare, Beasts, Fish, Foule, Rootes, and Berries." Indians were equally skilled at stalking humans. Prisoners had long been regarded as the chief spoils of native warfare and warriors returning from battle with captives in tow quickly increased their prestige within the village community. Because successful warriors were "the proudest Creature[s] on Earth," English traders found it relatively easy to enlist the natives in procuring slaves.[53]

The ways in which the various goods changed hands also bore the stamp of New World institutions. Many European traders, especially those who dealt with natives in the interior, discovered what Barlowe and Harriot had learned at Roanoke – namely that what Europeans perceived as commerce could take place only within the native context of friendship, gift giving, and reciprocity. Indians demonstrated a remarkable ability to maintain such institutions even in the face of the military, diplomatic, and biological turmoil of the eighteenth century.[54] When Thomas Griffiths went to seek clay from the Cherokees, he took along a Cherokee woman who had once been captured by other natives and subsequently ransomed by English officials. Her return to her people was to serve as a token of Griffiths' good will. As Griffiths noted, a group of Cherokee headmen were at first reluctant to allow him to travel to the clay pit. But because he "behaved like a True Brother, in taking care to conduct their Squaw safe home," the Indians eventually agreed to let him proceed. Even after he arrived at the pit, however, Griffiths could get no clay until he ate, drank, smoked, and "began to be familiar with these Strainge Copper Collour'd Gentry." Even then, Griffiths found that he still had to engage in more "Strong Talk" before the Indians allowed him to take their clay.[55]

Eighteenth-century traders also found that Indians (as they had at Roanoke) continued to employ European goods within the context of native culture. Indians had long since realized that the metal items the traders offered were

53. Mark Catesby, *The Natural History of Carolina, Florida, and the Bahama Islands*, 2 vols. (1747; reprint, Ann Arbor: University Microfilms International, 1977), vol.1, xxx; Smith, "Map of Virginia," in Barbour, *Complete Works of Smith*, vol. 1, 164; Lawson, *New Voyage*, 207.
54. The Choctaws' insistence on gift giving and their efforts to play off one European power against another are detailed in White, *Roots of Dependency*, ch. 3.
55. Anderson, "Cherokee Clay," 503, 505–6.

more useful as tools than charms. Metal cookware was better suited to endure the heat of the cooking fires whereas knives and axes eased the drudgery of girdling trees and skinning animals. Blankets and duffel did double duty as coats and bedclothes. But still, utility did not always determine demand. Well into the eighteenth century, Europeans provided the natives with decorative items such as mirrors, earbobs, and leather belts with buckles. Such "prestige goods" were in demand because they enabled Indian males to increase their status as astute traders and providers for their families.[56]

One item supplied by the traders was less benign when incorporated into native society. Those Englishmen who offered wine to Indians at Roanoke were harbingers of what became a widespread trade in alcohol, especially rum. Scholars still do not completely understand why liquor wreaked such havoc among Indians. At least a partial answer can be found within native culture. Warriors drank to bolster their courage and raise their self-esteem. Liquor also provided an excuse for otherwise heinous acts. Drunken natives who killed or wounded fellow villagers – normally a serious breach of local law – could, when sober, blame the deed either on demon rum or on the trader who supplied the insidious poison. The natives also drank to obtain "a dream-like state of religious possession" that seemed to enable them to commune with various deities. Consequently, rum became a valuable item at religious ceremonies and social gatherings. Liquor, like other trade goods, took on new functions and new meaning within the context of Indian culture.[57]

In other ways, however, alcohol was decidedly different from metal and cloth. Indians readily traded for knives, axes, and blankets, but their demand for such goods was finite. Once well supplied, they did not necessarily require more. Liquor, however, created its own infinite demand. One could not use rum without consuming it; alcohol had to be acquired in quantity again and again. Frequently, Indians who fully intended to trade animal skins or other forest products for tools and blankets could be induced by unscrupulous traders to accept alcohol instead.[58] When the rum was gone (often after a single night of what Europeans called "drunken Frolicks"), the natives had to go hunting again to acquire the goods they sought in the first place. Even if not a principal item of trade, liquor could be used to convince Indians to exchange other goods for less than fair value. When Thomas Griffiths went to Cherokee country in search of clay, he not only negotiated with the natives but also "heated 'em with Rum" and provided music for dancing. And although he claimed not to have made the Cherokees drunk, Griffiths did note that "when the Botle had gon

---

56. Hahn, "'Trade Do's Not Flourish,'" 344; Axtell, *European and Indian*, 254.
57. Quotation from Axtell, *European and Indian*, 257. Merrell, "Indians' New World," 549–50; White, *Roots of Dependency*, 84.
58. White, *Roots of Dependency*, 85.

about well . . . matters went on very Smooth between us" and he soon secured the material he sought.[59]

Although Indians continued to maintain some control over the ways in which goods were exchanged, their demand for liquor and other items gradually worked to undermine native independence. Indians had learned to use cloth, tools, and liquor, but not how to manufacture them. And, even if Indians had decided to abandon European goods in favor of precontact technology, they would have found it difficult to do so. East of the mountains, where contact with Europeans was more sustained and the Indian population decline more severe, Old World diseases took an especially heavy toll among elderly natives. The aged occupied important places in Indian society. After proving their ability during their youth, older men held many of the important political and religious positions. They made the critical decisions regarding warfare, designated days for feasting and fasting, and directed village rituals. Moreover, the elderly were generally the most skillful artisans, who practiced and taught conventional methods of constructing houses, canoes, baskets, and stone tools. By killing older Indians in disproportionate numbers, the new diseases gradually eroded the natives' cultural memory and restricted the dissemination of traditional lore. Watching these cherished relatives perish about them, Indians felt increasingly uneasy about the future. As one South Carolinian observed in 1763, the "daily decrease in their numbers [is] a circumstance that gives them much concern, however agreeable it may be to the selfish and all-grasping Europeans."[60]

Confronted with a demographic disaster and European encroachment, Indians of the coastal plain and piedmont (and later those farther west) pursued what their ancestors had always sought – survival. Now, however, survival meant finding a place within the rapidly expanding colonial economic system. Securing such a position meant producing commodities Europeans considered valuable. Perhaps Edmond Atkin, English Superintendent for Indian Affairs, explained it best in 1755 when he informed the Crown that "the policy of the Indians is Simple and Plain. 'Tis confined to Securing their personal Safety, a Supply of their Wants, and fair Usage."[61]

Within the framework of the European market economy, "a Supply of their Wants" took on new meaning. Before the arrival of traders and settlers, the natives had defined demand largely in terms of immediate need. Although Indians had sometimes pressured animal populations or destroyed plant life,

59. Quotations from Lawson, *New Voyage*, 211; and Anderson, "Cherokee Clay," 506.
60. Quotation from [Dr. John Milligan], "A Description of the Province of South Carolina," in B. R. Carroll, ed., *Historical Collections of South Carolina*, 2 vols. (New York: Harper Bros., 1836), vol. 2, 516.
61. Quotation from Edmond Atkin, *Indians of the Southern Colonial Frontier*, ed. Wilbur R. Jacobs (Columbia: University of South Carolina Press, 1954), 39. Hudson, "Why Indians Slaughtered Deer," 167–70; Merrell, "Indians' New World," 544.

their seasonal depredations had not been overly taxing on either. However, to acquire tools, cloth, liquor, and prestige goods, Indians now had to procure enough hides and other items to trade with Europeans and still meet their own needs.[62] Mark Catesby seems to have recognized this change when he wrote that before colonization, the natives "made no other use of the skins of deer, and other beasts, than to cloath themselves, their carcasses for Food, probably, them being of as much Value to them as the Skins." But, Catesby continued, "they now Barter the Skins to the Europeans for other Cloathing and Utensils they were before unacquainted with," their "Destruction of Deer and other Animals being chiefly for the Sake of their Skins." Across the southern colonies, the depopulation wrought by epidemic disease meant that fewer natives now stalked the animals, but those who did go into the forest carried with them a new survival ethic based on the requirements of the European market.[63]

They also went into the woods armed with European guns. At first, explorers and colonists refused to supply the natives with firearms, fearing the weapons would dramatically increase attacks on white settlements. Traders, however, cared less about warfare than about profit and soon found ways to circumvent official mandates. Guns became especially important to the Indian trade. Natives who had the new loud weapons could terrorize those who fought with bows and arrows. The Westos, a confederation of Indian groups who occupied what had once been Cofitachequi, provide a case in point. The Westos were among the first Carolina Indians to obtain guns, initially getting the weapons from Virginia and, after 1674, from Charles Town. Once armed, the Westos successfully attacked a number of neighboring Indians – the Cusabos, Yamasees, Creeks, Cherokees, and Catawbas – and took numerous prisoners for the slave traders. The Westos continued such raids until 1680 when they somehow ran afoul of the Charles Town traders and engaged in a war with the colonists. The Carolinians then stepped up the arms trade with other Indians who, in turn, helped defeat the Westos.[64]

Because guns became crucial to the slave trade and intertribal warfare, Indians were anxious to acquire the weapons and to learn how to use them. John Lawson found that when Indians "have bought a Piece and find it to Shoot any Ways crooked, they take the Barrel out of the Stock, cutting a Notch in a Tree, wherein they set it streight, sometimes shooting away above 100 Loads of Ammunition, before they bring the Gun to shoot according to their Mind." Lawson also thought Indians were excellent marksmen, reporting that some could hit a target at will "with a single Ball, missing but two Shoots [sic]

---

62. William Cronon, *Changes in the Land: Indians, Colonists, and the Ecology of New England* (New York: Hill & Wang, 1983), 98.
63. Catesby, *Natural History*, vol. 1, xi.
64. John T. Juricek, "The Westo Indians," *Ethnohistory*, 11 (1964), 134–8, 139; Corkran, *Carolina Indian Frontier*, 4–6.

in above forty." But even if adept at handling guns, Indians could not manufacture powder and shot or repair a broken weapon. Consequently, firearms, like liquor, worked to make Indians more dependent on traders and further tied the natives to the European economy.[65]

Together with their intricate knowledge of the woodlands, the natives' growing demand for guns, liquor, and other trade goods did not bode well for southern animals, especially the whitetail deer. As Harriot had discovered at Roanoke, deerskins stripped of their hair produced beautiful buff-colored leather that rivaled chamois in suppleness and durability. In the hands of European leatherworkers, the best North American deerskins became gloves; hides of lesser quality were stretched thin and fashioned into bookbindings.[66]

Like the natives, colonists also continued to rely on whitetails for food. Settlers who took time to learn deer-hunting from the Indians could enjoy remarkable success. Along Roanoke River, Byrd encountered a colonist named Epaphroditus Bainton who spent "most of his time in hunting and ranging the Woods, killing generally more than 100 Deer in a Year." Bainton's success owed much to his vigor (according to Byrd he was "young enough at 60 years of age to keep a Concubine, & to walk 25 miles a day") and his Indian-like habit of stalking the animals quietly on foot (he had once been thrown from a horse and had nearly broken his neck). But even more lethargic colonists who preferred to ride could put meat on their tables simply by trading with the Indians. George Alsop, a Maryland indentured servant, observed in 1666 that the "extreme glut and plenty" of deer "daily killed by the Indians and brought in to the English" made venison "the common provision the Inhabitants feed on." Indeed, the man to whom he was indentured (who traded regularly with the natives) once had some eighty deer cured and stored to feed his family and servants. According to Alsop, "before this Venison was brought to a period by eating, it so nauseated our appetites and stomachs, that plain bread was rather courted and desired than it."[67]

To meet demands for leather and venison, provide themselves with trade goods, and preserve their place within the expanding colonial system, Indians naturally had to kill more deer. Some contemporaries thought firearms greatly aided such commercial hunting. Mark Catesby remarked in 1731 that "the Use of Guns has enabled them [Indians] to slaughter far greater numbers of Deer and other Animals than they did with their primitive bows and arrows." Bow hunting did pose certain problems. At a range of only fifteen yards a whitetail

65. Quotation from Lawson, *New Voyage*, 33. Axtell, *European and Indian*, 259–60; Merrell, "Indians' New World," 550–1.
66. Usner, "Deerskin Trade," 85.
67. Byrd, *Dividing Line*, 157; George Alsop, "A Character of the Province of Maryland," in Clayton Hall, ed., *Narratives of Early Maryland*, Original Narratives of Early American History, gen. ed. J. Franklin Jameson (New York: Barnes & Noble, 1946), 345.

jumping at the twang of a bowstring can easily avoid an arrow traveling 150 feet per second. Guns, however, could prove equally unwieldy. Wet powder or mechanical problems could render firearms ineffective and, like the bowstring's twang, the click of a cocking mechanism or the report of the shot itself might alert deer to the presence of a human enemy. The one advantage guns did offer was "knockdown power." Unless an arrow severed the spine or lodged in the brain, it rarely dropped a deer in its tracks. Instead the animal ran through the woods until it collapsed from loss of blood. The shock effect of a lead ball could bring down deer more easily. Or, if an Indian missed his mark, the shot might break a bone, crippling the animal and preventing its escape.[68]

The ways in which Indians used firearms varied from place to place. Perhaps due to more level topography, coastal and piedmont natives seem to have been more inclined to use guns in conjunction with fire hunting. That method had always been used to trap and kill game in quantity and within the context of the fire hunt, guns probably served as little more than a substitute for traditional weapons. Other inland natives, including the Cherokees, apparently favored the "selective stalking technique" whereby individual hunters tracked deer alone. For these solitary hunters, guns might have provided a technological advantage because the weapons helped cut down the time it took to track a wounded whitetail. Overall, however, European firearms probably did not affect hunting as much as Catesby and other colonists thought.[69]

Whether driven by fire or stalked by individual Indians, South Atlantic deer populations now faced unprecedented hunting pressure. Whitetails are less polygamous than most mammals and some bucks mate only with one doe. The gestation period is long – about seven months – and a doe usually gives birth to two fawns. In the absence of predators, deer can reproduce quickly. (In one modern experiment four does and two bucks produced a herd of 160 deer in only six years.) With heavy hunting pressure, however, the deer's long gestation period and comparatively small number of offspring became liabilities. And human hunters were not the whitetails' only enemies. Natural predators, disease, parasitism, and available food also controlled the rate of increase.[70] As Indians stepped up their yearly kills, deer populations began to decline.

68. Quotation from Catesby, *Natural History*, vol. 1, xi. Harry D. Ruhl, "Hunting the Whitetail," in Walter P. Taylor, ed., *The Deer of North America* (Harrisburg, Pa.: Stackpole, 1958), 310.
69. Catesby, *Natural History*, vol. 1, xii; Albert E. Cowdrey, *This Land, This South: An Environmental History* (Lexington: University Press of Kentucky, 1983), 51–2; M. Thomas Hatley III, "The Dividing Path: The Direction of Cherokee Life in the Eighteenth Century," (Master's thesis, University of North Carolina at Chapel Hill, 1977), 38.
70. Walter V. Robertson, "Population Dynamics of White-Tailed Deer," in *White-Tailed Deer in the Southern Forest Habitat: Proceedings of a Symposium at Nacagdoches, Texas, March 25–6, 1969*, Southern Forest Experiment Station, Forest Service, United States Department of Agriculture (Nacagdoches, Tex.: Southern Forest Experiment Station, 1969), 5–6; Ernest Thompson Seton, *Lives of Game Animals*, 4 vols. (Watertown, Mass.: Branford, 1953), vol. 3, 276.

The more northerly coastal plain herds, doomed by their proximity to the James River traders, were first to dwindle. Traveling among the Tuscaroras in 1701, John Lawson reported "Venison very scarce to what it is amongst other Indians." One year later Indians in southeastern Virginia complained to the Virginia Council that their traditional hunting territory had been invaded by Tuscaroras seeking deer. Lawson believed the Tuscaroras' plight resulted from "the great Number of their People" who had grown "too populous for one Range."[71] The Englishman was partially correct. The Tuscaroras might not have encountered smallpox until 1707 and probably were more numerous than some groups to the southeast. But the shortage of deer more likely resulted from the Tuscaroras' contact with English traders, an association that had begun in 1650.[72]

Whereas Virginia Indians complained of Tuscarora encroachments, natives farther south faced even greater difficulties. Among the Indians most active in the Charles Town trade were the Yamasees, who had moved to the inner coastal plain of South Carolina (in part to be closer to English traders) in 1686. Over the next twenty years the Yamasees supplied Carolina traders with deerskins and with slaves captured in raids on the Spanish mission Indians to the south. But, by the first decade of the eighteenth century, both commodities were in short supply. Commercial hunting had severely decreased the whitetail population. Constant slave raids had similarly decimated the mission Indians. Traders, however, continued to provide the Yamasees with trade goods on credit and by 1711 the natives were deeply in debt to the merchants. When a census taken by the colonial government in 1715 convinced the Yamasees that they were about to be enslaved to make up the balance, the natives elected to wage war on the colony. Only an alliance between South Carolina and the Upper Creeks and Cherokees saved the colony from total destruction.[73]

As Indians fought colonists and each other, hunting declined and the deerskin trade contracted. Indeed, the Yamasee War was probably good for the deer population, allowing the animals to increase while the fighting raged. With the return of peace to the coastal plain and piedmont, deerskins again became an important export item. Between 1717 and 1719, some 17,000 to 24,000 skins annually left Charles Town. By the mid 1720s the yearly total had risen to more than sixty thousand; it climbed to eighty thousand in the early 1730s. As the trade again expanded, piedmont deer herds declined. In 1728 William Byrd II

---

71. Quotation from Lawson, *New Voyage*, 65. H. R. McIlwaine et al., eds., *Executive Journals of the Council of Colonial Virginia*, 6 vols. (Richmond: Dietz, 1925–66), vol. 2, 275. Merrell cites this in "Indians' New World," 552. Professor Merrell and I discussed this passage from Lawson before the article appeared, and I am indebted to him for this piece of corroborating evidence.

72. Parramore, "Tuscarora Ascendancy," 327 and n. 93.

73. Hahn, "'Trade Do's Not Flourish,'" 347–52.

admonished those journeying with him to the interior to bring along enough provisions for ten days, since it would take that long to reach an area where deer and other game still abounded. Likewise, during the middle decades of the century, Indians in the Catawba valley found their hunting grounds seriously depleted.[74]

Despite the continuing scarcity of deer east of the mountains, the trade in skins continued to grow. By the mid eighteenth century Charles Town was sending nearly 150,000 skins across the Atlantic. Charles Town exporters had deerskins because, as coastal plain and piedmont herds diminished, traders focused their energies on the west where deer were more abundant. Indians were more abundant there, too, and native allies became crucially important to the ongoing imperial struggle between England, France, and Spain. As the English presence in the interior became more pronounced and competition for commercial and military allies intensified, the Indians proved themselves astute diplomats, playing off one European power against another. Ironically, the imperial wars and diplomatic intrigue during the first half of the eighteenth century benefited both Indians and deer. Indians could use their numbers and military power as bargaining chips, forming alliances that ensured a supply of trade goods and, for a time, preserved traditional gift giving and reciprocity. Moreover, the shifting alliances and factionalism among the natives meant that Indians periodically went to war against both colonists and other Indians. Warfare curtailed hunting and deer populations had time to recover. As long as no single European power completely dominated the area, Indians retained a measure of independence, deer survived, and the trade went on.[75]

The Treaty of Paris in 1763 gave England title to East and West Florida and the lands east of the Mississippi, bringing peace to the interior and upsetting the precarious balance between hunting and fighting. Using Augusta as an entrepôt to the Creeks and Cherokees, Georgia traders avidly sought skins in the west. Indeed, Savannah emerged to challenge Charles Town as a shipping point for deerskins, exporting more than two million pounds (hides from half a million deer) between 1764 and 1773. From Pensacola in West Florida, British traders enjoyed easier access to Choctaw territory. South Atlantic and Gulf ports kept English traders well supplied with European goods, especially liquor, which now flowed more freely in the region.[76]

As the natives became dependent solely on British trade goods and traders

74. Converse D. Clowse, *Economic Beginnings of South Carolina, 1670–1730* (Columbia: University of South Carolina Press, 1971), 256–7; Byrd, *Dividing Line*, 141; Merrell, "Indians' New World," 554.
75. Crane, *Southern Frontier*, 111; White, *Roots of Dependency*, ch. 3.
76. White, *Roots of Dependency*, 69–85; Leila Sellars, *Charleston Business on the Eve of the American Revolution* (New York: Arno, 1970), 169; Robert McClung, *Lost Wild America* (New York: Morrow, 1969), 165; Phillips, *Fur Trade*, 1:341–2, 426.

continued to ply the Indians with rum, market hunting began again in earnest. By the mid 1760s, deer were scarce in Cherokee hunting grounds. Twenty years later (despite the disruptive warfare of the American Revolution) the extensive liquor trade among the Choctaws had led to shortages of whitetails in that region.[77] Complaints about the paucity of venison and skins continued to surface until the end of the century. While among the Yuchi Indians in 1797, Benjamin Hawkins, United States Agent for Indian Affairs, found "no game of any kind" and natives who had "suffered much . . . with hunger." A year later in Creek country, Hawkins noted that in such "extensive and wild country" a traveler would normally see "game in abundance." Yet, he concluded, "it is difficult for a good hunter, in passing through it, in any direction, to obtain enough for his support." In 1801 the Creek chieftain Mad Dog pointedly told a merchant from Panton, Leslie, and Company (a British firm then operating with Spanish permission out of West Florida) that "our deer and game is almost gone." Remembering happier times, Mad Dog continued, "When the Acorns fall deer are usually about, but where now are the deer?" His question was one that, two hundred years earlier, Thomas Harriot had thought would never be asked.[78]

While Indians struggled against food shortages, colonists pondered the economic problems associated with diminishing deer. In an effort to preserve the trade in leather and venison, colonial governments moved to restrict the hunting season. Virginia, where the colonial population was largest and where the trade had gone on longest, reacted first. Noting "the unseasonable killing" of deer "when poor and of Does bigg with young," Virginia legislators in 1699 made it illegal to kill whitetails between February 1 and July 1. In the following decades, Virginia moved to protect bucks in December as well. Other colonies passed similar legislation. South Carolina instituted a closed season on does and fawns from January through July and prohibited killing bucks in September, October, March, and April. Aimed directly at commercial hunting, the laws frequently allowed friendly Indians and all colonists to hunt for food, but not trade. Possession of out-of-season skins (often identifiable by their rusty hue) was prima facie evidence of a violation. Those caught in the act or with illegal

77. Gary C. Goodwin, *Cherokees in Transition: A Study of Changing Culture and Environment Prior to 1775* (The University of Chicago Department of Geography Research Paper no. 181, 1977), 98–99; White, *Roots of Dependency*, 87–9.

78. Quotations from "Letters of Benjamin Hawkins," *Collections of the Georgia Historical Society*, 9 vols. (Savannah: The Georgia Historical Society, 1840–1916), vol. 9, 73; Benjamin Hawkins, "A Sketch of the Creek Country in the Years 1798 and 1799," (reprint, New York: Krause Reprint, 1971), 24; and "Talk From the Indian Chief Mad Dog," *Florida Historical Quarterly*, 13 (1935), 165. William S. Coker and Thomas D. Watson, *Indian Traders of the Southeastern Spanish Borderlands: Panton, Leslie, & Company and John Forbes & Company, 1783–1847* (Pensacola: University of West Florida Press, 1986), chs. 1–3.

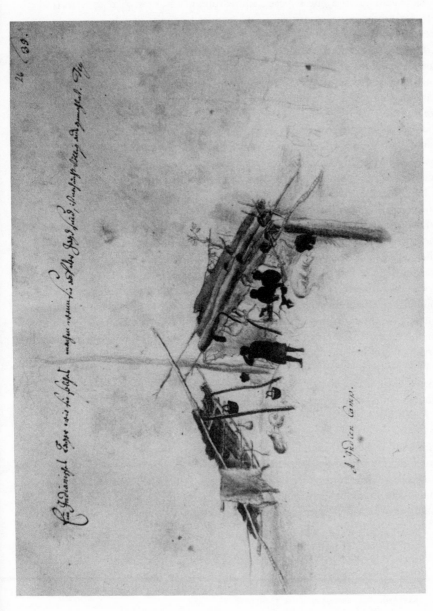

Figure 4.3. An Indian hunting camp with a temporary shelter made of saplings and cypress bark. Pet dogs frequently accompanied the hunters. The metal pots and deerskins suggest that these natives were securing hides for colonial traders. Drawing by Philip George Frederich von Reck, who traveled in Georgia in the 1730s. Reproduced by courtesy of the Royal Library, Copenhagen.

skins usually faced a fine for each animal unlawfully shot. A 1730 Maryland law, for example, levied a fine of four hundred pounds of tobacco for every illegal deer.[79]

As settlement spread into the inner coastal plain and piedmont, hunters in this backcountry proved especially difficult to control. Although farming was the principal occupation in the area, a large percentage of inland settlers in the Carolinas survived by killing game and trading skins. Many backcountry hunters were vagrants who squatted briefly on unowned land or wandered the countryside in search of deer. Others owned small plots, but simply preferred hunting to farming. The Cherokee War of 1760–1 increased the number of restless hunters in the Carolinas. In the wake of Indian attacks, militiamen deserted and settlers abandoned their farms for life in the woods.[80]

Backcountry hunters used a variety of techniques. Like the natives, white woodsmen frequently drove deer with fire in summer and autumn. William Eddis, the recently appointed governor of Maryland, noted in 1770 that backcountry settlers "were dexterous, during the winter season, in tracing their [the deers'] path through the snow; and from the animal's incapacity to exert speed under such circumstances, great multitudes of them were annually slaughtered and their carcasses left in the woods." Hunters throughout the southern colonies also pursued deer at night with torches fashioned from pine limbs. Like the modern poacher's trick of jacklighting, or "shining" deer, the torches temporarily blinded and paralyzed the animals which then became easy targets. Night hunting, however, had its drawbacks. Because the hunters fired only at a pair of eyes glowing in the distance, they sometimes shot cattle and horses. Such accidental kills only exacerbated tensions between the wandering hunters and settled farming colonists in the backcountry.[81]

Faced with complaints from settlers and fearing a shortage of deer, colonial governments eventually responded with more stringent measures. Legislators outlawed torchlight hunting and restricted woods burning. Lawmakers also struck directly at vagrant hunters. North Carolina's 1768 hunting law required those taking deer to produce certificates proving that they had "planted and tended five thousand corn hills ... in the preceding year or season" in the county in which they hunted. A year later South Carolina made it illegal for

79. Quotations from William Waller Hening, ed., *The Statutes at Large: being a collection of all the laws of Virginia, from the first session of the legislature, in the year 1619* (New York: R. & W. & G. Bartow, 1819–1823), vol. 3, 180. Thomas Cooper and David J. McCord, eds., *The Statutes at Large of South Carolina*, 10 vols. (Columbia, S.C.: A. S. Johnston, 1836–39), vol. 4, 310–11; William Kilty, *Laws of Maryland*, 2 vols. (Annapolis, 1800, Research Publications, Inc. microfilm), 1730: ch. 17, 1789: ch. 5, 1799: ch. 18.

80. Rachel N. Klein, "Ordering the Backcountry: The South Carolina Regulation," *William and Mary Quarterly*, 3d ser. 38 (1981), 668–70.

81. Quotation from William Eddis, *Letters From America*, ed. Aubrey C. Land (Cambridge, Mass.: Harvard University Press, 1969), 32. Klein, "Ordering the Backcountry," 671.

colonists to hunt more than seven miles from their homes.[82] Virginia took a more drastic step, imposing a four-year moratorium on commercial deer hunting in 1772. If the current depredations continued unchecked, the bill warned, "the inhabitants will not only be deprived of that wholesome and agreeable food, but the trade, in the article of skins will be greatly diminished." Virginians also feared for the sustenance of the College of William and Mary, which drew most of its revenue from a tax on skins. By 1799 Maryland had passed similar laws, barring hunting in certain counties for several years.[83]

William Eddis apparently had great faith in such conservation laws, noting that "apprehension of punishment may very greatly restrain if not totally eradicate an evil founded on cruelty and rapacity." But the exact impact of such measures remains an open question. Ideally, closed seasons offered two advantages. They kept deer protected for five months every year and offered some solace to both bucks and does during the rutting and birthing seasons. On the other hand, by allowing doe hunting in early fall, the regulations might have unwittingly contributed to the deaths of fawns still too young to survive without their mothers. And despite the restrictions on killing bucks, colonists and Indians could still legally hunt in November when whitetails beginning the rut were more approachable and easier to kill. Moreover, the very renewal and refinement of the laws and the eventual bans on commercial hunting in some areas suggest that the early regulations were difficult to enforce and perhaps ineffective.[84]

Yet deer never became extinct in the southern colonies. A decline in natural predators might have aided the deer's survival. For while colonists and Indians slaughtered hundreds of thousands of deer, settlers (with some assistance from the natives) waged a war of equal intensity on wolves and other carnivores that threatened both deer and livestock. As natural predators declined during the eighteenth century, the deer's capacity for reproduction – as well as the ebb and flow of Indian hunting and warfare – probably kept whitetails from disappearing completely. (With today's hunting regulations and low predator populations, deer easily survive high annual kills. In North Carolina, for example, hunters in 1987–8 legally took over seventy-eight thousand deer with no apparent long-term threat to the herds.)[85]

Although most concerned about the dearth of deer, eighteenth-century colonists found that market hunting had taken its toll on other animals,

82. James Iredell, *The Public Acts of the General Assembly of North Carolina* (Newbern, N.C., 1804), 69; Cooper and McCord, *Statutes at Large of South Carolina*, vol. 4, 310–11, 410–13, 719, vol. 5, 124.

83. Hening, *Statutes at Large of Virginia*, vol. 8, 592; Kilty, *Laws of Maryland*, 1730: ch. 17.

84. Quotation from Eddis, *Letters*, 32–3.

85. Statistics for 1987–8 are from "Big Game Tag Report Number 12," *Wildlife in North Carolina* 52:6 (June 1988).

including that most prized North American furbearer, the beaver. From the first, Europeans had marveled at the rodent's seemingly complex patterns of social organization. Reverend John Clayton, an English cleric who spent two years in Virginia and who was much interested in scientific matters, heard from contemporaries that beavers "have a very orderly government amongst them, in their works each knows his proper work, & station, & the overseers beat those young ones that loiter in their business, & will make them crie, & work stoutly." Likewise, William Byrd II thought that beavers "have more of Instinct, that Half-Brother of Reason, than any other Animal." Although beavers were not as socially and intellectually sophisticated as Clayton and Byrd believed, the animals' reproductive habits did differ from other rodents. Pairing for life, the adults mate in midwinter and give birth to four or five kits in early summer. The kits remain with their mothers for two years, during which time she generally bears no more offspring.[86]

This long cycle of parenting and low rate of reproduction meant that, like deer, beavers could be susceptible to overhunting. But beavers seem to have endured longer than deer. Both the Westos and the Tuscaroras supplied early English traders with beaver pelts; yet, John Lawson, who found venison scarce among the Tuscaroras, saw beaver dams wherever he traveled in the Carolinas. Likewise, William Byrd's surveying party frequently found it difficult to ford creeks that beavers had "render'd quite impassable for any creature but themselves." In part, beavers owed their survival to the southern climate. Thanks to the region's more temperate winters, the animals did not develop the same thick, luxurious coats as their northern cousins. As Byrd noted, fur from the southern colonies eventually proved less valuable than that from "the more Northern Countries where it is longer and finer." Indeed, the Westos and Tuscaroras might have been important to the southern beaver trade because they ranged widely and probably had contacts with Indians farther west and north who could provide better pelts.[87] For the most part, however, South Atlantic merchants seem to have preferred deer to beaver. In 1712 Virginia sent some forty-eight thousand beaver pelts across the Atlantic, but that seems to have been an exceptional year. Between 1699 and 1714, the colony averaged about two thousand skins annually. Charles Town averaged only six hundred furs per year during the same period, although in three different years (1699,

86. Quotations from Edmund Berkeley and Dorothy Smith Berkeley, eds., *The Reverend John Clayton: A Parson with a Scientific Mind, His Scientific Writings and Other Papers* (Charlottesville: University Press of Virginia for the Virginia Historical Society, 1965), 109–10; and Byrd, *Dividing Line*, 292. John O. Whitaker, Jr., *The Audubon Society Field Guide to North American Mammals* (New York: Knopf, 1980), 459; Leonard Lee Rue, III, *The World of the Beaver* (Philadelphia: Lippincott, 1964), 31–2.

87. Quotations from Lawson, *New Voyage*, 125; and Byrd, *Dividing Line*, 52, 294. Juricek, "Westo Indians," 154–5.

1700, and 1703) more than fourteen hundred beaver pelts left the southern port.[88]

Moreover, beavers were cunning adversaries. Primarily nocturnal, the animals lay "Snug in their Houses all day" and as Byrd observed, it was rare to see one during daylight. Some southern Indians (possibly the Westos) might have hunted beavers from canoes like natives farther north. But setting snares around ponds and streams to trap the rodents was probably a more common tactic. According to John Banister, a seventeenth-century Virginia naturalist, Indians rubbed their traps with a substance Englishmen knew as "wysoccan." Colonists never learned the exact formula for wysoccan (or wisokan). Banister reported that older Indian men kept the ingredients a secret in order to "awe the young ones."[89] Wysoccan could have come from a single source – milkweed is one possibility – but Indians probably derived the mixture from several plants that had a bitter taste. (The natives also used "wysoccan" to describe the bitter twang of European liquor.) On the snares wysoccan might have served either to lure beaver, disguise the traps, or perhaps mask any human scent left by the hunter.[90]

Beginning in the late seventeenth or early eighteenth century, however, Indian and English trappers began to rub their traps with castoreum, a pungent musky substance extracted from the sexual glands of the beaver. Castoreum proved a powerful attractor and, when used in conjunction with steel traps (apparently another innovation of the early eighteenth century), provided a more efficient means of trapping the wary rodents. This new technique might have allowed South Atlantic traders to acquire enough skins to turn a profit even if the pelts were thinner than those from the north. Castoreum itself was also in demand on the international market. Europeans used the smelly oil to manufacture perfume and several medicines. The use of castoreum on traps allowed more beaver to be taken, which, in turn, provided more castoreum for use at home and abroad.[91]

Whether attributable to castoreum and steel traps or simply to the general expansion of trade and settlement farther inland, beavers became noticeably scarce in the half century between 1730 and 1780. By the time William Bartram

88. Phillips, *Fur Trade*, vol. 1, 331; K. G. Davies, *The North Atlantic World in the Seventeenth Century* (St. Paul: University of Minnesota Press, 1974), 170.

89. Byrd, *Dividing Line*, 292; Joseph and Nesta Ewan, eds., *John Banister and His Natural History of Viriginia, 1678–1692* (Urbana: University of Illinois Press, 1970), 386.

90. Quinn, *Roanoke Voyages*, vol. 1, 444, vol. 2, 900; William L. Merrill and Christian F. Feest, "An Exchange of Botanical Information in the Early Contact Situation: Wisokan of the Southeastern Algonquians," *Economic Botany* 29 (1975), 178–82.

91. Robin F. Wells, "Castoreum and Steel Traps in Eastern North America," *American Anthropologist* 74 (1972), 479–80, 482; Christian F. Feest, "More on Castoreum and Traps in Eastern North America," *American Anthropologist* 77 (1975), 603; Ewan and Ewan, *John Banister*, 401. Thanks to Peter H. Wood for his helpful suggestions concerning castoreum.

explored the southern colonies in the mid 1770s, only "a few beavers" remained in the coastal plain and piedmont. When Governor John Drayton published his description of South Carolina in 1802, he could write that east of the mountains, "the beaver is but rarely to be met with."[92]

The demise of the beavers offered some benefits, however. Colonial millers might use abandoned beaver ponds as sites for their waterwheels, replacing dams of poplar and ash with walls of heavier material. But if no human tenant took over their upkeep, the dams fell into disrepair and the ponds behind them slowly dissipated, destroying acres of potential breeding grounds for malaria-carrying mosquitoes. On the other hand, unrestricted by beaver dams, inland streams probably flowed faster and cut deeper into their beds, speeding up erosion and increasing the chances of floods. Without beaver ponds to impede them, forest fires could spread more quickly and cover larger areas. Within the ever changing forest ecosystem, the decline of the industrious rodents probably had far-reaching implications that few southern colonists understood or took time to note.[93]

Although deer and beaver were the animals most often hunted for their hides, traders seldom turned up their noses at any well-dressed pelt. Black bears, whose skins sold for two dollars in western North Carolina by 1800, also became scarce in the settled regions.[94] Like bears, buffalo and elk enjoyed a certain amount of staying power against bows and arrows, but were probably more vulnerable to the shock and crippling effects of firearms. As settlers moved inland, piedmont herds (never large to begin with) fell victim to backcountry hunters. David Ramsay, who published a history of South Carolina in 1808, learned from an informant that in 1750 "three or four men with their dogs could kill from ten to twenty [buffalo] in a day." But, by 1763 Dr. John Milligan of South Carolina observed that "buffalo's are sometimes found in the woods near the mountains, but they are not so numerous as they were a few years ago." Forty years later Governor Drayton reported bison "entirely exterminated" in the coastal plain and piedmont. Likewise, by the 1770s Bartram could find "but few elks, and those only in the Appalachian mountains."[95]

92. William Bartram, *Travels of William Bartram*, ed. Mark Van Doren (Mineola, N.Y.: Dover, 1955), 231; John Drayton, *A View of South Carolina, As Respects Her Natural and Civil Concerns* (1802; reprint, Spartanburg, S.C.: Reprint, 1972), 88.

93. Byrd, *Dividing Line*, 292; Whitaker, *Field Guide to Mammals*, 460; Cowdrey, *This Land, This South*, 48.

94. François André Michaux, "Travels of François André Michaux," in Reuben G. Thwaites, ed., *Early Western Travels. 1748–1846*, 32 vols. (New York: AMS Press, 1966), vol. 3, 290; Catesby, *Natural History*, vol. 1, xxv–vi.

95. David Ramsay, *Ramsay's History of South Carolina From Its First Settlement in 1670 to the Year 1808*, 2 vols. (1858; reprint, Spartanburg S.C.: Reprint, 1960), vol. 2, 305; Milligan, "Description," in Carroll, *Historical Collections of South Carolina*, vol. 2, 482; Drayton, *View of South Carolina*, 88; Bartram, *Travels*, 231.

Smaller furbearers were also growing scarce in the settled regions. The muskrat, as its name suggests, not only provided a nice pelt, but also two small "stones" that gave off a pleasant musky scent. Europeans used the musk as an all-purpose freshener, especially well-suited to mask odors in clothing and bed linen. During his two-year sojourn in Virginia, John Clayton kept a live muskrat in a wooden chest, where "2 days before it died it was extraordinary odoriferous & scented the room very m[u]ch." Even after the animal's death, "the skin was very fragrant, [and] the stones also smeld very well." But its aromatic excretions (as well as its troublesome propensity for boring into colonists' dams) proved to be the muskrat's undoing. When Bartram traveled through the colonies, the animals could no longer be seen "in Carolina, Georgia, or Florida within one hundred miles of the seacoast." Otters, too, were now confined to the western backcountry. Only the scavenging opossum, which had endured eons of climatic change (and whose thin fur and seemingly filthy habits made its pelt undesirable), survived "in great abundance."[96]

Birds suffered less than mammals, but still felt the impact of market hunting. Wild turkeys became a staple of the meat trade. In South Carolina, natives brought the prodigious birds "many miles" to trade for goods worth but "two Pence Eng[lish] Value." Traveling through Virginia in 1759, the itinerant minister Andrew Burnaby saw Pamunkey Indians killing migratory wildfowl "a hundred dozen" at a time. The birds eventually turned up "at the tables of most of the planters." While in Georgia, Bartram feasted on "horseloads" of passenger pigeons taken by a local planter and his slaves. The hunters used techniques borrowed from the Indians, blinding the birds with torches and knocking them from their roosts with long poles. Although pigeons survived throughout the colonial period, similar practices and expanding urban meat markets would eventually wipe out the huge flocks. Even medicinal plants did not escape the effects of the Indian trade. By the end of the eighteenth century, Governor Drayton could report that "Ginseng has been so much sought by the Cherokee Indians for trade, that at this time it is by no means so plenty as it used to be in this state."[97]

As certain animals grew scarce and coastal and piedmont Indians became more dependent on colonists, English attitudes toward the natives began to change. In contrast to John Smith and other seventeenth-century colonists, Lawson berated those who still looked on Indians as "little better than Beasts in Humane Shape[s]." Adding that colonists "possess[ed] more Moral Deform-

96. Berkeley and Berkeley, *John Clayton*, 108; Bartram, *Travels*, 231.
97. John Archdale, "A New Description of that Fertile and Pleasant Province of Carolina," in Carroll, *Historical Collections of South Carolina*, vol. 2, 482; Andrew Burnaby, *Travels Through the Middle Settlements in North-America. In the Years 1759 and 1760. With Observations on the State of the Colonies*, 2d ed. (Ithaca, N.Y.: Great Seal Books, 1960), 30; Bartram, *Travels*, 231; Margaret Babcock Meriwether, ed., *The Carolinian Florist of Governor John Drayton of South Carolina, 1766–1822* (South Caroliniana Library, University of South Carolina, 1943), 109.

ities and Evils than these Savages do," Lawson urged settlers to learn native languages, religions, and customs. Such knowledge, he contended, would soon prove that, before contact, Indians had been "the freest People in the World." Robert Beverley in 1705 went even further in condemning his fellow Virginians, noting that "all the English have done since their going thither, has been to make some of these Native Pleasures [including hunting] more Scarce." This seemingly sudden concern for traditional Indian culture and precolonial subsistence arose in part because the natives of Virginia and coastal Carolina no longer seemed to pose a threat to English settlement. Although the Tuscaroras and Yamasees would prove otherwise, Lawson and Beverley tended to regard some Indians as curious, even pathetic, victims of the European incursion.[98]

Were Lawson and Beverley correct in laying the blame for the initial ecological disruption solely on themselves and other Europeans? Their argument has much to recommend it. Europeans not only initiated the contact, but also benefited (in terms of land and security) from the devastation wrought by Old World diseases. English traders made money from skins and slaves, while using liquor to keep Indians in chronic debt. Moreover, colonists made little effort to save native lives or curtail deer hunting until those problems threatened to undermine profits. By then, as colonial legislators discovered, the most serious ecological damage had already been done.

But in their indictment of Europeans, Lawson and Beverley might be guilty of painting too poetic a picture of precontact Indian life. Centuries before Europeans arrived on the South Atlantic shore, Indians had adapted to a number of potentially disruptive changes in the natural environment and in their way of life. They had, for example, combined agriculture with hunting and gathering to create subsistence patterns that afforded greater security. The natives sought to do the same with Europeans and their metal technology.[99] The newcomers were potential allies against other natives. Since metal hoes, axes, knives, kettles, and jewelry increased Indian prestige and made subsistence easier, the natives were more than willing to hunt both humans and animals to get the tools. Based on their experience and culture, Indians initially chose to become partners with Europeans in the search for skins and furs, an enterprise in which the natives' skills as hunters and woodsmen could be put to good use.

But although both groups participated willingly at first, biological and cultural forces combined to make the partnership unequal. Disease and liquor –

98. Lawson, *New Voyage*, 243; Robert Beverley, *The History and Present State of Virginia* (1705), ed. Louis B. Wright (Chapel Hill: University of North Carolina Press for the Institute of Early American History and Culture, 1947), 156; Nash, "Image," 224–6.
99. Neil Salisbury, "American Indians and American History," in Calvin Martin, ed., *The American Indian and the Problem of History* (New York: Oxford University Press, 1987), 50–2.

and the complex ways in which Indians reacted to both – made the natives progressively more dependent on European traders. Despite the natives' ongoing efforts to maintain traditional methods of exchange and their skill as diplomats, the English triumph in the interior eventually enveloped even the more populous Indian groups in the expanding colonial economy. It was a relationship that the natives who met the Roanoke explorers could not have foreseen, a relationship that cost countless animals and numerous Indians their lives.

Instead of seeking to assign guilt, it would perhaps be better to listen to the words of William Bartram, whose Quaker religion and work as a naturalist provided him with insights seldom shared by other colonists. While traveling in the backcountry, Bartram found "the wild country now almost depopulated." He observed "vast forests, expansive plains, and detached groves" filled with "heaps of white gnawed bones of ancient buffalo, elk, and deer, indiscriminately mixed with those of men, [and] half grown over with moss." Noting that the scene proved "rather disagreeable to a mind of delicate feelings and sensibilities," Bartram concluded that "some of these objects recognize past transactions and events, perhaps not altogether reconcilable to justice and humanity."[100] Modern Americans who share such delicate ecological sensibilities should not be too quick to condemn either colonists or Indians. Instead, they should view the destruction of wildlife as the understandable, although lamentable, result of a complex contest of cultures played out in a land of plenty.

100. Bartram, *Travels*, 263–4.

5

An accessible desert

If the waning supply of deer and beaver created problems for South Atlantic colonists, the decline in Indian numbers provided double compensation. Depopulating epidemic diseases not only reduced the threat of Indian attacks in parts of the coastal plain, but also left former village sites and their surrounding agricultural fields open for European settlement. Without Indian tenants to burn and seed them, the plots soon began the long process of reverting to forest, first sprouting weeds and grasses that in turn gave way to small trees and woody plants. Like the naturally occurring savannas, the grassy Indian fields proved especially appealing to early English colonists. For generations, their ancestors had equated dense dark forests with wildness and danger. Most Englishmen probably viewed uncut woodlands as something akin to Shakespeare's foreboding Forest of Arden: "a desert inaccessible under the shade of melancholy boughs." Such woods, Englishmen thought, were the proper home for animals, not humans. Even the term "savage," liberally applied to both "bestial" Indians and forest-dwelling Irishmen, derived from the Latin word "silva," meaning wood. With their meadowlike appearance, the former Indian plots offered a welcome psychological respite from the imaginary terror of the wildwood.[1]

The availability of Indian fields also meant that colonists might be spared the backbreaking work of clearing the forest. The prospect of such exhausting labor sometimes proved a powerful deterrent to those thinking of emigrating to the New World. The author of a 1650 tract promoting life in the southern colonies found it necessary to assure prospective settlers that they need not fear "that the Country is overgrowne with Woods, and consequently not in many Yeares to be penetrable for the Plough. For there are immense quantity of Indian fields cleared already to our hand, by the Natives, which till we grow over populous may every way be absolutely sufficient." Like most of those who wrote advertisements for the New World, the author overstated his case. Some early colonists along the Chesapeake and in the Carolinas enjoyed the security and ease of settling abandoned Indian land, but most Europeans had to clear their own plots. As Joel Gascoyne wrote in his 1682 treatise describing life in South

---

1. Keith Thomas, *Man and the Natural World: A History of the Modern Sensibility* (New York: Pantheon, 1983), 194–5.

Carolina, "the first thing requisite and necessary for the Settler to embrace, is to fell Timber, and to clear the Ground." In English eyes, agricultural clearing became the initial step in taming the wildwood or making the forest-desert accessible.[2]

English settlers who initially sought to grow Indian crops such as corn and tobacco simply adopted native methods for clearing new fields. Beginning as early as September and continuing through March, colonists removed bark from larger trees, a process that caused the trees to wither and die within two to three years. Settlers then burned off the underbrush and planted between and around the trunks. Like Indians, English farmers discovered that the standing trees did little to inhibit growth of their crops. This technique of girdling and burning not only saved time but also helped delay soil exhaustion. Even when stripped of their bark, the trees continued to return valuable material to the field. Moreover, when the trees finally fell, the rotting wood from their trunks added important organic matter to the ground. Commenting on such benefits in South Carolina, William De Brahm explained that, "Although most new Fields remain for a long time lumbered with the bodies of Trees for one or two years, this however does not hinder the Planters from cultivating the clear Spots; mean while, the Places thus covered with the Bodies of Trees, improve in Goodness of Soil." Throughout the colonial period, corn and tobacco continued to flourish among half-dead and downed timber.[3]

By the early eighteenth century, however, some colonists recognized the need for new techniques and more thoroughly cleared fields. William Byrd II noted that girdling and burning wasted or damaged much wood that might otherwise be used for fences or building material. Moreover, Byrd believed, the process made only limited use of the nitrogen-rich ash left over after the burn. When initially cleared, a field remained "rich enough of itself without such fertilizer" and leaving the ashes behind only squandered another potentially valuable commodity. During the mid eighteenth century, Virginians also began to plant more wheat, a grain usually sown broadcast in more thoroughly cleared

2. Quotations from Edward Williams, *Virginia, More especially the South Part Thereof, Richly and Truly Valued* (London, 1650), 4; and Joel Gascoyne, *A True Description of Carolina* (London, 1682), 2. Gloria L. Main, *Tobacco Colony: Life in Early Maryland, 1650–1720* (Princeton, N.J.: Princeton University Press, 1982), 6; Donald W. Meinig, *The Shaping of America*, Volume 1 *Atlantic America, 1492–1800* (New Haven, Conn.: Yale University Press, 1986), 151.

3. Quotation from John Gerar William De Brahm, *Report of the General Survey in the Southern District of North America*, ed. Louis De Vorsey, Jr. (Columbia: University of South Carolina Press, 1971), 94. James Adair was one European who recognized the benefits of Indian clearing techniques. (James Adair, *A History of the North-American Indians, Their Customs &c.*, ed. Samuel Cole Williams [Johnson City, Tenn.: Watauga Press, 1930], 434–5.) Similar practices and their ecological implications are described in William Cronon, *Changes in the Land: Indians, Colonists, and the Ecology of New England* (New York: Hill & Wang, 1983), 116–17.

and plowed fields. And, by mid century, many South Carolina planters grew indigo, another plant that did best in ground broken by plows.[4]

The inefficiency of girdling and burning, as well as the shift to different crops, led eighteenth-century colonists to employ other techniques. Using metal axes, settlers felled larger trees "about yard from the ground," a height that seemed to keep the stumps from sending out new shoots.[5] After colonists salvaged what they could for lumber, fencing, and firewood, the remaining underbrush could be burned in the accustomed manner and the ashes transported to other, older fields that needed the nitrogen. The remaining stumps and tangle of underground root systems still restricted the use of draft animals, but fields cleared in this fashion became accessible to the plow after several years. Colonists settling Georgia in the mid eighteenth century seem to have preferred this more thorough method of clearing. Only in the late eighteenth century, when migrating Virginians and Carolinians came into upper Georgia to grow tobacco, did girdling and burning become common practices in that colony.[6]

Even though they had access to metal technology, southern colonists would have found it difficult to clear the forest if they had not also enjoyed the advantage of an adequate labor force. Slaves greatly aided in conquering the wildwood. Africans not only provided labor, but also know-how. The use of fire as a clearing agent was a technique long employed in West Africa, and many of the slaves transported to the southern colonies already knew what Europeans had to learn from Indians.[7] During the early phases of clearing, black men and adolescents performed the laborious tasks of felling and splitting the larger trees. Once those trees came down, the men resumed other duties while women and children "cut down the brushes and Shrubs with Hoes and Hatchets" or hauled firewood. Burning a new field proved risky, so colonists often delayed that part of the operation until after dark, when winds had died down. De

4. William Byrd II, *The Natural History of Virginia or the Newly Discovered Eden*, ed. Richard Croom Beatty and William J. Malloy (Richmond, Va.: Dietz, 1940), 92–3; Harold B. Gill, Jr., "Wheat Culture in Colonial Virginia," *Agricultural History* 52 (1978), 381, 383–5; G. Terry Sharrer, "The Indigo Bonanza in South Carolina, 1740–90," *Technology and Culture* 12 (1971), 449–50.

5. Quotation from Hugh Jones, *The Present State of Virginia*, ed. Richard L. Morton (Chapel Hill: University of North Carolina Press, 1956), 77. Cronon, *Changes in the Land*, 116–17.

6. De Brahm, *General Survey*, 92–4; Thomas Nairne, *A Letter from South Carolina Giving an Account of the Soil, Air, Product, Trade, Government, Laws, Religion, People, Military Strength, Etc. of that Province* (1710; reprint, Ann Arbor, Mich.: University Microfilms, 1980), 49; "An Interview with James Freeman," in H. Roy Merrens, ed., *The Colonial South Carolina Scene: Contemporary Views, 1697–1744* (Columbia: University of South Carolina Press, 1977), 44; G. Melvin Herndon, "Forest Products of Colonial Georgia," *Journal of Forest History* 23 (1979), 134 n. 26.

7. Daniel C. Littlefield, *Rice and Slaves: Ethnicity and the Slave Trade in Colonial South Carolina* (Baton Rouge: Louisiana State University Press, 1981), 103–4.

Brahm offered this description of the process in South Carolina. "At Sun-set all Slaves leave their fields and retire to their Cottages to rest an hour; then all hands are turned out to lopping and fireing, which they continue until 9 o'Clock at night." The numerous small fires employed in clearing the fields conveniently afforded light for the whole process. Given the importance of slave labor in clearing the South Atlantic woods, the shift to more complex methods in the eighteenth century might have owed as much to increased black populations as to new crops and the inefficiency of girdling and burning.[8]

Aided by European technology and skilled African labor, colonists found it relatively easy to clear land that had been too heavily forested for the Indians' stone tools. Indeed, South Atlantic settlers (like colonists elsewhere) preferred to farm densely wooded areas, believing the abundance of natural vegetation offered proof of the soil's fertility. While traveling through the Indian villages of the North Carolina piedmont, Lawson saw the nearby oaks and concluded that "the Savages do, indeed, still possess the Flower of Carolina, the English [in the coastal plain] enjoying only the Fag-end of that fine Country." Mark Catesby echoed those sentiments in 1731, when he reported that some of the most coveted acreage lay in "Oak and Hiccory Land; those Trees, particularly the latter, being observed to grow mostly on good land."[9]

However vague they might appear, such notions had a sound basis in ecological fact. The huge oaks and hickories grew in the alluvial soils deposited by the slow-moving rivers of the coastal plain or in the darker clay and humic ground common to the piedmont and mountains. The giant trees also needed regular drenching rains, and where hardwoods flourished, prospective farmers could be assured of adequate moisture for their crops. Noting the dense foliage along Virginia's major rivers, Hugh Jones believed the best tobacco land could be found "where fine timber or grapevines grow." Grain also seemed to thrive in such soil. As Governor Drayton observed, "Whenever large rivers penetrate through these lands, there the adjacent soil is of excellent quality, favoring the growth of the heaviest timber; and is capable of producing from fifty to seventy bushels of Indian corn . . . to each acre."[10]

Where the water table intersected the coastal plain or where flat terrain

8. Quotation from De Brahm, *General Survey*, 93–4. See also "Johann Martin Bolzius Answers a Questionnaire on Carolina and Georgia," trans. and ed. Klaus G. Leowald, Beverly Starika, and Paul S. Taylor, *William and Mary Quarterly* 3d ser. 14 (1957), 257.

9. John Lawson, *A New Voyage to Carolina*, ed. Hugh Talmage Lefler (Chapel Hill: University of North Carolina Press, 1967), 61; Mark Catesby, *The Natural History of Carolina, Florida, and the Bahama Islands*, 2 vols. (1747; reprint, Ann Arbor, Mich.: University Microfilms, 1977), vol. 1, iv; Cronon, *Changes in the Land*, 114–15.

10. Jones, *Present State of Virginia*, 77; John Drayton, *A View of South Carolina, As Respects Her Natural and Civil Concerns* (1802; reprint, Spartanburg, S. C.: Reprint, 1972), 10; John L. Vankat, *The Natural Vegetation of North America: An Introduction* (New York: Wiley, 1979), 148–50; Cronon, *Changes in the Land*, 115.

encouraged coastal plain rivers and creeks to meander out of their banks, colonists found other valuable ground. Known as "inland swamps," these pockets of fertile land sprouted laurel oaks and other wetlands trees that caught the eyes of English farmers. Milder temperatures near the sea also offered a longer growing season, increasing the region's agricultural potential. In the late seventeenth and early eighteenth centuries, South Carolinians discovered that such conditions proved well suited for rice, a nutritious grain that flourished in the tropical climates of Asia and West Africa. Clearing southern swamps for rice required special techniques that were probably known to slaves (many of whom had grown the crop or seen it grown in their homeland), but which colonists had to learn. The creek or river that produced the quagmire first had to be dammed or diverted so that colonists and slaves could work on dry ground and so the fires could burn unimpeded. Most rice growers preferred to begin clearing in winter, when streams ran lower and cooler temperatures reduced the risk of snakebite in the reptile-infested swamps. Once the winter sun had dried the soil, clearing proceeded as usual. Slaves cut down the larger trees and fired the underbrush. They then hauled away the usable timber and ashes, leaving the trunks to rot. Any cane growing in the marshy ground probably had to be dug out by the roots, since fire made it sprout prolifically the following spring. When the weather warmed sufficiently, colonists sowed rice between the logs, releasing the dammed or diverted rivers to provide the necessary irrigation.[11]

Although rice adapted well to the inland swamps, those who grew the plants eventually came to prefer freshwater tidal swamps and marshlands. Virtually every major river from the lower Cape Fear in North Carolina south to the Okefenokee Swamp rose and fell with the tides and could be controlled with dikes and trunks. But colonists paid a high price for this convenience. These larger, wetter swamps sprouted huge white gum, cedar, and cypress trees that had to be cut, split, and hauled away before planters uncovered the "wet, deep, miry Soil" or "black greasy Mould" they coveted.[12]

Metal technology, African labor and know-how, and the increasing demand for farmland in the coastal plain and eastern piedmont eventually worked to change the complexion of the southern landscape. By 1648 Governor William Berkeley of Virginia reported "many thousand of Acres of cleer land . . . where the wood is all off of it." As the population of the Chesapeake region grew

11. De Brahm, *General Survey*, 72–3; Hugh Meredith, *An Account of the Cape Fear Country, 1731*, ed. Earl Gregg Swem (Perth Amboy, N.J.: Charles F. Hearman, 1922), 20–1; Duncan Clinch Heyward, *Seed From Madagascar* (Chapel Hill: University of North Carolina Press, 1937), 13; Peter H. Wood, *Black Majority: Negroes in Colonial South Carolina from 1670 through the Stono Rebellion* (New York: Norton, 1975), 35–7; Littlefield, *Rice and Slaves*, 104–5.

12. Quotation from Governor James Glen, "A Description of South Carolina," in B. R. Carroll, ed., *Historical Collections of South Carolina*, 2 vols. (New York: Harper Bros., 1836), vol. 2, 201. Heyward, *Seed From Madagascar*, 18.

Figure 5.1. Benjamin Henry Latrobe's 1798 watercolor of "An overseer doing his duty" shows slaves using fire and hoes to clear a stump-strewn field. A "worm" fence surrounds the plot. Reproduced by permission from the Maryland Historical Society, Baltimore.

during the eighteenth century, more the of area's trees fell to settlers' fires and axes. Much of the tidewater region probably came to resemble Hugh Jones's 1724 description of Virginia. Perhaps still fearful of the uncharted wildwood, Jones characterized the colony as "one continued forest," but happily noted "patches of some hundred acres here and there cleared." Farther south, settlement and population growth proceeded more slowly and colonists initially brought less land under cultivation. Even so, the demand for alluvial soil and swampland encouraged the removal of timber along major streams. Joel Gascoyne's map of South Carolina drawn in 1682 described the territory along the lower Ashley River and the entire region between Stono and Edisto rivers as "land taken up." Edward Crisp, who charted Charles Town and the adjacent areas almost thirty years later, took care to list each landholder along the major waterways. His map shows English holdings extending to the upper reaches of the Ashley and Cooper rivers and along the major tributaries. Where no names appeared, Crisp drew trees, perhaps an indication that colonists were removing the timber along creeks and rivers.[13]

One of the most immediate effects of such deforestation was to reduce the amount of land available to the already diminishing animal populations. By 1731 Mark Catesby had discovered that black bears "fly the Company of Man, their greatest Enemy, and as the Inhabitants advance in their Settlements, the bears &c. retreat further into the woods." Although colonists avidly sought bears for meat and skins, the beasts' disappearance from settled regions also resulted from the high value placed on oak and hickory regions. Dependent on the mast-bearing trees and fish resources of the older forests and river bottomlands, the once ubiquitous bears disappeared as colonists moved into what appeared to be promising farmland. Wolves and panthers, that also needed vast areas of unbroken older forests, followed bears into the backcountry. Other creatures residing in the eastern forests suffered as well. In clearing oak and hickory forests, settlers disturbed acres of potential pigeon roosts and turkey habitat. Animals relocating to avoid colonists still found themselves at the mercy of Indian hunters who sought pelts and meat to exchange with

13. Governor William Berkeley, "A New Description of Virginia," in Peter Force, comp., *Tracts and Other Papers, Relating Principally to the Origin, Settlement, and Progress of the Colonies in North America, from the Discovery of the Country to the Year 1776,* 4 vols. (Washington, D.C., 1836–46), vol. 2, Tract VIII, 14; Jones, *Present State of Virginia,* 56; Gascoyne, *True Description* (map is included as frontispiece to the book); Edward Crisp, "A Compleat Description of the Province of Carolina," Library of Congress, Geography and Map Division. De Brahm also observed clearing along rivers, noting in 1764 that "all Lands upon and along the Sea Coast, upon and between Navigable Streams and Rivers are occupied, and at this time become private property" (De Brahm, *General Survey,* 72).

traders. Along with market hunting, habitat destruction became a major factor in the decline of game animals.[14]

Agricultural clearing did not always prove detrimental to wildlife. Partly cleared colonial fields provided an almost ideal environment for upland birds, especially bobwhite quail. Weeds and grasses that grew around stumps and logs or along fence lines offered the birds suitable cover. Moreover, by clearing away the larger trees, colonial farmers drove away foxes, wolves, and other predators that might have fed on the birds. In the absence of such natural enemies, other grass and seed-eating animals flourished on agricultural sites. Rabbits and mice became regular raiders of both fields and storehouses. Another animal that probably benefited from colonial farming was the opossum. Although possums sometimes roam through dense woodlands, they prefer cultivated areas where trees border weedy, old fields. The possum's gestation period is shorter than any other North American mammal (twelve to thirteen days) and in the South, females give birth to two litters per year. Given such remarkable fecundity (and the limited value of their pelts), possum populations must have increased as settlers provided the age-old marsupials with suitable habitats.[15]

The impact of agricultural clearing on the most valuable animal, the white-tailed deer, is difficult to gauge. Early Chesapeake planters who primarily grew tobacco and corn might exhaust their fields in as little as three to five years. Those colonists then moved on to clear fresh ground, leaving the old plots to begin the long process of forest succession. The annual grasses, herbs, and pioneer trees that invaded the old fields would have provided browse for whitetails. But abandoned fields also proved attractive to colonists' cattle. Constant grazing by livestock could effectively forestall succession, leaving a sort of natural pasture that was well suited for cattle, but less appropriate for deer. Moreover, hunting by Indians and colonists reduced deer populations so drastically that the ecological impact of any new habitats provided by colonial agriculture might well have been negligible. Writing of Edisto Island in 1808, David Ramsay noted the "cleared state" of the land and observed that any deer

14. Quotation from Catesby, *Natural History*, vol. 1, xxv. Jonathon L. Richardson, *Dimensions of Ecology* (Baltimore: Williams & Wilkins, 1977), 40; Peter Matthiessen, *Wildlife in America* (New York: Viking, 1959), 69; W. W. Ward, "Clearcutting in the Northeastern Hardwood Forests," in Eleanor C. J. Horwitz, ed., *Clearcutting: A View From the Top* (Washington, D.C.: Acropolis, 1974), 72–3.
15. Herbert L. Stoddard, *The Bobwhite Quail: Its Habits, Preservation and Increase* (New York: Scribner, 1931), 8–9, 349–50; Richardson, *Dimensions*, 140; Roger A. Caras, *North-American Mammals: Fur-Bearing Animals of the United States and Canada* (New York: Gallahad Books, 1967), 14–15.

who should "venture to stroll from the neighboring main and surrounding inlets" were "instantly hunted down."[16]

Fluctuations in animal populations were not the only changes observed by eighteenth-century colonists. Landon Carter, one of the wealthiest planters in Virginia, thought he detected a fundamental change in the Chesapeake climate. Carter was extremely observant of the natural world. Like most of the so-called great planters he spent many of his waking hours inspecting his holdings, keeping detailed records of the land and everything it produced. Fascinated with, and dependent upon, the fickle southern weather, Carter paid particular attention to temperature, rainfall, wind, and storms. In 1770 he noted in his diary that "this climate is so changing [that] unless it returns to his former state Virginia will be no Tobacco colony." The spring, Carter believed, now remained "cold even into the summer" and, as he observed in 1771, the change of seasons inevitably brought temperatures "too hot and drie for any [crops] to stand." Constantly concerned about the state of his tobacco and other cash crops, Carter may have overstated the seriousness of the changes he perceived. Moreover, the winter of 1770 was colder than normal in the Chesapeake and the freezing temperatures probably contributed to Carter's theory. His advanced age (early sixties) and failing health might also have increased his sensitivity to cold and dampness.[17]

But in a curious sort of way, Carter was correct. Around the cleared fields of his plantations, the climate was changing. By 1770 Chesapeake farmers had adopted new techniques that allowed for more thorough clearing of their tracts. Carter, like other Chesapeake colonists, had also begun to grow more wheat, which required more extensive clearing and plowing. Modern plant ecologists are well aware of the influence of such forest removal on temperatures. In densely wooded areas such as the oak and hickory lands colonists preferred, the crowns of the trees form an almost unbroken canopy that controls and moderates air temperature. The canopy intercepts incoming solar radiation, and because the green foliage does not warm as rapidly as the soil and ground

16. Quotation from David Ramsay, *Ramsay's History of South Carolina From its First Settlement in 1670 to the Year 1808,* 2 vols. (1958; reprint, Spartanburg, S.C.: Reprint, 1960), vol. 2, 285. On competition between deer and cattle see Neil W. Hosley, "Management of the White-tailed Deer in its Environment," in Walter P. Taylor, ed., *The Deer of North America* (Harrisburg, Pa.: Stackpole, 1956), 210.

17. Quotations from Jack P. Greene, ed., *The Diary of Colonel Landon Carter of Sabine Hall, 1752–1778,* 2 vols. (Charlottesville: University Press of Virginia, 1965), vol. 1, 433, vol. 2, 634–5. T. H. Breen, *Tobacco Culture: The Mentality of the Great Tidewater Planters on the Eve of Revolution* (Princeton, N.J.: Princeton University Press, 1985), 177–82. Breen suggests that such comments also reflect the planters' concern about low tobacco prices and their increasing debts.

litter, summer temperatures remain lower on the ground than at the tops of the trees. During the cold months, the canopy thins, but the trees still restrict the sun's heat from rising off the soil and ground litter, keeping average winter readings higher. Agricultural clearing, whether practiced in the colonial period or in the twentieth century, creates more severe temperature fluctuations. Without the forest canopy to moderate extremes, summer temperatures become hotter and winter readings colder. Thus, the springs were colder and summers warmer around Carter's fields. Such changes sprang not from any dramatic alteration in the overall climate, but rather from the ways in which the deforested plantation tracts reacted to the usual weather patterns.[18]

Carter's observations also convinced him that Virginia's frosts now came earlier and stayed longer than ever before, a trend he attributed to the fluctuating temperatures. But the early frosts on his fields might also have resulted in part from deforestation. Within any standing forest, the earliest and latest frosts occur in small openings and low-lying concave areas. At night, these regions rapidly radiate heat to the atmosphere. The continuous, upward flow of warm air creates a constant draft that not only cools the cleared patches, but also attracts cold air from the surrounding forest. Known as "frost pockets," such areas are slow to sprout new trees, and modern foresters often find it difficult to reseed them because the lower temperatures interfere with sprouting and flowering. In similar fashion, cleared fields sent much of the accumulated daytime heat back to the atmosphere so that it did indeed frost earlier in Carter's fields than in other areas.[19]

Once the shading effect of the forest canopy was eliminated, the surface soil warmed quickly during the summer and soon dried out completely. During the first two or three years after clearing, the warming trend proved beneficial to crops. Gradual heating caused organic material to decay faster, releasing nutrients into the field. The effect was especially evident in the darker soils of the oak and hickory regions, where the sun's radiation helped release nutrients stored in the thick layers of raw humus. This seemingly increased fertility

18. David H. Moehring, "Climatic Elements in the Southern Forests," in Norman E. Linnartz, ed., *The Ecology of Southern Forests, 17th Forestry Symposium* (Baton Rouge: Louisiana State University Press, 1968), 10; Mark J. Schroeder and Charles S. Buck, "Fire Weather," *United States Department of Agriculture Handbook no. 360* (Washington, D.C.: United States Department of Agriculture, Forestry Service, 1970), 30; Carville V. Earle, *The Evolution of a Tidewater Settlement System: All Hallow's Parish, Maryland, 1650–1783* (University of Chicago Department of Geography Research paper no. 170, 1975), 34. Cronon (*Changes in the Land*, 122–3) notes these climatic changes in colonial New England, and it seems likely that such alterations also occurred in the southern colonies, especially as colonists adopted more efficient and thorough clearing techniques.

19. Greene, *Carter Diary*, vol. 2, 635; Moehring, "Climatic Elements," 10.

further justified colonists' faith in heavily forested regions which, when newly
cleared, revealed "a stratum of rich black mould."[20] In later years, however, the
intense heat of the southern summer created problems for colonial farmers.
Lacking the necessary humus to absorb and retain ground water, fields dried to
a hard-packed surface that resisted even the most efficient plows and hardiest
draft animals. The ground water that did accumulate after a rain evaporated
quickly and only increased the hardening effect. Carter discovered that, like the
sun, "prodigious rains" "baked the ground excessively," making the summers
drier than in times past.[21]

During winter and early spring, deforestation seemed to create the opposite
effect. Carter spoke of the excessive wetness of the winter, noting that the "land
runs into cohesion with every little moisture." For the most part, wetter winters
were only a seasonal illusion. In the long run, removing the forest cover from
plantation tracts speeded evaporation and kept soil drier throughout the year.
Winter and early spring appeared wetter because, without broadleaf trees to
regulate ground temperatures, the soil froze to a greater depth than in the
surrounding forests. As fields warmed during the temperate winter days, the
land became muddy and difficult to till. Because the ground sometimes froze
again at night, most of the moisture remained trapped in the soil, to be released
once more the following day. The lack of shade also meant that the infrequent
snows melted more rapidly, adding still more water to the miry ground. When
the warmer temperatures of late spring finally ended the messy cycle of freezing
and thawing, fields could no longer retain the ground water, and it soon
evaporated or ran off into nearby streams.[22]

The annual spring thaw also increased runoff from wooded areas, but there
the forest itself helped regulate the flow. Newly budding broadleaf trees
combined with thick evergreens to break up and scatter the spring rains over a
broader plain. In addition, humus and accumulated ground litter not only
trapped moisture, but also held the topsoil in place. In cleared fields, however,
rains fell unimpeded and carried topsoil into adjacent streams, filling them with
sediment. Once deposited in the streambed, sediment reduced the carrying
capacity of streams and rivers. With fewer beaver dams to trap debris and settle
it out in ponds, the flow rate increased. In cleared regions, small streams might

20. Quotation from Harry J. Carman and Rexford Tugwell, eds., *American Husbandry* (New York:
Columbia University Press, 1939), 164. Ward, "Northeastern Hardwood Forests," in Horwitz,
Clearcutting, 66–8.
21. Quotation from Greene, *Carter Diary*, vol. 1, 612. Cronon, *Changes in the Land*, 122–3.
22. Quotation from Greene, *Carter Diary*, vol. 1, 462. Charles W. Ralston, "Clearcutting of Public
Forests in the Southern Pine Region," in Horwitz, *Clearcutting*, 95; Cronon, *Changes in the
Land*, 122–4.

reach flood level with every prolonged rain, whereas larger rivers overflowed their banks more often and caused greater damage.[23]

In the southern colonies, such effects were most pronounced in the piedmont, where stream valleys were narrower and subject to flooding. During the eighteenth century, as colonists moved into and cleared portions of Virginia's hilly up-country, flush piedmont streams sometimes roared across the fall line into the coastal plain and flooded more level terrain. Such spring floods or freshets could wreak havoc in the tidal estuaries. Destructive freshets struck the region in 1685, 1724, 1738, and 1752, culminating in the worst flood in Chesapeake history in 1771. That freshet exceeded the regular tides by over forty feet, destroying tobacco warehouses, some six thousand hogsheads of tobacco, and a number of large ships. Sediment carried by the flood waters clogged channels and altered the courses of several streams. Contemporary estimates placed damages from the 1771 freshet at two million pounds sterling.[24]

Agricultural clearing intensified other effects of the storms that brought the floods. One of the chief ecological functions of the standing forest is to reduce the effects of wind on the surrounding countryside. In wooded areas, the crowns of larger trees catch and dissipate the violent gusts of winter and spring so that vegetation near the ground remains protected from the icy blasts. But if no forests stand in their way, winds can gather speed over level terrain and cause extensive damage to exposed fields.[25] More than once, Carter found his winter fodder "blown into stemms" by such tempests. In 1775, the anonymous author of *American Husbandry*, a treatise on New World agriculture, urged those settling in the Ohio Valley to preserve a stand of trees as shelter from the northwest wind. Under no circumstances, the writer warned, should those farmers repeat the mistakes of southern colonists who had "attack[ed] all the timber around their houses with such undistinguishing rage, as not to leave themselves ... a tree within sight."[26]

The climatic changes associated with deforestation were local variations and more prominent in the late eighteenth-century Chesapeake, where more land was thoroughly cleared and higher latitude made for more dramatic seasonal variation. But not all timber cutting resulted directly from the desire for open farmland. In all the English colonies, settlers and the Crown regarded the American forest as both enemy and friend. The dense woods harbored wild

23. Cronon, *Changes in the Land*, 123–5; Joseph Kittredge, *Forest Influences* (New York: McGraw-Hill, 1948), 271; Richard Lee, *Forest Hydrology*, (New York: Columbia University Press, 1980), 280–1.
24. Arthur Pierce Middleton, *Tobacco Coast: A Maritime History of ChesapeakeBay in the Colonial Era* (1953; reprint, Baltimore, Md.: Johns Hopkins University Press, 1984), 57–9.
25. Cronon, *Changes in the Land*, 122–3.
26. Greene, *Carter Diary*, vol. 1, 381–2; Carman and Tugwell, *American Husbandry*, 226.

creatures (human and otherwise) and stood in the way of agriculture; yet, at the same time, the forests promised to create a lucrative market in timber products. Unlike the gold and silver the Spanish retrieved from the New World, trees could be procured with the most basic tools and a comparatively small labor force. In contrast to fur traders, would-be lumbermen needed no guns, liquor, or blankets to trade with Indians.[27]

Among Englishmen already accustomed to local wood shortages in their homeland, the ready availability of "faire, straight, tall, and as good timber as any can be" engendered dreams of a wood supply to rival that of the heavily forested Baltic countries. The author of one early promotional tract boldly predicted that southern trees would soon "finde a speedy Market, since the decay of Timber is a defect growne universall in Europe, and the commodity such a necessary Staple, that no civil Nation can be conveniently without it." The Jamestown colonists wasted little time in trying to fulfill such prophecy. The first ships to leave Virginia for England carried pine, oak, and other trees to be used in the construction of houses and vessels.[28]

Optimism and ambition notwithstanding, it soon proved much too costly to ship whole trees or freshly cut logs across the Atlantic. The cargo simply weighed too much and took up space that could be devoted to more profitable items such as tobacco and skins.[29] In the southern colonies, the lumber industry first developed locally as an outgrowth of agricultural clearing. In addition to farmland, newly arriving colonists required some sort of temporary shelter, both for themselves and their servants or slaves. Wood from the cleared plots quickly found its way into such structures. Thomas Nairne's instructions for building a "plantation" in South Carolina reflected the link between agriculture and the production of finished lumber.

> If anyone desires to make a plantation, in this Province, out of the Woods, the first thing to be done is, after having cutt down a few Trees, to split Palissades, or Clapboards, and therewith make small Houses or Hutts, to shelther the Slaves. After that, whilst some servants are cleaning the land,

27. Cronon, *Changes in the Land,* 109; K. G. Davies, *The North Atlantic World in the Seventeenth Century* (Minneapolis: University of Minnesota Press, 1974), 193.
28. Quotations from Thomas Harriot, "A Briefe and True Report of the Newfound Land of Virginia," in David B. Quinn, ed., *The Roanoke Voyages,* 2 vols. (London: The Hakluyt Society, 1955), vol. 1, 363; and Williams, *Virginia Richly Valued,* 41. On early timber exports from Virginia, see Berkeley, "New Description," in Force, *Tracts,* vol. 2: Tract VII, 5; and William Strachey, *The Historie of Travell into Virginia Brittania,* ed. Louis B. Wright and Virginia Freund (London: Hakluyt Society, 1953), 130.
29. Robert G. Albion, *Forests and Sea Power* (Cambridge, Mass.: Harvard University Press, 1926), 240; Cronon, *Changes in the Land,* 109.

others are to be employed in squaring or sawing Wall-plats, Posts, Boards, and Shingles, for a small House for the Family, which usually serves for a Kitchin afterwards, when they are in better circumstances to build a larger [dwelling].[30]

Early settlers who followed Nairne's instructions sawed or hewed their building materials by hand, but those who demanded finished lumber in quantity soon resorted to more efficient methods. As early as 1650, promotional writers urged that "the Saw mill may be taken into consideration" so that "Timber for building houses, and shipping may be more speedily prepared." In the southern colonies, as elsewhere, the term sawmill could apply to almost any sort of lumber production. Throughout the colonial period, much lumber was prepared on plantations, where specially trained slaves sawed planks by hand. Water-powered mills like those in England required a substantial investment in capital and labor. Water mills were in use in all the southern colonies by the mid eighteenth century, but usually belonged to large landowners with enough capital and labor to build and supply such an operation. In the upper Cape Fear valley of North Carolina, however, emigrant[?] Scottish Highlanders pooled their resources to build community mills and then divided the profits among the investors. Early Georgia, too, had community sawmills, supported in part by funds from the colony's Trustees (founders). For large landowners, a sawmill proved doubly advantageous. It not only provided lumber for the plantation, but also gave slaves another task to perform in the off-season when crops needed less attention.[31]

Although much less productive than modern lumber yards, water-powered colonial mills might still turn out several hundred board feet of finished wood a day. Such comparatively efficient production eventually helped create the timber export business early explorers and colonists had envisioned. Because it weighed less and took up less space than freshly cut logs and tree trunks, finished lumber could be shipped at a cheaper rate. Moreover, colonists discovered a ready market for wood products much closer to home. In the West Indies the clearing of vast tracts for sugar plantations created a wood shortage so severe that colonists in Barbados once tried to annex the island of St. Lucia in order to gain access to a new supply of timber. The close proximity of a Caribbean market further cut shipping costs so that by the mid eighteenth

30. Nairne, *Letter*, 49.
31. Quotation from Williams, *Virginia Richly Valued*, 5. Cronon, *Changes in the Land*, 109; H. Roy Merrens, *Colonial North Carolina in the Eighteenth Century* (Chapel Hill: University of North Carolina Press, 1964), 100; G. Melvin Herndon, "Timber Products of Colonial Georgia," *Georgia Historical Quarterly* 57 (1973), 57.

century, timber leaving the major southern ports went "largely to the West Indies."[32]

Unlike agricultural clearing, which placed an equal bounty on every tree standing in the way of the plow, the export market required wood to suit the specific needs of the buyer. In all the English colonies, such demand meant selectively cutting certain trees in greater numbers. Because their export business relied heavily on rum, molasses, and raw sugar, Caribbean merchants needed a continuous supply of materials for constructing barrels and hogsheads in which to ship their merchandise. The staves usually came from the strong, durable, and slightly pliable oaks common to eastern America. Any oak could be cut into staves, but colonists generally preferred to harvest white oak because it grew larger than most species and yielded more staves per tree. Some Southerners still refer to the trees as stave oaks, modern testimony to their importance in barrel making.[33]

In deforested parts of the West Indies, white oak was also in demand as a building material. Its dense, hard wood proved especially suitable for framing and rafters. White oak logs could be riven into "clapboard," the colonial term for siding.[34] Together with the high value farmers placed on its habitat, commercial demand for white oak gradually led to shortages of larger trees in settled regions. Among those who witnessed the effects of colonial lumbering on southern oaks were the French naturalist André Michaux and his son François André Michaux. During the 1780s and 1790s, André Michaux traveled widely in eastern America, ranging as far north as Quebec and west to the Ohio country. But his particular interest was the flora of the southern colonies. One of Michaux's prize possessions was his garden near Charles Town, where he transplanted specimens from his forest excursions. By 1801 André Michaux had published a book on American oaks and planned a multivolume work that would include virtually all the trees in North America. Michaux died before he could publish this second work, but his son François André Michaux took up his father's task and brought out the five-volume *North American Sylva* between 1810 and 1813. Drawing on his father's work, the younger Michaux (who also traveled in the South) noted that by the late

32. Quotation from Carman and Tugwell, *American Husbandry*, 163. For a contemporary account of sawmill production, see De Brahm, *General Survey*, 94. See also Cronon, *Changes in the Land*, 119. The growth of the West Indian lumber trade can also be charted through legislation fixing the dimensions of the various timber products and laws providing for lumber inspection. See J. P. Kinney, *The Development of Forest Law in America Including Forest Legislation in America Prior to March 4, 1789* (New York: Arno, 1972), 386–7.

33. Cronon, *Changes in the Land*, 111–12; Davies, *North Atlantic World*, 193; Merrens, *Colonial North Carolina*, 102–3; Elbert L. Little, *The Audubon Society Field Guide to North American Trees, Eastern Region* (New York: Knopf, 1980), 383.

34. G. Melvin Herndon, ed., *William Tatham and the Culture of Tobacco* (Coral Gables, Fla.: University of Miami Press, 1969), 32.

eighteenth century, white oak was "less employed than formerly in building only because it is more scarce and costly."[35]

In addition to white oak, coopers required more pliable wood that could be bent into hoops and fitted around the ends of barrels to hold the staves in place. Few trees proved better suited to that purpose than the various species of hickories that grew alongside oaks in the southern uplands. Because hickory wood hardens as it ages, hoops could be fashioned only from the more pliable saplings, and coopers seldom used wood from trees more than twelve feet tall. Moreover, merchants found it difficult to lay in a store of saplings because cut trees seemed particularly prone to attack by insects and decay. By selectively and continuously cutting the saplings, colonial lumbermen effectively slowed the regeneration process. As with white oaks, the Michauxs found small hickories "scarce in all parts of the country which [had] been long settled."[36]

Colonists who cleared bottomlands and tidal swamps discovered a market for two other trees: bald cypress and Atlantic white cedar. Because both species flourish in damp, low-lying areas, they produce wood that easily withstands repeated wetting and drying. Colonists also noticed that cedar and cypress logs proved "extraordinarily light, and free to rive," traits that, combined with their durability, made them excellent roofing material. As John Lawson wrote of white cedar, "The best Shingles for Houses are made of this Wood, it being no Strain to the Roof, and never rots." Like the production of oak staves and hickory hoops, shingle making began as a plantation industry. Landowners with access to the prized trees taught their slaves to rive shingles in winter, when they had fewer crops to tend and were already engaged in clearing the woods for new fields. During the eighteenth century, making shingles for export became an important part of the lumber business in the southern colonies.[37]

The growing importance of shingle making along the South Atlantic coast probably resulted in part from the depletion of cedar supplies farther north. By the mid eighteenth century, travelers in New England and the Middle Colonies found cedar stands diminishing. Such scarcities stemmed from the cedar's peculiar means of regenerating. The trees grow best in swampy ground, yet they require a dry, exposed seedbed in order to sprout. Most swamps produce thick stands of trees that shade the soil, meaning that cedars gain a toehold only after the canopy thins, either from a sudden recession of the impounded waters or, more commonly, from fire. But in order to create appropriate conditions for

35. Quotation from François André Michaux, *The North American Sylva; Or a Description of the Forest Trees of the United States, Canada, and Nova Scotia*, trans. J. Jay Smith, 5 vols. (Philadelphia: Rice, Rutter, and Co., 1865), vol. 1, 24. U. P. Hedrick, *A History of Horticulture in America to 1860* (New York: Oxford University Press, 1950), 192.
36. Michaux, *North American Sylva*, vol. 1, 138.
37. Lawson, *New Voyage*, 103; Merrens, *Colonial North Carolina*, 105–6.

a white cedar forest, such fires must occur only when the water table is high enough to keep cedar seeds (which are encased in tiny cones) from burning. Because they depend on some natural clearing agent, white cedars, like pines, are typical of the early stages of forest succession and eventually give way to a broadleaf forest of bays and other hardwoods.[38]

South Atlantic colonists took to their new role in the trade with vigor. Planters advertising land for sale tried to attract buyers with promises of "seadar and sypress swamps" that might supplement their incomes. In North Carolina, such land could be found in quantity to the north of Albemarle Sound in the vicinity of Great Dismal Swamp. Together with the availability of trees, the region's comparatively high population density made it a center of shingle production. Also rich in raw material, the Cape Fear valley offered the convenience of a larger slave population and it too became important in the trade. In those and other low-lying areas of the coastal plain, colonists soon added Atlantic white cedar and cypress to the list of diminishing trees.[39]

Cedars, oaks, and hickories were also cut for export in New England and the Middle Colonies, but several trees unique to the South also found their way to market. One of these was southern live oak, which became important to the shipbuilding industry. As David Ramsay explained, ships made of water-resistant live oak might "last upwards of forty years, [even] though employed in the destructive climate of the West Indies, and in carrying sugars, than which nothing is more trying to the timbers." Because it grew only in a narrow band across the dunelands and barrier islands, the live oak soon fell victim to selective cutting. The shift to cotton production in the late eighteenth century took an even greater toll as South Carolinians removed the trees to plant valuable sea-island cotton. Like most of their species, live oaks grow slowly and are typical of the latter stages of forest succession. Once destroyed, the trees seldom replaced themselves; by 1800 lumbermen found it increasingly "difficult to procure sticks of considerable size in the Southern States."[40]

Valuable as they might be, however, neither oaks, hickories, nor cedars could measure up to that most valuable southern tree, the longleaf pine. "Fine-

38. Cronon, *Changes in the Land*, 113; Merrens, *Colonial North Carolina*, 105–6; Murray F. Buell and Robert L. Cain, "The Successional Role of Southern White Cedar, *Chamaecypaius Thyoides*, in Southeastern North Carolina," *Ecology* 24 (1943), 91–4.

39. Quotation from "Thomas Smith to Burrell Massinerd, London, 7 November, 1705," in Merrens, *Colonial South Carolina Scene*, 23; idem, *Colonial North Carolina*, 105–6; Peter C. Stewart, "The Shingle and Lumber Industries in the Great Dismal," *Journal of Forest History* (April 1981), 98–100; Cecil C. Frost, "Historical Overview of Atlantic White Cedar in the Carolinas," in Aimlee D. Laderman, ed., *Atlantic White Cedar Wetlands* (Boulder, Colo.: Westview, 1987), 260–1.

40. Quotations from Ramsay, *Ramsay's History of South Carolina*, vol. 2, 148; and Michaux, *North American Sylva*, vol. 1, 54. Albert E. Cowdrey, *This Land, This South: An Environmental History* (Lexington: University Press of Kentucky, 1983), 53.

grained and susceptible of bright polish," longleaf pine planks proved ideal for ceilings, floors, and interior walls. Strong and durable, it also made excellent deck planking for ships. Most important, the trees seemed inexhaustible, stretching from southern Virginia and across the rest of the South in an almost unbroken hundred-mile-wide band.[41]

Because colonial farmers shied away from the sandy soils in which the trees flourished, pine logs could not be acquired as a convenient by-product of agricultural clearing. Procuring finished pine lumber in quantity required special techniques best suited to large estates that housed many slaves. During winter, when the sap reached its lowest ebb, planters of sufficient means set up temporary camps in the longleaf forests. William Bartram witnessed one such operation along the Savannah River. Written in his always poetic style, Bartram's description calls to mind modern logging camps of the Pacific Northwest. The slaves, he reported, stood "mounted on the massive timber logs, [while] the regular strokes of their gleaming axes re-echoed in the deep forests." The "timber landing" to which the slaves brought the felled trees rested on a bluff sixty to seventy feet above the stream. Slaves rolled logs off the high embankment into the river, roped them together in rafts, and floated them some fifty miles to Savannah. Wherever large streams intersected the long-leaf forests, colonists set up similar operations. John Collet's map of North Carolina, drawn in 1770, shows most of the sawmills situated along the Cape Fear, Neuse, and their major tributaries – perfect locations for tapping the colony's plentiful supply of longleaf pines.[42]

Colonists and the Crown not only valued pines for their lumber, but also for their thick, straw-colored sap, known to Englishmen as resin or turpentine. Englishmen found hundreds of uses for pine sap. Spirits of turpentine, the volatile liquid constituent of the resin, had a wide variety of medicinal uses. Applied externally, its natural heating properties helped relieve sore joints and muscles; taken internally in small doses, it served as a laxative and diuretic. Those who could afford it used spirits of turpentine to drive fleas from their stables and bedrooms. Rosin, the solid part of the sap, might be fashioned into candles or blended with lye to produce medicinal soap.[43]

But Englishmen most valued pines for two other products: tar and pitch. Soldiers used pine tar to lubricate wheels of wagons and field artillery. Farmers used tar as a preservative for fence posts and applied it to seed corn to deter

41. Michaux, *North American Sylva*, vol. 3, 107–8.
42. William Bartram, *Travels of William Bartram*, ed. Mark Van Doren (New York: Dover, 1955), 256–7; John Collet, "A Compleat Map of North Carolina from an Actual Survey by Capt. Collet, Governor of Ft. Johnston," Library of Congress, Geography and Map Division; Merrens, *Colonial North Carolina*, 98–101.
43. Thomas Gamble, *Naval Stores: History, Production, Distillation, and Consumption* (Savannah: Review Publishing and Printing Company, 1921), 29–30.

birds and rodents. Water that had been allowed to stand on tar was believed to be an effective remedy for coughs and respiratory diseases in both livestock and humans. During the colonial period, however, the Crown sought tar mainly for its uses in shipbuilding. Rope used as rigging first had to be coated with tar to prevent weathering and fraying. Pitch, an even heavier, stickier substance obtained by boiling down tar, provided a protective coating for the hulls of wooden ships. Because of their importance to the maritime industry, tar, pitch, and the crude resin or turpentine that produced them came to be known as "naval stores."[44]

The earliest explorers along the South Atlantic coast were quick to recognize the potential of the pinelands. The Frenchmen who established the tiny and short-lived outpost at Charlesfort in 1562 used resin from nearby pines in constructing a ship. Early English colonists also realized that the scaly-barked conifers were a prime resource. Before colonization, England relied primarily on the Baltic countries to furnish the Royal Navy with tar and pitch. The expansive pinelands of the South Atlantic coastal plain promised to alleviate that dependence, and investors in the Jamestown colony urged settlers to make immediate use of the trees. When he arrived in Virginia with the "second supply," Christopher Newport brought with him a number of Poles and "Dutchmen" to instruct colonists in the manufacture of tar and pitch. After Virginia became a crown colony in 1624, Charles I continued to call for the production of naval stores, demanding in 1632 that colonists send samples of their tar and pitch to England for inspection. Charles II went even further, authorizing Governor William Berkeley to ship three hundred tons of tobacco to England duty-free if the governor could also send over a like amount of tar, pitch, and other commodities.[45]

Despite such encouragement from across the Atlantic, the naval stores industry was slow to take hold in Virginia. During the early years of colonization, the high profits made from tobacco exports led to the neglect of other commodities. But the slow development of tar and pitch production also has an ecological explanation. The loblolly and Virginia pines growing near Jamestown and in the surrounding vicinity produced only a thick resin that, although it contained "turpentine in abundance," required much time and effort to distill. Moreover, both species grew best in old Indian fields or other cleared areas, meaning that, at the time of colonization, pure stands suitable for large-scale production were sparsely distributed. John Pory clearly defined the

44. Sinclair Snow, "Naval Stores in Colonial Virginia," *Virginia Magazine of History and Biography* 72 (1964), 75–6.
45. "Rene Laudonniere's account of the First French Settlement at Charlesfort," in David B. Quinn, ed., *New American World: A Documentary History of North America to 1612*, 5 vols. (New York: Arno Press and Hector Bye, Inc., 1979), vol. 2, 306; Snow, "Naval Stores in Virginia," 78–82.

problem in 1620, when he noted that "in Poland a principall country for that comidity, there be whole forests of pytch trees" that grew "for fower and five hundred myles together." But, in eastern Virginia, Pory observed, the "same kinde of trees grow but . . . skatteringe here one and there one, and may indeed be employed to that use but w[i]th greate labor, and as greate losse."[46]

Colonists settling farther south had better luck. In the Carolinas, colonists encountered pure stands of longleaf pines perfect for commercial exploitation. Those trees produced a thinner resin that, as William Byrd explained in 1728, "abound[ed] more with Turpentine and consequently Yield[ed] more Tarr, than either the Yellow [loblolly] or the White Pine."[46] In addition, the milder winters common to the southern coastal plain meant that valuable resin flowed up to "6 mo[nth]s. longer than in Virginia and the more Northern plantations."[47]

Settlement of the Carolinas and access to the longleaf pine forests coincided with a new and urgent demand for tar and pitch in England. In 1689 the Stockholm Tar Company received a monopoly for the naval stores trade and the price of pitch and tar from the Baltic region rose dramatically. As hostilities between England and France increased during the years that followed, those commodities became even more scarce and costly. The Great Northern War between Russia and Sweden, which lasted from 1699 to 1721, further restricted tar and pitch sales so that trade between England and the Baltic countries eventually fell off by 80 percent. In response to this crisis, Parliament passed legislation in 1705 that provided bounties of four pounds per ton on American tar and pitch and three pounds per ton on rosin and turpentine. For a time, Parliament's tactics stimulated production throughout the colonies. By 1715 America was supplying roughly half of England's need for naval stores. By 1722 competition from North and South Carolina producers had lowered the price of Baltic tar from fifty to twelve shillings per barrel. In 1729, after complaints about the quality of American tar, Parliament cut back on the bounties. That change and the emergence of rice culture in South Carolina substantially reduced that colony's exports of naval stores during the 1730s. But even if they could not depend on Parliament for support, southern colonists continued to produce tar, pitch, and turpentine. North Carolina, which never developed a single-crop economy like its neighbors to the north and south, led the southern colonies in exports of naval stores. Virginia, despite its slow start and lack of

46. Quotation from John Pory, "A Letter to Sir Edwin Sandys, June 12, 1620," in Susan Myra Kingsbury, ed., *The Records of the Virginia Company of London*, 4 vols. (Washington, D.C.: Government Printing Office, 1906–1935), vol. 3, 303. Snow, "Naval Stores in Virginia," 78–9; W. W. Ashe, "The Forests, Forest Lands, and Forest Products of Eastern North Carolina," *North Carolina Geological Survey Bulletin No. 5* (Raleigh, 1894), 73.

47. William Byrd II, *Histories of the Dividing Line Betwixt Virginia and North Carolina*, ed. William K. Boyd (1929; reprint, Mineola, N.Y.: Dover, 1967), 90.

longleaf pines, ranked second, followed by South Carolina, Georgia, and Maryland.[48]

Due to the demand for tar and pitch, virtually any southern colonist who could get to a stand of pines could make naval stores; ownership was not necessarily a prerequisite for access. North Carolina farmers settling in or near the longleaf forest sometimes tapped trees that legally belonged to speculators or other planters. But, as with pine lumber, producing turpentine, tar, and pitch in quantity usually required significant numbers of slaves and vast tracts of pine-laden land, preferably near a navigable stream. And not just any slaves would do. Skilled labor was essential, not only for acquiring the product, but also for packing it in barrels and shipping it downstream to the port towns. Writing in 1741, James Murray, a North Carolina planter, told one of the colony's leading landholders that "If you intend to do any business here, a Cooper and a Craft that will carry about 100 barrels will be absolutely necessary. I have suffer'd much for want of them, and that want of Craft and negroes will be a great obstruction in securing the Quantity of Naval Stores at this time that otherwise I might do."[49]

To acquire raw turpentine (resin), colonists employed at least two techniques. In winter, when they had fewer demands on their time, colonists sent their slaves into the pine forests to cut two or more deep grooves in a standing tree so that the cuts converged near the base, where colonists installed several planks to act as a trough for the resin. A second and more common method was to cut large rectangular notches, called "boxes," on both sides of larger longleaf pines. The valuable sap collected on the flat bottom edge of the box, where, as John Brickell noted, "the Negroes with Ladles take it out and put it into Barrels."[50]

Separating resin into spirits of turpentine and rosin required that raw sap be placed in large copper kettles, one part resin to four parts water. The entire mixture then had to be boiled until it separated into a "thin and clear Oil like Water" (spirits of turpentine) and the solid rosin that remained at the bottom of the vats. Because the distillation process demanded much labor and had to be

48. Justin Williams, "English Mercantilism and Carolina Naval Stores," *Journal of Southern History* 1 (1935), 171–2; Clarence L. Ver Steeg, *Origins of a Southern Mosaic: Studies of Early Carolina and Georgia* (Athens: University of Georgia Press, 1975), 121; Francis Yonge, "A View of the Trade of South-Carolina With Proposals humbly Offer'd for Improving the Same," in Merrens, *Colonial South Carolina Scene*, 69–70; G. Melvin Herndon, "Naval Stores in Colonial Georgia," *Georgia Historical Quarterly* 52 (1968), 433.
49. Quotation from Nina M. Tiffany, ed., *Letters of James Murray, Loyalist* (Boston, 1910), 64. Merrens, *Colonial North Carolina*, 89; Percival Perry, "The Naval Stores Industry in the Old South," *Journal of Southern History* 34 (1968), 512; Wood, *Black Majority*, 112.
50. John Brickell, *The Natural History of North Carolina* (1737; reprint, Murfreesboro, N.C.: Johnson Reprint, 1969), 265; Wood, *Black Majority*, 112.

COLLECTING THE CRUDE TURPENTINE.

Figure 5.2. A nineteenth- or early twentieth-century engraving showing the techniques used to extract resin or crude turpentine from longleaf pines. Though the clothing and tools of the workers are modern, the trees probably look much like those tapped during the colonial period. Reproduced by courtesy of the North Carolina Department of Cultural Resources, Division of Archives and History, Raleigh.

done in spring, when slaves had other duties to perform, most early colonists chose not to produce the finished products. Instead, they shipped the barrels of raw sap to England for distillation. As Brickell remarked, "The Rosin is very scarce in these parts, few giving themselves the trouble." Not until the late eighteenth century did colonists begin to distill their own spirits and rosin in quantity.[51]

Although raw turpentine production did not require that trees be cut down, the process had many other ecological implications. Most of the sap accumulated in July and August, a prime fire season in the coastal plain. Rarely more than twelve inches from the ground and filled with volatile resin, the boxes became especially susceptible to lightning fires or blazes kindled through "the carelessness of travelers and wagoners." Without thick bark to retard the flames, the fires burned through to the heartwood, either consuming the whole tree or damaging it so severely that it soon died. Destructive wildfires in turpentine "orchards" could easily be identified by the thick black smoke of burning resin, an ominous signal that the owner of the trees would be out of business for the season.[52]

To reduce the risk of wildfire, some settlers practiced a technique known as "raking the faces." Periodically during the fire season and once or twice in winter, colonists or their slaves raked twigs, dead needles, and other debris from around the bases of boxed trees. These small, cleared circles served as miniature firebreaks that prevented stray flames and sparks from igniting the boxes. In the late eighteenth century, turpentine producers added a new twist to the technique. Once the orchard had been raked, colonists sometimes set light ground fires designed to consume ground litter and render the site less susceptible to an uncontrolled blaze. Although the practice helped protect larger pines, it proved disastrous for young trees. Not yet fire-resistant, seedlings and small saplings perished along with the ground litter. A winter burn might also destroy the seed crop, crippling the forest's ability to reproduce itself.[53]

Even if they escaped damage from wildfire, boxed or grooved trees seldom survived for long. When the pines stopped producing resin in quantity,

51. Brickell, *Natural History*, 267; Gamble, *Naval Stores*, 18.
52. Quotation from Michaux, *North American Sylva*, vol. 3, 111. Brickell, *Natural History*, 26; Norman R. Hawley, "Burning in a Naval Stores Forest," *Proceedings of the Tall Timbers Fire Ecology Conference* 3 (1964), 83–4; Stephen J. Pyne, *Fire in America: A Cultural History of Wildland and Rural Fire* (Princeton, N.J.: Princeton University Press, 1982), 149.
53. Hawley, "Burning," 84; Charles Mohr, *Timber Pines of the Southern United States* (Washington, D.C.: Government Printing Office, 1894), 62. One of the more interesting features of naval stores production is the lack of change in the techniques used to tap the trees. Not until the mid nineteenth century, when metal cups replaced boxes, did practices begin to differ substantially from those used in the colonial period. The risks of fire and the methods for coping with it remained essentially unaltered.

colonists moved on to tap other trees, leaving the dry boxes and grooves behind. In much the same way as they collected sap, abandoned cuts often filled with rainwater, increasing the likelihood of attack by fungi and decay. Trees damaged by naval stores production also attracted bark and wood-boring beetles. François André Michaux might have seen trees boxed for turpentine when he reported that insects had left "extensive tracts of the finest pines . . . covered only with dead trees."[54]

Pitch and tar production exacted an even greater toll. During the early years of colonization, the Crown urged Virginia settlers to learn the "East Country" method of distilling tar, a technique used on the firs of the Baltic countries. The East Country method called for bark to be removed from standing trees to a point eight feet above the ground. The trees then had to be left undisturbed for at least a year until the barked area became saturated with sap, whereupon the trees were cut and the pitchy lower trunks burned to produce tar.[55]

Although widely regarded as the best means for procuring high-quality tar, the East Country method required time and energy that South Atlantic colonists preferred to devote to agricultural commodities such as tobacco and rice. Consequently, early settlers chose another, less demanding technique. Colonists or their slaves first sought a slightly elevated mound or knoll on which they dug a circular pit. Four to six feet away, they scooped out another, shallower depression connected to the first by a narrow ditch. Known as a kiln, the entire structure was lined with clay to facilitate the flow of tar. During winter, colonists sent their slaves into the pine forest to gather dead, dry pine boughs called lightwood. They placed the wood in the pit and covered it with clay or sod, leaving small openings near the bottom of the woodpile. The "tar-burners" then set the highly volatile wood on fire, but because the holes at the base of the kiln afforded only a slight draft, the pile smoldered for weeks. Slaves tended the kilns constantly, making sure the fire did not go out or burn too hot. Tar, produced by the slow combustion, collected at the center of the pit and flowed through the ditch to the receptacle, where it could be ladled into barrels for export or boiled into pitch.[56]

Kiln tar proved much inferior to that extracted by the East Country method. The high temperatures of the kilns led to the accumulation of wood acids in the tar. When applied to ship's rigging, those acids sometimes weakened or "burned" the very ropes the tar was supposed to protect. Tar from the southern colonies also retained clay residue from the kilns, which affected its purity. Despite the Crown's continuing efforts to discourage them, colonists

54. Michaux, *North American Sylva*, vol. 3, 110; Mohr, *Timber Pines*, 72; A. W. Schorger and H. S. Betts, "The Naval Stores Industry," *United States Department of Agriculture Bulletin No. 229* (Washington, D.C.: United States Department of Agriculture, 1915), 25–7.
55. Snow, "Naval Stores in Virginia," 78.
56. Brickell, *Natural History*, 265–6; Mohr, *Timber Pines*, 68; Wood, *Black Majority*, 112–13.

found the kilns too convenient to abandon. Kilns could be fired at almost any time of year, allowing slaves to tend crops or take care of other, more demanding seasonal chores.[57]

Kilns consumed pine at an alarming rate. By 1753 North Carolina annually exported about 61,528 barrels of tar and 12,052 barrels of pitch. Because it took almost a full cord of lightwood to make a barrel of tar and one-third to one-half again as much to produce pitch, North Carolinians were probably processing some seventy-five thousand cords of pine per year – the equivalent of a stack of wood 4 feet high, 4 feet wide, and 113 miles long. Because colonists preferred dry light wood for the kilns, slaves did not need to cut living trees to feed the furnaces. The use of deadwood allowed tar burners to recycle pines that had initially been used for other purposes. John Brickell reported that colonists often sent their slaves into abandoned turpentine orchards to split those dead and dying trees into usable lightwood. Likewise, smaller branches and residue from pines cut for lumber and those toppled by wind or ice could be salvaged for the kilns.[58]

At seventy-five thousand cords per year, however, colonists who produced naval stores in quantity could still strip a pine forest of suitable wood. Exactly how fast a tract of pines became depleted depended on a number of factors, including the size and number of trees. But a colonist with ten slaves who produced turpentine, tar, and pitch might have been able to exhaust one thousand acres of pines in as little as three years.[59] By the last quarter of the eighteenth century, anyone traveling through the longleaf forests could witness the effects of naval stores production. Ebenezer Hazard, who journeyed through the coastal plain in 1777 and 1778, thought it "very dangerous riding in No. Carolina when the Winds blow hard, for you ride all the Way through Pines, many of which have been 'boxed' to get the Turpentine out & others have been so much burned by burning the Woods that a high Wind is very apt to overset them."[60]

The long-term effects on the pinelands were less obvious. Longleaf pines

57. Governor Robert Johnson, "A Governor Answers a Questionnaire, 1719/20," in Merrens, *Colonial South Carolina Scene,* 65; Ashe, "Forests, Forest Lands, and Forest Products," 75; Brickell, *Natural History,* 265.

58. Gamble, *Naval Stores,* 21; Mohr, *Timber Pines,* 67–8. My description of the amount as one giant cord of wood is drawn from Cronon's similar treatment of firewood in New England (Cronon, *Changes in the Land,* 120). Brickell, *Natural History,* 265.

59. Lewis Cecil Gray, *History of Agriculture in the Southern United States to 1860,* 2 vols. (1932; reprint, Gloucester, Mass.: Peter Smith, 1958), vol. 1, 111; Converse D. Clowse, *Economic Beginnings of South Carolina, 1670–1730* (Columbia: University of South Carolina Press, 1971), 178. This estimate is based on naval stores industries in East Florida between 1763 and 1783. The same might have held true farther north.

60. Hugh B. Johnston, ed., "The Journal of Ebenezer Hazard in North Carolina, 1777 and 1778," *North Carolina Historical Review* 36 (1959), 375–6.

produce abundant seed crops only every three to four years and up to 90 percent of those usually fall victim to squirrels, turkeys, and other animals. During the early stages of its growth, the longleaf is also particularly sensitive to competition from other plants, and seedlings are often crowded out by perennial grasses and herbs. Colonists further restricted pine reproduction by choosing the largest trees for their sawmills and turpentine orchards. Such trees generally grew only in older pine forests where smaller hardwoods (harbingers of the next stage of forest succession) had already moved in beneath the lofty conifers. Cutting pines reduced competition for the sprouting oaks and hickories, "releasing" them to dominate the site.[61]

But the vastness of the pinelands and the seasonal nature of lumbering and the naval stores industry effectively reduced the threat of shortages during the colonial period. Southerners probably did not begin to realize the implications of unrestricted production until the mid nineteenth century, when improved overland transportation made it economically feasible to tap trees farther inland and copper stills eliminated some of the labor involved in turpentine distillation. By 1850 the formerly pure longleaf forests of northeastern North Carolina had given way to small tracts of oak mingled with stands of loblolly pine. The still-visible mounds of ancient tar kilns gave silent testimony to colonial exploitation, prompting one nineteenth-century observer to note that "the distribution of no tree has been more affected than that of the long-leaf pine by the transformation from a wilderness to a civilized country."[62]

Late eighteenth- and nineteenth-century observers also recognized that the depletion of oak, hickory, cedar, cypress, and pine did not result solely from commercial production. In addition to supplying other markets, South Atlantic colonists also had to cut trees to meet their own needs. Indeed, settlers probably cut more timber for use at home than they shipped abroad. Like their Caribbean counterparts, colonists required clapboard, shingles, and planking for their dwellings. As James Murray's description of his naval stores operation suggests, those who dealt in resinous produce needed many barrels and consequently an abundance of staves. Other products made equally great demands on the forests. In addition to lumber for their houses, Chesapeake tobacco planters needed staves for hogsheads in which to ship their crop as well as finished lumber for boats, carts, coffins, and furniture. Because the coastal plain lacked a ready supply of building stone, planters also relied on wood from nearby forests for barns and the numerous curing houses and outbuildings common to tobacco plantations. Residents of South Carolina and Georgia

61. Thomas C. Croker, Jr., "Ecology of an Ideal Forest Community in the Longleaf-Slash Pine Region," in Linnartz, *Ecology of Southern Forests*, 77; Ralston, "Southern Pine Region," in Horwitz, *Clearcutting*, 86–7.
62. Ashe, "Forests, Forest Lands, and Forest Products," 18.

needed barrels for shipping rice and naval stores as well as large wooden vats in which to process indigo.[63]

Colonists with access to large forested tracts met such demands with white oak, cypress, cedar, and longleaf pine. But by the mid eighteenth century, local scarcities and rising prices forced newly arriving settlers and those of lesser means to use inferior materials. In North Carolina, inland settlers cut the smaller, more porous scarlet oaks for staves and clapboard. In the Virginia piedmont, colonists built their houses with spongy loblolly planks, accepting the inconvenience of buckling floors as a trade-off for less expensive boards. Throughout the English South, settlers found myriad uses for other trees. Dugout canoes, used extensively for travel along the rivers of the South Carolina and Georgia low country, were hewn from white cedar or cypress. Posts made from cabbage palmetto proved highly resistant to the ravages of sea worms and became the preferred material for docks and wharves. During the American Revolution colonists also used soft palmetto posts to build forts, discovering that the wood "close[d] on the passage of the [musket or cannon] ball, without splitting."[64]

For Englishmen fearful of the wilderness and its "savage" inhabitants, the chief symbols of civility were the fences that surrounded colonial fields. Due to its communal nature, Indian agriculture required no fixed boundaries, and during the early years of colonization, fences helped distinguish well-kept English fields from the tangled, though highly productive, Indian plots. In England, farmers often used hedges to surround their fields, but South Atlantic colonists found such enclosures impractical. Hedges took too long to grow and could not be moved to new fields when the plots no longer produced. And unlike colonists in New England, those in the English South lacked the raw material to enclose their fields with stone walls. Besides, as Mark Catesby pointed out, settlers would be foolish to ignore "the facility of making wooden fences in a country abounding in trees."[65]

South Atlantic colonists employed several types of fences. During the early years of settlement, one popular technique was to lay a large, whole tree trunk on the ground and to drive several stakes on both sides so the stakes crossed at the top forming a fork. An additional rail could then be laid lengthwise through the forked stakes. The large bottom rail discouraged wandering hogs and burrowing animals from entering under the fence, whereas the higher rail worked to deter cattle. A second and perhaps more permanent structure was

63. Cowdrey, *This Land, This South*, 54; Earle, *Evolution of a Settlement Pattern*, 34.
64. Quotation from Michaux, *North American Sylva*, vol. 3, 2. Lawson, *New Voyage*, 99, 103; Michaux, *North American Sylva*, vol. 3, 91; Wood, *Black Majority*, 123–4.
65. Quotation from Catesby, *Natural History*, vol. 1, xvi. On English hedges and New England stone walls, see Cronon, *Changes in the Land*, 119–20.

the post and rail fence, constructed by driving posts and attaching rails at appropriate intervals.[66]

Over the course of several years, enough posts, rails and fallen trunks to supply a large estate could consume many trees, but initially, the temporary nature of colonial fences must have worked to conserve wood. Because they needed to stand only until the field became exhausted, fences could be constructed from any timber that resisted weathering for about five years. Colonists in the coastal plain relied on pine, even employing valuable longleaf rails when they could be had in sufficient quantity. Farther inland, planters built their fences of oak, black walnut, and chestnut, eschewing hickory because it often rotted in as little as three years. When colonial farmers cleared other fields, those fences still in good repair could be dismantled and assembled at the new site. Moreover, spreading the demand for material among several varieties of trees helped limit selective overcutting of a single species.[67]

European visitors to England's southern colonies decried such seemingly haphazard fencing practices, arguing that the ready availability of wood offered all the more reason to erect permanent enclosures. By the mid eighteenth century, continuing complaints and the destructive habits of wandering livestock prompted colonial lawmakers to pass mandatory fencing regulations. The laws generally required fences three to six feet high around cleared ground. According to North Carolina's law, "the peace and harmony of every neighbourhood" depended on such "good and sufficient fences."[68]

In the backcountry, away from the watchful eye of the local authorities, colonists sometimes ignored the regulations, but farther east, in more densely settled areas, planters now had to erect more and longer lasting fences. The new laws probably contributed to the growing popularity of a third type of enclosure: the worm, or Virginia rail, fence. Like the earliest structures, worm fences might employ rails supported by crossed poles. Such enclosures could also be constructed without posts simply by laying three or more split rails atop one another at sharp angles so that they stretched in a zigzag pattern around cultivated fields. This second technique helped alleviate problems caused by decaying posts, which were generally the first parts of a fence to give way. But even if the posts could be eliminated, the rails of these more permanent

66. Darrett B. and Anita H. Rutman, *A Place in Time: Middlesex County, Virginia 1650–1750* (New York: Norton, 1984), 65; Robert D. Mitchell, *Commercialism and Frontier: Perspectives on the Early Shenandoah Valley* (Charlottesville: University Press of Virginia, 1977), 136–7.

67. Lawson, *New Voyage*, 99; Michaux, *North American Sylva*, vol. 1, 67–9, vol. 2, 85. De Brahm reported that on a large estate a single slave might split as many as "100 Rails a day" for fencing (De Brahm, *General Survey*, 94).

68. Quotation from James Iredell, *The Public Acts of the General Assembly of North Carolina* (Newbern, N.C.: Martin and Ogden, 1804), 245. Lillian M. Willson, *Forest Conservation in Colonial Times* (St. Paul, Minn.: Forest Products History Foundation, 1948), 11.

structures had to be split from water- and rot-resistant woods such as cypress, cedar, longleaf pine, white oak, and live oak, placing a greater demand on these already diminishing species.[69]

Although colonists required lumber for building and rails for fencing, much of the timber cut for local use went to heat their houses and cook their food. In the South Atlantic colonies, as in other parts of North America, early settlers and promotional writers marveled at the availability of wood "proper for fireing." Blessed with abundant forest resources, colonists shunned other fuels. As early as 1701, Lawson reported the discovery of coal in the Virginia piedmont and believed similar deposits might be found in the Carolinas. Yet he saw no real need for such resources, noting that the "Plenty of Wood (which is much the better Fuel) makes us not inquisitive after Coal-Mines." Unlike Indians, who had relied almost exclusively on deadfalls, colonists cut their firewood from the standing forest. In summer, when only the cooking fires needed stoking, settlers sent their children or younger slaves to cut and gather wood from forested plots reserved especially for that purpose. In winter, when they needed it most, colonists augmented supplies from their woodlots with timber cut during agricultural clearing.[70]

Some of the German colonists who immigrated to England's southern colonies might have burned their wood in cast-iron stoves that consumed the fuel slowly and efficiently. Englishmen, however, preferred open fireplaces that, as modern wood burners know, sent much of the warm air they generated up the chimney. By the last quarter of the eighteenth century, colonists who lived in coastal towns were running short of fuel. David Ramsay estimated that the citizens of Charleston annually used some thirty thousand cords of wood for heating and cooking.[71] Within six years of the founding of Georgia, colonists reported "no more free wood in Savannah," noting that "it must be bought from the plantations for which reason fire-wood is already right expensive." By 1770 William Eddis could write that despite "the extensive forests that abound throughout this vast continent, fuel is an expensive article in all the considerable towns."[72]

69. Mitchell, *Commercialism and Frontier*, 136–7; [Janet Schaw], *Journal of a Lady of Quality; Being the Narrative of a Journey from Scotland to the West Indies, North Carolina, and Portugal, in the years 1774 to 1776*, ed. Evangeline Walker Andrews and Charles McLean Andrews (New Haven, Conn.: Yale University Press, 1927) 163, 163n.

70. Quotations from Brickell, *Natural History*, 265; and Lawson, *New Voyage*, 90. De Brahm, *General Survey*, 94; Cronon, *Changes in the Land*, 120.

71. Cronon, *Changes in the Land*, 120; Earle, *Evolution of Settlement System*, 33–4; Ramsay, *Ramsay's History of South Carolina*, vol. 2, 190, 190n.

72. George Fenwick Jones and Renate Wilson, eds., *Detailed Reports on the Salzburger Emigrants Who Settled America ... Edited by Samuel Urlsperger*, 8 vols. to date (Athens: University of Georgia Press, 1968–), vol. 5, 147; William Eddis, *Letters From America*, ed. Aubrey C. Land (Cambridge, Mass.: Harvard University Press, 1969), 21.

Town dwellers were not the only ones to experience wood scarcities. The box frame and clapboard houses typical of the Virginia and Maryland countryside proved especially drafty and difficult to heat. Jasper Danckaerts, who traveled in the region in 1679 and 1680, noted that the siding on such dwellings was "not usually laid so close together, as to prevent you from sticking a finger between them, in consequence of their not being well joined, or the boards being crooked." Although some colonists caulked the boards with clay or other material, Danckaerts still noted that "if you are not so close to the fire as almost to burn yourself, you cannot keep warm, for the wind blows through them everywhere."[73] The larger, eighteenth-century "big houses" and estates of the great tidewater planters also required much fuel. In addition to providing for his family, the landowner had to furnish heat for slave quarters and wood for cooking fires, creating a huge demand for firewood. During the colder-than-usual winter of 1770, Landon Carter took time to reflect on the requirements of his several estates. Restating his belief that Virginia's climate had changed, he noted that

> We now have full 3/4 of the year in which we are obliged to keep constant fires; we must fence our ground with rails build and repair our houses with timber and every cooking room must have its fire the year through. Add to this the natural deaths of trees and the violence of the gusts that blows them down and I must think that in a few years the lower parts of this Colony will be without firewood.[74]

Such observations concerning the availability of firewood reflected local conditions, not a large-scale decline in timber resources. Farther inland, vast tracts of timber still stood untouched. Although he complained that South Carolinians wasted much wood, David Ramsay noted in 1808 that "the day is far distant when Carolina, stript of its trees, will resemble the south of Europe, and some of the more populous settlements in the northern States." Even on Landon Carter's plantations, plenty of trees remained intact. The problems he and other writers sensed, like the shortages associated with commercial lumbering, resulted from selective cutting. Cordwood cut from the seemingly infinite supply of pines resisted fire when green, and when allowed to season, it burned so fast that it constantly had to be replaced with fresh fuel. Consequently, colonists located their woodlots in hardwood forests, where they

73. Bartlett Burleigh James and J. Franklin Jameson, eds., *Journal of Jasper Danckaerts, 1679–1680*, Original Narratives of Early American History, gen. ed. J. Franklin Jameson (New York: Barnes & Noble, 1913), 97, 96; Main, *Tobacco Colony*, 141–4.

74. Greene, *Carter Diary*, vol. 1, 382. In 1777, Carter reported that a single snowy day made it difficult for his slaves to gather wood and threatened to create a shortage. Such comments might indicate that his estates never had an overly abundant supply of firewood (Greene, *Carter Diary*, vol. 2, 1084).

could obtain various species of oak, or preferably, hickory. Those woods produced "an ardent heat," leaving "a heavy, compact and long-lived coal." Cutting such trees for fuel only added to the scarcities created by the demand for staves, hoops, clapboard, fencing, and ship timber. Carter saw two possible solutions. In contrast to Lawson seventy years earlier, Carter hoped colonists would be "happy in discovering mines of coal." Failing that, he could only hope for some efficient method for burning the pines that covered his old fields.[75]

The immediate solution to local wood shortages proved much easier and ecologically less sound than either of Carter's proposals. Colonists who lacked a ready supply of firewood simply bought it from those who had more. Inland settlers cut the valuable hardwood and either hauled it overland or more commonly floated it down rivers to more heavily settled regions. As the author of *American Husbandry* wrote in 1775, "In the management of their woods, they [southern colonists] have shown the same inattention to futurity as their [northern] neighbors; so that in the old settled parts of the provinces, they begin to fear a want of that useful commodity, and would have felt it long ago, had they not such an immense inland navigation to supply them." The continuing growth of the trade can be charted through legislation designed to regulate the sale of wood. By 1784 all the South Atlantic colonies had passed laws defining a standard cord of marketable firewood as a stack eight feet long, four feet broad, and four feet high.[76]

The extensive use of rivers to transport timber products and firewood had other ecological implications. To save labor and expense, colonists often removed trees from the adjacent banks and slopes so that (as William Bartram discovered) the logs could be rolled or dragged into the streams. In much the same way as it affected agricultural fields, eliminating the forest canopy caused water temperatures to grow warmer and increased evaporation. Removing timber from the drainage basin also meant that rainwater ran off more rapidly at all seasons and that soil dried out quicker. Rivers might rise during spring freshets, but overall the basin became drier, causing water levels to drop in major streams and their tributaries. Silt accumulated from increased erosion added to the effect, raising the level of the streambed and making waterways shallower than ever before.[77] In the heat of the southern summer, coastal plain streams often ran low anyway, and removing the timber along the banks only compounded the effect. In 1765 North Carolina Governor William Tryon

75. Quotations from Ramsay, *Ramsay's History of South Carolina*, vol. 2, 190; Michaux, *North American Sylva*, vol. 1, 91; and Greene, *Carter Diary*, vol. 1, 382. Cronon, *Changes in the Land*, 121.

76. Quotation from Carman and Tugwell, *American Husbandry*, 189. On the growth of the firewood trade and corresponding legislation, see Kinney, *Development of Forest Law*, 381.

77. Lee, *Forest Hydrology*, 111–29; Cronon, *Changes in the Land*, 124–5.

noted that "in the Summer Months," most of the Cape Fear sawmills were "obliged to lay still for want of Water." William De Brahm also discovered that rivers dammed for sawmills in Georgia sometimes "disappeared two or three years after being chosen, and left the mills dry."[78]

Such fluctuations in temperature and water levels also might have worked to deplete fish populations. Some smaller streams no longer ran deep or cool enough to attract perch, trout, and other inland species. In some cases, the water that powered colonial mills first had to be collected behind log or stone dams, which restricted spawning runs of saltwater fish. Even if no mill dams stood in their way, migrating fish sometimes had to negotiate permanent logjams created by rafts of timber or naval stores that broke apart on their way to market.[79]

Fishing techniques used by colonists and their slaves must have compounded the problem. South Carolina colonists discovered that Africans were especially adept at using small dugout canoes to fish the numerous rivers and creeks of the low country. Slaves from coastal regions of West Africa were also skilled at casting large nets that could corral large numbers of migrating ocean species. Like Indians, slaves in South Carolina knew how to dam small creeks and saturate the water with herbal poisons to stupefy fish. Europeans and Africans also took fish with spears, gigs, and harpoons as well as with hooks and lines. Lower water levels and stream obstructions in settled regions probably made it easier to concentrate fish within a smaller area where they could be killed in quantity, making such techniques more destructive than similar tactics employed by Indians.[80]

Recognizing the potential depletion of a valuable resource, colonial governments responded with legislation similar to that prompted by the fur trade. In 1680 Virginia established an off-season during which no fish could legally be taken with harpoons or gigs. South Carolina outlawed fish poisoning in 1726. Legislators also attempted to strike at the root of the problem by forcing those who built dams or otherwise obstructed streams to provide passageways for spawning fish. But, as John Bartram (William's father and himself a well-known naturalist) observed, "the english lives chiefly on meat and fowl"; the timber industry proved much too valuable to give up in favor of sturgeon and other fish. One South Carolina statute designed to limit the effects of stream obstructions carefully explained that nothing in the stated regulations should "be construed to prevent the proprietors of lands on the said creek from erecting mills and building mill dams across the same." Writing in 1766, John Bartram wondered if nearby rivers might become like streams farther north,

78. William S. Powell, ed., "Tryon's 'Book' on North Carolina," *North Carolina Historical Review* 34 (1957), 412; De Brahm, *General Survey*, 165.
79. [Schaw], *Journal of a Lady of Quality*, 184–5, 185n.
80. Wood, *Black Majority*, 123; Cowdrey, *This Land, This South*, 57.

Figure 5.3. Log dams like this one, drawn by Benjamin Henry Latrobe in 1798, made it difficult for some ocean fish to return to their freshwater spawning grounds. Reproduced by permission from the Maryland Historical Society, Baltimore.

where fish "abounded formerly when ye Indians lived much on them & was very numerous[;] & now there is not ye 100th or perhaps ye 1000[th part of the] fish to be found."[81]

Initial efforts to control other problems created by deforestation came not from colonial legislatures, but from the Crown. Feeling the pinch of wood scarcities and running short of ship timber, the English government attempted to preserve the best American wood for its own use. Using a conservation technique employed in England, the Crown commissioned surveyors or foresters to emblazon the most useful American trees with an inverted *v*. English officials first applied this broad arrow policy (so named because of the shape of the markings) to New England white pines, valued as masts for ships. The broad arrow came to the South Atlantic colonies in 1729, where foresters used it chiefly to protect the dwindling supply of live oak. Although the English government eventually intended to harvest the trees it preserved, the broad arrow might have slowed selective cutting if the Crown had been able to administer it. But, like most other mercantile legislation, the laws proved virtually impossible to enforce. The West Indian market was too close and smugglers too numerous and crafty for the Crown's agents. The steady renewal of such regulations until the American Revolution suggests their ineffectiveness. Because those who ignored the broad arrow appeared in admiralty court without benefit of a jury, the policy became a sore point with colonial merchants and, instead of aiding the Royal Navy, only contributed to the growing rift between Britain and America.[82]

Most colonists probably thought the Crown overly cautious in its concern for American trees, but the British government could sometimes be as cavalier as the colonists about the future of the southern timber supply. The same 1705 Act of Parliament that encouraged naval stores production made it illegal to cut or destroy "a pitch pine tree or a tar tree" under twelve inches in diameter that was not within a fence or enclosure. The statute also called for a fine of ten pounds for setting woods fires in turpentine orchards without first giving public notice. But that act's primary purpose was to slow destruction of pines in New England, Rhode Island, New York, and New Jersey, not along the South Atlantic.[83]

Not until 1799, when the fledgling United States Navy faced the specter of

81. Quotations from John Bartram, "Diary of a Journey Through the Carolinas, Georgia, and Florida From July 1, 1765 to April 10, 1776," *Transactions of the American Philosophical Society,* new series, 23 part 1 (December 1942), 55; and Thomas Cooper and David J. McCord, eds., *The Statutes at Large of South Carolina,* 10 vols. (Columbia, S.C.: A. S. Johnston, 1836–9), vol. 5, 278–9. Cowdrey, *This Land, This South,* 57.

82. Cronon, *Changes in the Land,* 110–11; Cowdrey, *This Land, This South,* 53–4.

83. Kinney, *Development of Forest Law,* 392.

a prolonged commercial war with France, did American authorities make a concerted effort to preserve timber along the South Atlantic coast. Empowered by Congress to purchase and preserve lands that contained wood suitable for ships and naval stores, the United States government bought two islands off the Georgia coast, both of which contained valuable supplies of oak and pine. Later laws sought similar protection for timberland acquired by way of the Louisiana Purchase and the Florida cession, indications of growing anxiety over trends established during the colonial period.[84]

Like the measures designed to protect fur bearing animals, such concern came too late to affect the ways in which colonists used the woodlands. Long before the Louisiana Territory and Florida officially became part of English America, the forests of the South Atlantic colonies had been drastically altered. By selectively cutting oak, hickory, cedar, and other timber, colonists had removed many of the trees that had first attracted settlers to the region. Even the pinelands, once described by William Strachey as "infinite," had already begun to shrink. The wolves and panthers that frightened early explorers had begun to move farther west in search of undisturbed habitat. Sturgeon and other ocean going fish no longer ran the rivers and creeks in abundance. Agricultural clearing had created local variations in weather and had increased the chances for damage by floods or wind.[85]

Unlike the destruction of wildlife, in which colonists and Indians shared, change in the forests was primarily the work of Europeans and their slaves, spawned by an inherent desire to civilize and reap the benefits of the wild. But civility involved more than driving out wild creatures and wild men. For Europeans, the land remained a "desert" until it was converted into a mirror image of the European countryside. In their terminology, the land had to be "cultivated."[86] It had to yield Old World crops and become home to Old World animals. Those innovations would bring even greater ecological change, but colonists thought that was a small price to pay for making their New World desert accessible and productive.

84. Ibid., 237–40.
85. Quotation from Strachey, *Historie of Travell*, 130. Merrens, *Colonial North Carolina*, 107.
86. Thomas, *Man and the Natural World*, 254–5.

6

The price of civility

The first English settlers along the South Atlantic coast believed it would be relatively easy to transplant Old World agriculture into the new land. Promotional writers told of a warm climate and rich soil, which promised to yield exotic crops and quick wealth for colonial planters. Such claims were not entirely advertising hyperbole. Parts of coastal South Carolina and Georgia were capable of producing tropical fruits. Frenchmen attempting to colonize Florida and southern Georgia in the 1560s may have planted a number of warm-weather delicacies, including oranges, lemons, figs, and olives. In those regions, some of the trees apparently survived, even in the absence of human care. Either Spanish or French colonists introduced peaches into Florida. Indians soon developed a taste for that sweet fruit and transplanted it farther north. By the time English explorers made it to the interior of Georgia and the Carolinas, peaches were flourishing in the woods.[1]

Hoping to duplicate such success farther north, the Roanoke colonists planted sugarcane, oranges, and lemons alongside such traditional English favorites as wheat, barley, and oats. At Jamestown, the first settlers planted their gardens with lemons, pineapples, and olives. Even when early experiments with such crops failed, colonists did not give up on exotic species. Noting that sugarcane did not seem to flourish along the North Carolina coast, Thomas Harriot wondered if the roots might have been damaged in transport or if colonists had arrived too late in the year to set the delicate plants.[2]

Harriot believed in the viability of such crops because he, like many Englishmen, thought that the South Atlantic climate resembled that of the Mediterranean coast, a notion based on the premise that the two areas lay in similar latitudes and therefore must have identical temperatures. This fallacy

1. E. Merton Coulter, ed., *The Journal of William Stephens, 1741–1743*, 2 vols. (Athens: University of Georgia Press, 1958), vol. 1, 240; U. P. Hedrick, *A History of Horticulture in America to 1860* (New York: Oxford University Press, 1950), 104, 118–19, 132–3; Alfred W. Crosby, *Ecological Imperialism: The Biological Expansion of Europe, 900–1900* (New York: Cambridge University Press, 1986), 156–7.
2. Thomas Harriot, "A Briefe and True Report of the Newfound Land of Virginia," in David B. Quinn, ed., *The Roanoke Voyages*, 2 vols. (London: The Hakluyt Society, 1955), vol. 1, 336; [Gabriel Archer?] "The Description of the Now Discovered River and Country of Virginia, with the Liklyhood of Ensuing Ritches, by Englands Ayd and Industry," *Virginia Magazine of History and Biography* 14:4 (April 1907), 375.

persisted during the first years of colonization because early writers tended to describe the entire southeastern coast as "tropical" in the hope of attracting more colonists to the region.[3] The initial English expeditions, which usually took place during the warm months, inadvertently helped confirm the myth. While exploring Virginia in mid-May, Christopher Newport's party concluded that the climate closely resembled that of the West Indies, with warm days and cool nights the typical weather pattern. It took a seasoned world traveler and veteran of colonization like John Smith to correct such reports. As Smith noted, the summers could be as hot as those in Spain, but the "extreame sharpe" cold of winter along the Chesapeake could also be as biting and penetrating as any the settlers had known in Europe.[4]

Those who lingered very long in Virginia found that Smith was right. In the Chesapeake region, tropical fruit could not survive the killing frosts. Nor did wheat, barley, or other English crops seem to do particularly well at first. Forced to subsist on fish and wild game as their provisions dwindled, the Jamestown colonists came to realize that not just their livelihood but their very survival hinged on developing a system of subsistence agriculture. Chronic shortages of supplies between 1607 and 1612 taught the colony's leaders a hard lesson: English settlers had to eat before they could sell.[5]

Fortunately for Virginians and other colonists, the North American climate provided its own subsistence crop, one which Indians had grown for centuries – corn. American corn offered several important advantages over traditional European grains. Corn could be grown in almost any soil, even in the sands of the coastal plain. Ecologists also recognize corn as a viable pioneer crop, meaning that it grows well on partially cleared land, a prime consideration for settlers who initially planted between standing trees. Perhaps equally important, corn did not shatter when it ripened and could be harvested in autumn,

3. Carl Ortwin Sauer, *Sixteenth-Century North America* (Berkeley: University of California Press, 1971), 279–80.
4. John Smith, "A Map of Virginia With a Description of the Countrey, the Commodities, People, Government and Religion," (1612) in Philip L. Barbour, ed., *The Complete Works of Captain John Smith (1580–1631)*, 3 vols. (Chapel Hill: University of North Carolina Press for the Institute of Early American History and Culture, 1986), vol. 1, 143. [Archer?], "Now Discovered River," 375.
5. Lewis Cecil Gray, *History of Agriculture in the Southern United States to 1860*, 2 vols. (Gloucester, Mass.: Peter Smith, 1958), vol. 1, 17–18. Some recent studies suggest that colonists' tales of starvation might have been exaggerated in an effort to force England to send more supplies. Disease also contributed to the mortality rate, a point addressed later in this chapter. For a discussion of starvation, disease, and possible exaggerated reports, see Carville V. Earle, "Environment, Disease, and Mortality in Early Virginia," in Thad W. Tate and David L. Ammerman, eds., *The Chesapeake in the Seventeenth Century: Essays on Anglo-American Society* (Chapel Hill: University of North Carolina Press for the Institute of Early American History and Culture, 1979), 96–125.

freeing colonists and slaves to tend and gather other crops during the summer. Once taken from the stalk, the grain could be husked by hand and pounded into meal with the aid of a simple mortar and pestle. Wheat, barley, and other European grains required threshing and usually had to be ground with elaborate water-powered stone wheels.[6]

Realizing that corn might effectively reduce the threat of food shortages, the Jamestown colonists learned the basics of its cultivation from the natives. Like the Indians, early Virginians began planting the grain in March and harvested it throughout the summer. Colonists settling farther south also relied on corn. Noting the abundance of "Indian corn or Maize" grown by Carolina settlers, John Lawson described it as "the most useful Grain in the World," adding that "had it not been for the Fruitfulness of this Species, it would have proved very difficult to have settled some of the Plantations in America."[7]

The initial shift from Old World grains and tropical fruits to corn set the tone for early agriculture in England's southern colonies. During the seventeenth and the early eighteenth centuries, farmers in the Chesapeake and Carolinas concentrated less on accepted European theories and more on what their experience in the New World taught them. In addition to corn, Chesapeake colonists soon learned to cultivate other indigenous crops, such as beans and squash. The European foodstuffs they transplanted were primarily vegetables that flourished in temperate, not tropical, climates. In 1613 Alexander Whittaker, minister of the Virginia colony's Henrico congregation, noted that a number of Old World crops thrived in Virginia, but instead of lemons, olives, and oranges, he listed peas, cabbages, and carrots.[8]

But colonists' dreams of agricultural profits did not die with the frostbitten fruit trees and sugarcane. Unlike Indians, colonists hoped to do more than simply survive from season to season. The same European economic system that required deerskins, timber, and naval stores also encouraged the development of cash crops for export. For Indians, farming had remained an end in itself. For the first colonists, subsistence only laid the basis for commercial agriculture. Even in the higher latitudes of the Chesapeake and North Carolina, where oranges and lemons could not flourish, the land produced other exotic

6. Gray, *History of Agriculture*, vol. 1, 161. William Stephens, secretary of the Georgia colony, was one writer who commented on the advantages of harvesting late corn. In September 1739, Stephens noted that it was "common among many old Planters, after their Corn is so bent down, to let it hang till the rest of their Crop, whether Pease, rice, &c. are all housed." (William Stephens, *A Journal of the Proceedings in Georgia Beginning October 20, 1737*, 2 vols. [1742; reprint Ann Arbor, Mich.: University Microfilms, 1966], vol. 2, 120).

7. Alexander Whittaker, *Good Newes From Virginia* (London, 1613), 23; John Lawson, *A New Voyage to Carolina*, ed. Hugh Talmage Lefler, (Chapel Hill: University of North Carolina Press, 1967), 81.

8. Whittaker, *Good Newes*, 23.

crops, many of which did not grow in the northern latitudes of New England or the mother country.[9]

The Roanoke colonists discovered that the coastal Indians already grew one crop that might be of value in Europe. Harriot described it as "an herbe" of "precious estimation" among the natives. He recommended the plant for export on the basis of its supposed therapeutic value. Once "dried and brought into powder," Harriot reported, the herb could be burned to produce medicinal smoke that purged "superfluous fleame and other gross humors," leaving those who used it "notably improved in health." Indians called the plant "uppewoc"; Englishmen knew it by its Spanish name, "tobacco." Thanks to Harriot's treatise and similar claims for the plant's medicinal properties, New World tobacco (most of which initially came to England from Spanish vessels captured by privateers) became a fashionable social habit among Englishmen of sufficient means to purchase it.[10]

Virginians searching for a cash crop also recognized the possible merits of tobacco. When John Rolfe's experiments in 1612 produced a milder, better tasting strain of the weed, American tobacco quickly emerged as a "poor man's luxury," enjoyed by virtually all classes of Englishmen. Early shipments of tobacco brought such immense profits that in 1616 Virginia Governor Thomas Dale found it necessary to decree that those who planted the crop must also grow two acres of corn for their families and male servants – a wise decision given the settlers' ongoing fascination with exotic exports. Even with that restriction, however, the tobacco business boomed. By 1627 Virginians exported five hundred thousand pounds of the weed annually. Tobacco's success owed as much to its ecological adaptation to the southern climate as to the high prices it brought in England. Like corn, tobacco could be grown in almost any soil and thrived in hills between trees, stumps, and downed timber. Unlike lemons and oranges, tobacco required neither extended periods of tropical heat nor regular drenching rains.[11] With the founding of new colonies, tobacco agriculture spread north into Maryland and south into northeastern North Carolina. From

9. Gray, *History of Agriculture*, vol. 1, 21–4; K. G. Davies, *The North Atlantic World in the Seventeenth Century* (Minneapolis: University of Minnesota Press, 1974), 141–4.

10. Harriot, "Briefe and the True Report," in Quinn, *Roanoke Voyages*, vol. 1, 344–5. On the capture of tobacco prizes by English privateers, see Davies, *North Atlantic World*, 145.

11. Davies, *North Atlantic World*, 145. Perhaps the best evidence of tobacco's adaptability to tidewater soils is John Smith's testimony that during the height of the tobacco boom, settlers planted the weed in "the market-place, and streets, and all other spare places" in and around Jamestown. (Barbour, *Complete Works of Smith*, vol. 2, 262.) For a short, secondary account of the early tobacco boom, see Edmund S. Morgan, "The First American Boom 1618 to 1630," *William and Mary Quarterly*, 3d ser., 18 (1971), 169–98. See also Allan Kulikoff, *Tobacco and Slaves: The Development of Southern Cultures in the Chesapeake, 1680–1800* (Chapel Hill: University of North Carolina Press for the Institute of Early American History and Culture, 1986), 30–2.

Figure 6.1. The supposedly therapeutic plant that exacted many an hour of backbreaking labor from Indian slaves, white servants, and Africans. From Jonathan Carver, *A Treatise on the Culture of the Tobacco Plant* (London, 1779). Earl Gregg Swem Library, College of William and Mary.

the upper reaches of Chesapeake Bay to Albemarle Sound, the eastern flatlands became a "tobacco coast." There, the weed remained a primary staple, though during the eighteenth century it would increasingly share that role with wheat.[12]

Colonists who came to the southern reaches of the coastal plain also had to learn the agricultural lessons of the South Atlantic climate. After a group of Massachusetts Bay Puritans failed in their attempt to locate a colony on the lower Cape Fear River, settlers from Barbados came to the area in 1664 hoping to produce citrus fruits and olive oil. That enterprise, too, was unsuccessful. In 1670 Barbadians came back, eventually settling Charles Town on a river they called "Ashley." Here, too, they tried a number of crops, including tobacco.[13]

But tobacco prices depended on demand in Europe, and at the time of South Carolina's founding, prices for the weed were low and going lower. Moreover, the colony lay too far north to produce sugar, another profitable staple with which the settlers were familiar. Consequently, during the first decades of colonization, South Carolinians survived by trading with the Indians, raising livestock, and selling forest products. Not until the early eighteenth century did rice become South Carolina's principal export crop. Some southern Indians had gathered several species of wild American rice, but did not grow it as a subsistence crop. South Carolinians probably learned domestic rice cultivation from their slaves, some of whom had either grown the crop or seen it grown along the rivers of West Africa. Slaves knew how to plant the grain by making small impressions with their heels and how to separate the husks from threshed rice by "fanning" it in the wind. Nurtured by African labor and know-how, rice grew well in the semicleared inland and tidal swamps. More shallow-rooted than either corn or tobacco, rice plants easily took hold in boggy ground that contained the stumps and roots of the natural vegetation. By the 1730s Carolina rice planters were growing the grain as far north as the lower Cape Fear River in North Carolina.[14]

Early settlers in South Carolina also brought seeds for what would become the colony's other major export crop: indigo. Like rice, indigo grew wild in

---

12. Donald W. Meinig, *The Shaping of America* Volume 1, *Atlantic America, 1492–1800* (New Haven, Conn.: Yale University Press, 1986), 150–60. Meinig refers to this part of the colonial south as "Greater Virginia." "Tobacco Coast" is the phrase employed by Arthur Pierce Middleton in *Tobacco Coast: A Maritime History of Chesapeake Bay in the Colonial Era* (1953; reprint Baltimore, Md.: Johns Hopkins University Press, 1984).

13. William S. Powell, ed., *Ye Countie of Albemarle in North Carolina* (Raleigh: State Department of Archives and History, 1958), xxvi–xxvii; Peter H. Wood, *Black Majority: Negroes in Colonial South Carolina from 1670 through the Stono Rebellion* (New York: Norton, 1974), 17–20; Meinig, *Atlantic America*, 172–4.

14. Davies, *North Atlantic World*, 192; Wood, *Black Majority*, 28–34, 108–114, 56–62; James M. Clifton, "Golden Grains of White: Rice Planting on the Lower Cape Fear," *North Carolina Historical Review* 50 (1973), 365–6.

parts of the American South, but the species best suited for making the deep blue dye Englishmen coveted came from the West Indies. Experiments with the West Indian variety began immediately, but colonists did not cultivate the crop in earnest until the 1740s, when a series of commercial wars with France cut off the supply of indigo from the French West Indies. Even then indigo might not have developed into a suitable cash crop had it not been for the efforts of a recent immigrant from the Caribbean named Eliza Lucas. Well versed in the methods of cultivation used on her father's estate in Antigua, she grew several crops of indigo solely for seed and distributed it among neighboring planters. In 1745 the British government took a hand in encouraging the crop, offering a bounty on indigo produced in the colonies. Like rice, indigo cultivation benefited greatly from African labor and know-how. Slaves who worked indigo fields used a slight variation of the techniques employed to plant rice, first hoeing the soil with a mattock, dropping in the seeds, and replacing the dirt with their heels.[15]

Although corn, tobacco, rice, and indigo initially dominated southern agriculture, settlers did not completely ignore other crops. In sharp contrast to their attitudes toward thick forests and uncut woodlands, Europeans professed a fondness for groves of trees that reflected human habitation, especially orchards and vineyards. Colonists eventually augmented the wild peach groves with other fruits. In 1710 Thomas Nairne reported that South Carolinians had transplanted a number of tasty delicacies, including "Grapes from the Maderas, and elsewhere . . . apples, Pears, Quinces, [and] Figs." The most intriguing orchards, however, were developed from both imported and indigenous mulberry trees, on which some colonists tried to raise silkworms. Settlers in Virginia experimented with worms as early as 1610, but the comparatively high profits to be made from tobacco diverted farmers' interest to that commodity. In similar fashion, rice culture worked to turn South Carolina colonists away from raising caterpillars.[16]

In Georgia, fruits and worms got a more systematic trial. The colony's Trustees at first sought to make it a land of sober, virtuous small farmers. Both slavery and rum were initially outlawed. According to the Trustees' plans, Georgia's principal crops were to be grapes for making wine, various tropical fruits, mulberry trees, and silk. But, like colonists farther north, Georgians

---

15. Gray, *History of Agriculture*, vol. 1, 73–4; G. Terry Sharrer, "The Indigo Bonanza in South Carolina, 1740–1790," *Technology and Culture* 12 (1971), 448, 449–50.

16. Quotation from Thomas Nairne, *A Letter from South Carolina Giving an Account of the Soil, Air, Product, Trade, Government, Laws, Religion, People, Military Strength, Etc, of that Province* (1710; reprint, Ann Arbor, Mich.: University Microfilms, 1980), 9. Gray, *History of Agriculture*, vol. 1, 187–8. On the European, particularly English, affinity for orchards, see Keith Thomas, *Man and the Natural World: A History of the Modern Sensibility* (New York: Pantheon, 1983), 204–5. On the spread of fruit trees in the colonial south, see Hedrick, *History of Horticulture*, 104, 32.

discovered that lofty agricultural visions did not necessarily correspond to climatic realities. Olive trees, carefully nurtured for eight years in the Trustees' experimental garden, eventually bloomed and bore fruit, but the olives withered and dropped off before they could be harvested. Settlers along the coast continued to grow oranges, but the trees would not grow farther inland, and even along the coast, the fruit frequently fell victim to killing frosts. Georgia did manage to export some raw silk, but as in other southern colonies, field crops eventually carried the day. The prohibition on slavery officially ended in 1750, and a year later the Trustees gave over proprietorship of the colony to the Crown. Once slavery became legal, Georgia settlers, too, began to grow rice and indigo in quantity, so that the pattern of agriculture established in South Carolina eventually dominated the outer coastal plain from the Cape Fear to the Altamaha rivers.[17]

By the time Georgia was settled, colonial agriculture was making its way farther inland. Between 1720 and 1770, colonists steadily moved into the southern up-country. Some of the settlers were former indentured servants or late-arriving English colonists who could find no suitable land in the coastal plain. But many of the immigrants came from the Middle Colonies, primarily Pennsylvania. The new colonists took up residence in the Shenandoah Valley or in the sandhills and piedmont farther south, regions known to coastal planters as "Back Parts," "Back Settlements," or "the backcountry."[18] According to one contemporary observer, the migrants represented "A mix'd Medley from all Countries." Scotch-Irish, Germans, Welsh, Swiss, English Quakers, and other groups frequently carved out small, ethnically homogeneous neighborhoods in the upland forests. They spoke a wide variety of European dialects, and travelers in the region often commented on the odd phrases and shrill accents of backwoods speech. Backcountry settlers first grew corn and other subsistence crops, but also might tend small plots of wheat, tobacco, and indigo.[19]

17. James C. Bonner, *A History of Georgia Agriculture, 1732–1860* (Athens: University of Georgia Press, 1964), ch. 2, see especially, 18–23; Meinig, *Atlantic America*, 181–2. Meinig's term for this part of the colonial south is "Greater Carolina."

18. Robert D. Mitchell, *Commercialism and Frontier: Perspectives on the Early Shenandoah Valley* (Charlottesville: University Press of Virginia, 1977), 18, 28; Carl Bridenbaugh, *Myths and Realities: Societies of the Colonial South* (New York: Atheneum, 1970), 120–1, 128–9. Settlement of the Shenandoah Valley was influenced by migration from both Pennsylvania and Virginia. Consequently, a case can be made for considering the Valley as a separate area. However, for the purposes of an overview, I have, like Bridenbaugh, chosen to include it as part of the backcountry.

19. Quotation from: Richard Hooker, ed., *The Carolina Backcountry on the Eve of Revolution: The Journal of Charles Woodmason* (Chapel Hill: University of North Carolina Press for the Institute of Early American History and Culture, 1953), 6. Bridenbaugh, *Myths and Realities*, 122–8, 131–2; Arthur R. Hall, "Soil Erosion and Agriculture in the Southern Piedmont: A History" (Ph.D. thesis, Duke University, 1948), 76.

The various types of agriculture and the many dialects that characterized the South Atlantic region suggest that European colonists were culturally and linguistically as diverse as the region's earliest Indian inhabitants. Moreover, many crops grown for subsistence or export either grew wild or had been domesticated by the natives. Some of the techniques employed by colonial farmers also resembled those of the Indians. Using methods adapted from the natives, Chesapeake tobacco planters scraped the soil into mounds. Young seedlings were then transplanted to the fields – one plant to each mound. Continual hoeing kept out weeds and maintained the crop. Corn, too, flourished in similar small mounds of earth. Delicate rice plants also had to be tilled by hand. Indigo and wheat usually were sown in more thoroughly cleared and plowed fields. But well into the eighteenth century, colonists found Indian farming methods to be as effective and efficient as European techniques.[20]

Only a few colonists, however, paid lip service to such similarities. Most European settlers believed their system of agriculture brought new order and stability to the South Atlantic landscape. Writing in 1751, Governor James Glen found reason to thank God that South Carolina no longer lay in "its uncultivated condition, overgrown with woods, overrun with wild beasts, and swarming with native Indians." Instead, Glen continued, the region could now be regarded "as an undoubted part of the British dominions, as one of the fairest provinces belonging to our Imperial Crown."[21]

The change Glen perceived had less to do with types of crops and farming techniques than with the ways in which colonists apportioned their acreage. To take advantage of the land's many resources, Indians had moved from region to region, gathering or harvesting the available foods. Colonists preferred to remain in one location and bring the land's resources to their farms. Toward that end, farmers divided their arable land into several separate fields, each of which usually produced a single, specific food or commercial staple. Colonists planted their crops in straight rows, leaving about six feet of ground between each hill and like distance between the rows. Except for the remaining trees or stumps, the crops stood alone "like the rows of trees in an orchard," and in the

20. Carville V. Earle, *The Evolution of a Tidewater Settlement System: All Hallow's Parish, Maryland, 1650–1783* (The University of Chicago Department of Geography Research Paper no. 170, 1975), 30; Darrett B. and Anita H. Rutman, *A Place in Time: Middlesex County, Virginia 1650–1750* (New York: Norton, 1984), 40–1; Timothy H. Breen, *Tobacco Culture: The Mentality of the Great Tidewater Planters on the Eve of Revolution* (Princeton, N.J.: Princeton University Press, 1985), 46–8; Albert E. Cowdrey, *This Land, This South: An Environmental History* (Lexington: University Press of Kentucky, 1983), 55; Sharrer, "Indigo Bonanza," 449; Harold B. Gill, Jr., "Wheat Culture in Colonial Virginia," *Agricultural History* 52 (1978), 383–4.
21. Governor James Glen, "An Attempt Towards an Estimate of the Value of South Carolina," in H. Roy Merrens, ed., *The Colonial South Carolina Scene: Contemporary Views, 1697–1744* (Columbia: University of South Carolina Press, 1977), 178.

minds of colonists, this system of monoculture (one crop per field) provided a civilized alternative to the disheveled multicrop Indian fields.[22]

Although single-crop fields appealed to the settlers' sense of civility, the new practice created a variety of problems. Indigenous animals favored the new agriculture almost as much as colonists. Alligators, snakes, and muskrats frequently took up residence in the banks and dikes of South Carolina rice fields. By burrowing or boring into the soft earth, those animals could cause the banks or floodgates to give way. Mature fields could be destroyed by such an untimely dousing.[23]

Larger and more orderly plots of corn and other subsistence crops also provided new food sources for creatures of the nearby forests. John Brickell reported that bears became so enamored of colonists' potatoes that the beasts "seldom fail[ed] to destroy and root out" any field they discovered. Deer found newly sprouting corn and grain fields so appealing that some Virginia planters set rows of sharpened sticks inside their fences. Invading whitetails that vaulted the enclosures impaled themselves on the spikes, providing colonists with another source of venison and skins. Local weather conditions might intensify such invasions. The Moravians, who settled Wachovia in the North Carolina piedmont, noted that a particularly late frost in 1774 seemed to limit the amount of mast available in the forests. As a result "larger and smaller wild creatures – field mice, squirrels, raccoons, possums, bears, – and the feathered tribe, were driven into the fields and did much damage, especially to the corn."[24]

Planters had several ways of dealing with such varmints. From either their slaves or the Indians, some Carolina planters learned to hollow out and hang gourds in order to attract nesting purple martins. As John Lawson noted, the

---

22. Quotation from "An Interview with James Freeman," in Merrens, *Colonial South Carolina Scene*, 45. As Merrens notes in his introduction, this piece, although clearly directed at prospective settlers, is "one of the more credible and charming specimens of promotional literature." On monoculture, see William Cronon, *Changes in the Land: Indians, Colonists, and the Ecology of New England* (New York: Hill & Wang, 1983), 150.

23. Julia Floyd Smith, *Slavery and Rice Culture in Low Country Georgia, 1750–1860* (Knoxville: University of Tennessee Press, 1985), 50.

24. Quotations from John Brickell, *The Natural History of North Carolina* (1737; reprint, Murfreesboro, N.C.: Johnson Reprint, 1969), 111; Robert Beverley, *The History and Present State of Virginia* (1705), ed. Louis B. Wright (Chapel Hill: University of North Carolina Press for the Institute of Early American History and Culture, 1947), 308–9; and Adelaide L. Fries et. al., eds., *Records of the Moravians in North Carolina*, 11 vols. (Raleigh: North Carolina Historical Commission, 1922–69), vol. 2, 816, 818. E. L. Jones, "Creative Disruptions in American Agriculture," *Agricultural History* 48 (1974), 513. Early colonists in Georgia also complained of various pests in their cornfields. For an example, see Clarence L. Ver Steeg, ed., *A True and Historical Narrative of the Colony of Georgia By Pat. Talifer and Others With Comments by the Earl of Egmont* (Athens: University of Georgia Press, 1960), 138.

martins were "very Warlike Bird[s]" and might "beat the Crows from the Plantations." But most colonists did not rely on the pests' natural enemies. Noting that "crows and squirrels do great damage to crops of corn," the Virginia Assembly in 1734 required taxpayers in certain counties to present local authorities with a number of crows' heads or "squirrel's scalps" proportionate to the colonists' taxable wealth. Those who failed to meet their quota had a make up the difference in tobacco – one pound for every head or scalp they could not produce. Both crows and squirrels could be most easily captured when young and some planters organized special hunts during the nesting seasons. In 1770 Landon Carter set aside one April Sunday solely for the capture of young crows, offering each of his slaves an extra half pound of meat for every six heads they procured. County justices who collected the trophies from such hunts were under strict orders to bury the heads, lest some unscrupulous taxpayer try to turn in the same scalps more than once.[25]

Squirrels and crows plagued colonial farmers at all seasons, but other marauders appeared only at harvest time. Lured from the forests by ripening fruit, thousands of Carolina parakeets arrived in early autumn to sample the wares of colonial orchards. Although such invasions could be disastrous, most colonists found it easy to destroy parakeets because the birds refused to scatter when settlers fired their guns into the flocks. Alexander Wilson, a Scottish naturalist and friend of William Bartram, once fired into a flock of parakeets along the Kentucky River. "Showers of them fell," he reported, "yet the affection of the survivors seemed rather to increase; for after a few circuits around the place they again alighted near me, looking down at their slaughtered companions with such manifest symptoms of sympathy and concern as entirely disarmed me." Parakeets survived along the South Atlantic throughout the colonial period but, doomed by such remarkable sociability, they, too, eventually went the way of the passenger pigeon. Writing in the early twentieth century, one ornithologist listed "slaughter by agriculturalists" as the primary cause of the parakeet's disappearance.[26]

Even more destructive than parakeets were the great flocks of bobolinks that descended on Carolina and Georgia rice fields during their spring and fall

25. Quotation from Lawson, *New Voyage*, 149. Peter H. Wood notes that "It is impossible to say" whether this information disseminated from Indians or slaves. (Wood, *Black Majority*, 21.) William Waller Hening, ed., *The Statutes at Large of Virginia; being a Collection of all the laws of Virginia from the first session of the legislature, in the year 1619*, 13 vols. (New York: R. & W. and C. Bartow, 1819–23), vol. 8, 389; Jack P. Greene, ed., *The Diary of Colonel Landon Carter of Sabine Hall, 1752–1778*, 2 vols. (Charlottesville: University Press of Virginia, 1965), vol. 1, 390.

26. Alexander Wilson and Frank M. Chapman, quoted in Peter Mathiessen, *Wildlife in America* (New York: Viking, 1959), 115, 181. For a contemporary account of parakeets invading colonial orchards, see Mark Catesby, *The Natural History of Carolina, Florida, and the Bahama Islands*, 2 vols. (1747; reprint, Ann Arbor, Mich.: University Microfilms, 1977), vol. 1, 11.

Figure 6.2. Illustrations by naturalist Alexander Wilson. The large bird at the top is a Carolina parakeet. From Alexander Wilson, *American Ornithology; or the Natural History of the Birds of the United States* (Philadelphia, 1811), Vol. 3, Pl. 26. Earl Gregg Swem Library, College of William and Mary.

Figure 6.3. A pair of bobolinks making a meal of Carolina rice. Drawn by Mark Catesby. Reproduced by permission from Colonial Williamsburg Foundation Library, Special Collections.

migrations. In spring, bobolinks left their winter home in South America and headed up the southern coast en route to summer breeding grounds farther north. The birds usually reached the rice fields in May and might completely destroy a newly sprouting crop. In August or September, the birds again passed through rice country as they returned to South America. If the bobolinks arrived when the maturing rice was still "soft and milky," the birds gorged themselves until they could barely fly. Indeed, bobolinks eventually came to depend on American rice crops to sustain them during their autumn migrations. Today, rice grown in the southern United States supplies about 76 percent of the bobolink's food between September and October.[27]

Planters relied on slaves to help fend off such seasonal invaders. Applying techniques that must have been well known in the rice country of Africa, slaves used clappers or other noisemakers to scare the bobolinks. Slaves also built fires along the river banks in an attempt to smoke out the birds from the fields. If those techniques failed, planters went after the birds with guns. Like parakeets, bobolinks often refused to abandon their feeding grounds in the face of gunfire and could be killed by the hundreds. Fattened on rice, the birds proved a tasty seasonal addition to the plantation table, prompting Mark Catesby to note that rice birds were "esteemed in Carolina the greatest delicacy of all other birds." South Carolina legislators gave planters another motive for hunting bobolinks by offering bounties on the feathered pests. Bobolinks apparently never faced the threat of extinction, but such hunts must have reduced the size of the flocks.[28]

In part, the birds survived because colonists eventually found effective ways to deter bobolinks without killing them. Because the ricebirds came at predictable seasons, planters could sometimes prepare for the onslaught. By planting in early June, rice growers could be sure their late-maturing crop would escape both the spring and fall bobolink invasions. But rice planted so late usually yielded less than crops set in March or April. If they hoped to make a suitable profit, colonists could set aside only a small fraction (perhaps about one-fifth) of their crop from the birds. By the late eighteenth and early nineteenth centuries (after the shift to the tidal swamps made it easier to control water) planters developed other ways to stave off the bobolinks. Before the rice began to mature and well in advance of the expected fall invasion, slaves flooded the fields with what planters described as "intermediate water." The sudden

27. Catesby, *Natural History*, vol. 1, 14; Duncan Clinch Heyward, *Seed from Madagascar* (Chapel Hill: University of North Carolina Press, 1937), 31; David Doar, *Rice and Rice Planting in the South Carolina Low Country* (Charleston: The Charleston Museum, 1936), 27; Brooke Meanley, *Blackbirds and the Southern Rice Crop* (Washington, D.C.: United States Department of the Interior, Fish and Wildlife Service, 1971), 39.

28. Smith, *Slavery and Rice Culture*, 50; Catesby, *Natural History*, vol. 1, 14; Doar, *Rice and Rice Planting*, 27; Matthiessen, *Wildlife in America*, 125. On bounties for rice birds, see Cowdrey, *This Land, This South*, 49.

dousing forced the plants to sprout "water roots" and set the field's overall growth back about ten days. If properly timed, the process prevented rice from reaching the milky stage until the bobolinks had moved on.[29]

A number of indigenous insects also found colonial fields to be ideal food sources. Landon Carter frequently complained of damage from grasshoppers, noting that they seemed to prefer "the cleanest ground" of his oldest and best-kept tobacco fields. On one occasion, Carter reported, "millions" of grass-hoppers destroyed a twenty-acre turnip field in the space of "one night and a day." The tobacco flea beetle, known to planters as "the Flie," was also a menace in Chesapeake fields. Tobacco planters had to be particularly wary of hornworms, the larvae of the sphinx moth. As William Tatham, who published a treatise on tobacco agriculture, wrote in 1800, "The act of destroying these worms is termed worming the tobacco, which is a very nauseous occupation, and takes up much labour. It is performed by picking everything of this kind off the respective leaves with the hand, and destroying it with the foot."[30]

Farther south, grasshoppers and caterpillars attacked indigo fields. There, slaves picked off the insects and either mashed them between their fingers or drowned them in lime water. Chickens turned into an indigo field could also help destroy the worms. Rice, too, attracted crawling pests. "Rice worms," small, inch-long, green and white caterpillars, could move into a dry field and cut the delicate rice plants right to the ground. Sometimes a simple flooding would cure such an infestation. At other times, slaves had to go into the field and remove the worms.[31]

Not all the pests flying or crawling around colonial farms came from surrounding fields and forests. A number of troublesome Old World animals accompanied colonists across the Atlantic. Black rats, frequent passengers in the holds of European ships, first came ashore at Jamestown in 1609, where they immediately destroyed the colonists' winter supply of grain. The prolific rodents multiplied so fast that by 1737 John Brickell found rats "in great plenty all over the Province, and as mischievous in these parts, as in any part of the World, destroying Corn, Fruit, and many other things." The common house mouse, another stowaway on European vessels, became equally well established by the early eighteenth century.[32]

29. Heyward, *Seed from Madagascar*, 32; Alice R. Huger Smith, *A Carolina Rice Plantation of the Fifties* (New York: Morrow, 1936), 29.

30. Greene, *Carter Diary*, vol. 1, 435, vol. 2, 721; Edmund and Dorothy Smith Berkeley, eds., *The Reverend John Clayton, A Parson With a Scientific Mind: His Scientific Writings and Other Related Papers* (Charlottesville: University Press of Virginia, 1965), 65; G. Melvin Herndon, ed., *William Tatham and the Culture of Tobacco* (Coral Gables, Fla.: University of Miami Press, 1969), 22.

31. Sharrer, "Indigo Bonanza," 450; Doar, *Rice and Rice Planting*, 27.

32. Brickell, *Natural History*, 130. Barbour, *Complete Works of Smith*, vol. 2, 212; Alfred W. Crosby, "Ecological Imperialism: The Overseas Migration of Western Europeans as a Biological Phenomenon," *Texas Quarterly* 30 (1978), 15–18.

Insects, too, made the transatlantic trip. The honeybee, which usually aided European crops and provided a new food for bears, flourished across the South, reaching the Mississippi River by the 1790s. Although settlers welcomed this immigrant, southern Indians labeled it "the white man's fly" and considered its approach an ominous harbinger of encroaching European settlement.[33] Colonists were less enthusiastic about the immigration of the cockroach, which seemed to thrive in the hot swampy environs of the outer coastal plain. The Hessian fly, an introduced insect whose larvae ravaged New England wheat crops during the last quarter of the eighteenth century, might have destroyed some southern grain during the colonial period. But the insects probably did their greatest damage after 1800, when they swept into wheat fields in the Virginia piedmont and later followed migrating Southerners into Texas and the Great Plains.[34]

Eighteenth-century wheat crops did, however, suffer from several imported Old World fungus parasites collectively known to colonists as "rust." The most destructive of these fungi, stem rust, grew on wheat stems and leaves, where it consumed much of the water and nutrients needed by the developing kernels. As a result, kernels shriveled to half their normal size and were often blown out with the chaff during threshing. By the mid eighteenth century, New England wheat farmers had discovered that their rust problems resulted in part from the barberry bush, an imported ornamental shrub. The bush served as an alternate host for the fungus, allowing its spores to survive the winter and infect maturing wheat the following spring. Several New England colonies passed laws calling for eradication of the barberries, a campaign undertaken again by the United States Department of Agriculture in the early twentieth century.[35]

But South Atlantic farmers found no such botanical scapegoat. Because the southern winter seldom produced temperatures severe enough to kill the

33. Quotation from Thomas Jefferson, *Notes on the State of Virginia* (1787), ed. William Peden (Chapel Hill: University of North Carolina Press, 1958), 72. For contemporary accounts of the westward migration of honeybees, see Johann David Schoepf, *Travels in the Confederation* (1783–84), trans. and ed. Alfred J. Morrison (New York: Bergman, 1968), 105; and Benjamin Hawkins, "Letters of Benjamin Hawkins," in *Collections of the Georgia Historical Society*, 9 vols. (Savannah: The Georgia Historical Society, 1840–1916), vol. 9, 40. See also Crosby, "Ecological Imperialism," 115.

34. "Itinerant Observations in America," in *Collections of the Georgia Historical Society*, vol. 4, 13; Cronon, *Changes in the Land*, 153; United States Department of Agriculture, *Third Report of the United States Entomological Commission* (Washington, D.C.: United States Department of Agriculture, 1883), 199, 221, 227.

35. Frederick Wallman, *Plant Diseases: An Introduction for the Layman* (Garden City, N.Y.: Natural History, 1971), 13. John H. Martin and S. C. Salmon, "The Rusts of Wheat, Oats, Barley, and Rye," in United States Department of Agriculture, *Plant Diseases: The Yearbook of Agriculture, 1953* (Washington, D.C.: United States Department of Agriculture, 1953), 330–1; Cronon, *Changes in the Land*, 154–5.

fungus, rust needed no alternate host. And during the warm wet springs common to Virginia, the fungus spread more rapidly than in the north. Always interested in any natural phenomenon that threatened his crops, Landon Carter spent much time and energy trying to understand wheat rust. Each time the fungus struck his fields he advanced a new theory, attributing it on different occasions to soil, insects, or some "constitution of air." Perhaps aware of the barberry discovery in New England, Carter watched for rust on neighboring plants, especially blackberries. There he observed a related, but different, fungus (known to botanists as "blackberry rust") and developed still another theory. Noting that the rust seemed to appear on the blackberries overnight, Carter thought the disease might "be owing to some peculiar quality in the night air which receiving the rays of the sun so immediately upon it, it does as through a lens or burning glass scorch the leaves up." For all his efforts, however, Carter apparently never discovered a means of effectively controlling rust. Like other farmers across colonial America, he had to accept European parasites as the inevitable ecological consequence of growing European crops.[36]

For colonists like Carter who resided in the South Atlantic coastal plain, another more serious threat to their well-being came from Old World parasites carried by indigenous mosquitoes. European settlers felt the effects of such organisms in the form of "intermittent agues," or "fevers"; modern doctors recognize the ailment as malaria. Anopheline mosquitoes capable of carrying the parasites probably flourished in the American South long before colonization, but the insects remained relatively harmless until the arrival of Europeans.[37]

Some of the first explorers and would-be colonists to reach the South Atlantic coast probably brought with them a species of parasite capable of causing a mild form of malaria. Known to scientists as *Plasmodium vivax*, the species was fairly widespread in Europe. Once injected into the blood of a healthy person, the parasites made their way to the liver, where they multiplied, and then returned to the bloodstream to prey on red blood cells. *P. vivax* primarily attacks young blood cells. As their bodies marshaled defenses against the invasion, afflicted Europeans felt the fever, chills, and aching limbs characteristic of infection. If their bodies' natural defenses succeeded in driving the parasites from the blood, the victims recovered after a short debilitation. The parasites, however, lived on, returning to the liver to multiply and attack

36. Quotations from Greene, *Carter Diary*, vol. 2, 694, 698–9. R. E. Wilkinson and H. E. Jaques, *How to Know the Weeds*, 3d ed. (Dubuque, Iowa: William C. Brown, 1979), 67; *Plant Diseases: Yearbook, 1953*, 330–1; Joseph C. Arthur, *The Plant Rusts (Urendinales)* (New York: Wiley, 1929), 35; Cronon, *Changes in the Land*, 155.

37. Saul Jarco, "Some Observations on Disease in Prehistoric North America," *Bulletin of the History of Medicine* 38 (1964), 9; F. L. Dunn, "On the Antiquity of Malaria in the Western Hemisphere," *Human Biology* 37 (1965), 391–2.

again in eight to ten months. This classic malarial cycle of recovery and relapse might persist for several years before the victim acquired immunity to the infecting strain of parasite.[38]

But even though some Europeans carried vivax malaria, the disease must have been slow to become entrenched along the South Atlantic seaboard. A single individual who carried the parasites could spread the disease only if he suffered a relapse during the warm months when anophelines were abroad. At least one of the mosquitoes that imbibed the tainted blood would then have to survive for weeks while the parasites developed within the insect's system. Assuming appropriate weather, the infected mosquito could then pass the organisms to another human. Odds for propagating the cycle improved if several victims relapsed simultaneously within range of the local anophelines.[39]

Many of the initial efforts at colonization were small and probably provided relatively few carriers. And even if a colony became infected, malaria did not necessarily become endemic to that locality. Ayllon's expedition, for example, may have suffered from the disease and could have passed it via mosquitoes to nearby Indians. But the seminomadic habits of the coastal natives were not conducive to spreading malaria. The disease probably disappeared when the Spanish left the area. The story seems much the same along the South Atlantic coast throughout the sixteenth and into the seventeenth century. Some colonists and Indians suffered from malaria, but the outbreaks must have been sporadic and short-lived. The well-documented health problems that affected every colony during its formative years probably owed more to dysentery, salt poisoning, typhoid fever, and dietary deficiencies than to mosquito-borne parasites.[40]

Gradually, however, the pattern of infection began to change. As Indian populations dwindled and the more sedentary Europeans settled along the coastal rivers, random occurrences of malaria gave way to longer, well-defined seasonal outbreaks that afflicted specific locales. Colonists who contracted the disease during the summer and fall tended to relapse the following spring, providing the anophelines with a reservoir of parasites on which to draw. As

38. Darrett B. and Anita H. Rutman, "Of Agues and Fevers: Malaria in the Early Chesapeake," *William and Mary Quarterly*, 3d ser. 33 (1976), 34, 40; Kenneth F. Kiple and Virginia Himmelsteib King, *Another Dimension to the Black Diaspora* (New York: Cambridge University Press, 1981), 15, 51; Kenneth F. Kiple, *The Caribbean Slave: A Biological History* (New York: Cambridge University Press, 1984), 14–15.

39. Rutman and Rutman, "Agues and Fevers," 36–7, 42; St. Julien Ravenel Childs, *Malaria and Colonization in the Carolina Low Country, 1526–1696*, The Johns Hopkins University Studies in Historical and Political Science, ser. 59, no. 1 (Baltimore: The Johns Hopkins Press, 1940), 16.

40. Childs, *Malaria and Colonization*, 51–2, 109–10; Earle, "Environment, Disease," 48–51; Gerald L. Cates, "'The Seasoning': Disease and Death Among the First Colonists of Georgia," *Georgia Historical Quarterly* 64 (1980), 148–51, 155.

mosquitoes proliferated during the hot, muggy months, other settlers became infected. Newly arriving immigrants who lacked immunity to the local strains of parasites were especially vulnerable and most newcomers underwent a "seasoning" or period of sickness during their first summer and autumn in the New World. In addition, some colonists undoubtedly brought new strains of *P. vivax* from Europe, which helped sustain the cycle of transmission from man-to-mosquito-to-man. Aided by immigration, vivax malaria probably became endemic in the Chesapeake before 1650 and along South Carolina's Ashley River by 1680. Settlers attributed malarial symptoms to a variety of causes, but clearly understood the nature of the affliction. John Clayton offered a typical contemporary explanation in 1688 when he reported that during September, "many fall sick, this being the time of an Endemical sickness, for Seasonings, Cachexes, Fluxes, Scorbutical Dropsies, Gripes and the like."[41]

Even as Clayton wrote, the "seasoning" was becoming much worse for some colonists. During the second half of the seventeenth century, another much more virulent form of malarial parasite invaded the coastal plain. Known as *Plasmodium falciparum*, the organisms probably originated in West Africa and came to the Americas in the blood of imported slaves and slave traders. Unlike the more benign *P. vivax*, *P. falciparum* attacks both young and mature red blood cells and can cause clotting of blood vessels leading to internal organs or the brain. Falciparum malaria can kill up to 25 percent of its victims whereas vivax malaria generally claims 5 percent or less.[42]

Although both forms of malaria can be fatal, the disease more often is a "debilitator," not a "killer." Usually a malarial attack weakens the victim's overall resistance to disease, paving the way for other contagions that are the more immediate cause of death. Working in tandem with malaria, dysentery, typhoid fever, influenza, pneumonia, and a variety of respiratory infections became wholesale killers of colonists. Some settlers were more vulnerable than others. Pregnant women were especially prone to malarial infection, as were children aged five to ten. Among adult males, newly arriving immigrants who lacked immunity to the local strains of parasites were most susceptible to a serious bout with seasoning or fever.[43]

Because malaria took its heaviest toll among the new, the young, and the pregnant, its overall effect was to lower life expectancy and retard population growth. The best place to observe some of the effects of endemic malaria is

41. Quotation from Berkeley and Berkeley, *John Clayton*, 45. Rutman and Rutman, "Agues and Fevers," 38–9; Childs, *Malaria and Colonization*, 202.
42. Kiple and King, *Another Dimension*, 15; Wood, *Black Majority*, 87; Rutman and Rutman, "Agues and Fevers," 50.
43. Quotations from Rutman and Rutman, "Agues and Fevers," 50–2; Lorena S. Walsh and Russell R. Menard, "Death in the Chesapeake: Two Life Tables for Men in Early Colonial Maryland," *Maryland Historical Magazine* 69 (1974), 226–7.

the seventeenth-century Chesapeake, where historians have done systematic studies of population growth. Due to the labor demands of tobacco agriculture, that region absorbed white immigrant servants by the thousands. These new arrivals provided a continuous supply of fresh nonimmune hosts for *P. vivax* and *P. falciparum*. In addition, immigrants frequently carried other contagious ailments, creating a disease environment in which epidemics of influenza or some other malady could, in conjunction with malaria, carry off newcomer and native-born colonist alike.

Anyone residing in the Chesapeake during the seventeenth century could expect a short and sickly life. A twenty-year-old male who immigrated to Virginia or Maryland usually did not live much past forty. Native-born males, who had some immunity to vivax malaria, but initially not to falciparum malaria, lived slightly longer, but still could expect to die a few years shy of age fifty. By contrast, men in the more healthful environs of New England might live to age sixty and beyond. The peculiar susceptibility of expectant mothers, together with a general shortage of women, worked to keep Chesapeake birth rates low. Fertility improved somewhat over the course of the century, but deaths among newcomers still exceeded births. Not until the 1690s, after an entire generation had acquired some immunity to the endemic strains of falciparum malaria and immigration slackened, did the male death rate begin to drop significantly. Only then did native-born settlers begin to outnumber immigrants within the white population.[44]

Information available for other parts of the coastal plain also suggests that endemic malaria was a greater threat to colonists who lived in areas that had been settled early and attracted a steady stream of immigrants. In seventeenth-century Charles Town, the disease seems to have been at its worst during the 1680s, a decade that saw both increased immigration and the introduction of falciparum malaria. The town appears to have grown healthier when immigration declined a bit in the 1690s and the local population gained immunity. However, the disease still remained a problem in the countryside and probably contributed to a high mortality rate and slow growth within South Carolina's white population during the early eighteenth century.[45]

Malaria might also have been endemic in the swamps of northeastern North Carolina during the seventeenth century. But without major ports, that region attracted comparatively few immigrants directly from overseas. Many of the settlers came from the Chesapeake, where they might already have undergone a

44. Walsh and Menard, "Death in the Chesapeake," 214–15; Daniel Blake Smith, "Mortality and Family in the Colonial Chesapeake," *Journal of Interdisciplinary History* 8 (1978), 416–18; Rutman and Rutman, "Agues and Fevers," 48–51; Kulikoff, *Tobacco and Slaves*, 32–3, 42, 61.
45. Childs, *Malaria and Colonization*, 208, 253; H. Roy Merrens and George D. Terry, "Dying in Paradise: Malaria, Mortality, and the Perceptual Environment in Colonial South Carolina," *Journal of Southern History* 50 (1984), 541–50; Wood, *Black Majority*, 69, 143–4.

seasoning. Moreover, these new Carolinians were less likely to be exposed to other killing contagions brought from Europe. Consequently, colonists in the Albemarle region achieved a measure of longevity more quickly than their Chesapeake counterparts. In Perquimans County, North Carolina mortality rates were high during the early years of settlement, but men born during the last quarter of the seventeenth century, who made it to age twenty, frequently lived to age fifty and sometimes beyond.[46]

Once malaria became established along the coast, colonists unwittingly contributed to its propagation and spread. Although the various species of anophelines vary in habits and biting characteristics, they also share some important traits, one of which is that they rarely range more than a mile or two from their watery breeding sites. By the turn of the century, declining beaver populations had begun to reduce the number of natural ponds available to mosquitoes. But colonists provided other habitats that brought the insects into contact with humans. Removing timber along the already sluggish coastal plain rivers or in swamps allowed more sunlight to reach the water and must have increased the growth of certain algae on which anopheline larvae feed. The dams associated with sawmills only compounded the problem by adding still another source of slow-moving water exposed to the sun.[47]

Just as tobacco crops lured grasshoppers and hornworms, flooded rice fields provided acres of new, mosquito-breeding grounds in South Carolina and along the lower Cape Fear. Indigo production, too, encouraged the winged pests. To produce dye, indigo plants had to be fermented in huge wooden vats (usually made from pine or cypress) and then spread on fields to dry. Both the vats and the putrid drying plants attracted flies and mosquitoes in abundance. Aided by such practices, malarial parasites continued to infect colonists throughout the eighteenth century. Georgia provides a case in point. Sporadic outbreaks of malaria may have contributed to mortality there in the 1730s and 1740s, but the disease probably did not become endemic until after 1750, when royal officials rescinded the previous ban on slavery and Georgians began to import Africans, clear land, and grow rice in quantity.[48]

Due to the seasonal nature of malaria, the disease could take a white labor

46. James M. Gallman, "Mortality Among White Males: Colonial North Carolina," *Social Science History* 4 (August 1980), 303–4, 309–10.

47. Rutman and Rutman, "Agues and Fevers," 36; Cates, "'The Seasoning,'" 152–3.

48. Wood, *Black Majority*, 75; Sharrer, "Indigo Bonanza," 451. In 1774, the Georgia General Assembly passed legislation requiring that after steeping, indigo be buried at least two inches underground or "otherwise effectually destroyed." Such a law was necessary due to the "pernicious effects ... from the number of flies which are engendered by leaving the weed ... to rot above ground." (Horatio Marbury and William H. Crawford, Esqrs., *Digest of the Laws of the State of Georgia From Its Settlement As a British Province in 1775 to the Session of the General Assembly in 1800. Inclusive* [Savannah, 1802], 270). Cates, "'The Seasoning,'" 152.

force out of the fields precisely at the time of harvest, an inconvenience a number of smaller seventeenth-century Chesapeake planters must have experienced.[49] By the early eighteenth century, however, most of the wealthier South Atlantic planters were gradually acquiring black slaves to tend their crops and lumbering operations. Slaves imported from the West Indies and later directly from Africa had their own problems adjusting to the New World disease environment. In the cooler climes of the Chesapeake, perhaps as many as one in four slaves succumbed to respiratory infections during their first winter and spring on a tidewater plantation. And, like Europeans, slaves were susceptible to smallpox, pneumonia, and influenza.[50] But slaves fared much better than their masters around mosquito-infested rice fields, rivers, and millponds.

Because many slaves came from the malarious environment of West Africa, they had developed better biological defenses against the troublesome parasites. In Africa, where malaria flourished, a future slave was likely to have hosted and survived numerous strains of the parasite, thereby acquiring more protective antibodies than the typical colonist. In addition, most slaves also had a measure of genetic protection. Modern studies link resistance to vivax to certain anomalies of red blood cells, characteristics that are rare in non-blacks.[51]

Some slaves also carried genetic protection against the more lethal falciparum. Resistance to falciparum is also tied to certain blood characteristics. One of these is sickle-cell trait, a condition in which one carries the gene to produce sickle-shaped cells, but exhibits no symptoms. A second, much more serious condition involving the sickling gene is "sickle-cell disease," a type of anemia that sometimes develops in children when both parents carry the trait. Both sickle-cell trait and sickle-cell anemia afford some protection against falciparum, but sickle-cell anemia itself generally causes death before the victim is twenty years old. A third blood characteristic that affords some protection is a blood enzyme deficiency, known to doctors as "G6PD deficiency." Scientists have also identified many variations of both sickle-cell trait and G6PD deficiencies, which also seem to offer some protection.[52]

Exactly how these characteristics provide such defenses remains unclear, but unlike resistance to vivax, protection against falciparum is not racial. Sickle-shaped cells and the blood enzyme deficiency are not confined to blacks, but

49. Rutman and Rutman, "Agues and Fevers," 56–7.
50. Russell R. Menard, "From Servants to Slaves: The Transformation of the Chesapeake Labor System," *Southern Studies* 16 (1977), 355–90; idem, "The Africanization of the Low Country Labor Force," in Winthrop D. Jordan and Sheila L. Skemp. eds., *Race and Family in the Colonial South* (Jackson: University Press of Mississippi, 1987), 81–103; Kulikoff, *Tobacco and Slaves*, 37–44; Wood, *Black Majority*, ch. 5.
51. Wood, *Black Majority*, 88–90; Kiple, *Caribbean Slave*, 16–17.
52. Kiple, *Caribbean Slave*, 15–17.

are found in non-Negroid races that have inhabited malarious environments for long periods. Historian Kenneth H. Kiple has estimated that perhaps 25 percent of West African slaves coming to the Americas carried the sickle-cell trait and another 25 percent, the G6PD deficiency. Because these traits can be passed along genetically, both newly arriving slaves and their offspring were much better equipped than their masters to escape autumnal infection. Although planters could use African biological defenses to good advantage and sometimes cited these characteristics as justification for using slave labor, colonists paid a high medical price for the privilege. Even if tolerant of both forms of malaria, newly arriving blacks served as carriers for new strains of falciparum, and malaria remained a serious problem throughout the South well after cessation of the slave trade.[53]

Malaria was not the only mosquito-borne disease to cause problems in the South Atlantic coastal plain. By 1700 some colonists had encountered another deadly seasonal menace: yellow fever. Whereas malaria results from a protozoic parasite, yellow fever is caused by a virus carried by another mosquito, the female *Aedes aegypti*. As with malaria, the initial symptoms of yellow fever infection are general sluggishness, chills, fever, and perhaps a severe backache or headache. But yellow fever is frequently a killer. Some victims recover after the initial symptoms and gain immunity, but more commonly, the patient hemorrhages internally, lapses into a coma, and dies. As historian John Duffy has suggested, yellow fever ranked as "one of the most deadly and terrifying" of all the infections to strike colonial North America.[54]

Unlike the anopheline carriers of malaria, *A. aegypti* probably was not native to the Americas, and the same seems to hold true for the lethal virus it carries. Most evidence points to Africa as the source of both vector and contagion. Aedes has a short range and is extremely sensitive to cold temperatures. Moreover, to spread yellow fever, a female aedes has to bite an afflicted human within three days of infection and then survive twelve to eighteen days while the virus incubates. For those reasons, both mosquito and virus were slow to come to the New World. Not until the mid seventeenth century, when faster slaving vessels afforded aedes a quicker Atlantic crossing and burgeoning Caribbean populations provided adequate human hosts, did the virus make a documented appearance in the West Indies. From there it took another fifty years to reach the South Atlantic region, where the first documented outbreak occurred in Charles Town in 1699.[55]

Once introduced into the region, however, yellow fever became a regular visitor to the South Carolina coast. Charles Town suffered at least seven major

53. Ibid., 17; Wood, *Black Majority*, 91.
54. John Duffy, *Epidemics in Colonial America* (Baton Rouge: Louisiana State University Press, 1953), 138; Kiple and King, *Another Dimension*, 29.
55. Kiple and King, *Another Dimension*, 31–6.

epidemics during the eighteenth century. Each time, the virus was a dreaded transient brought in by vessels from the West Indies. Each time, it struck in summer and lasted until the first killing frosts destroyed the infecting mosquitoes. And each time, Charles Town's residents added up the dead: 179 in 1699; at least 140 in 1706; 8 to 12 daily in 1732; 544 in 1799.[56]

Charles Town's peculiar susceptibility was not simply the result of its warm weather or the city's importance as a port of call for West Indian vessels. Yellow fever could and did strike farther north, afflicting New York, Boston, and Philadelphia throughout the eighteenth century. What Charles Town had in common with those cities was not climate, but rather the necessary population density to support the aedes mosquito in its constant search for blood meals. A 1708 population estimate placed Charles Town's population at three thousand persons living in 250 houses. By 1799 the city housed over sixteen thousand people. The growing population, confined in a relatively small space, created ideal conditions for perpetuating an epidemic. Rain barrels, mudholes, ditches, and the other man-made reservoirs common to emerging colonial municipalities provided appropriate freshwater breeding grounds near human habitation.[57]

The aedes could not survive the killing frosts, and unlike malaria, yellow fever never became endemic to the South Atlantic region. Nor does it appear to have been much of a problem anywhere except Charles Town. Outbreaks of ailments with similar symptoms occurred occasionally along the Chesapeake, but nothing that can be identified specifically as yellow fever. Due to the short range of the aedes, most rural residents of the southern colonies were never in danger of infection unless they visited the port city. And even if they became infected in town and then returned to a plantation, the disease could not be passed on to others without the necessary mosquito vector. Throughout most of the English South, people simply did not live close enough together to sustain the virus. It was not until well into the nineteenth century that New Orleans and Savannah took their places alongside Charleston as potential epidemic sites.[58]

As with the seasonal outbreaks of malaria, colonists noticed that yellow fever rarely killed as many blacks as whites. Those blacks who contracted the contagion usually survived with only a comparatively mild bout of sickness. In part, blacks benefited from acquired immunity. Slaves born in West Africa were likely to have been exposed to the disease during childhood, a time during which the body is best equipped to fight off the malady. If an African child survived such an initial encounter (usually with only mild sickness),

56. Duffy, *Epidemics*, 142–63; Wood, *Black Majority*, 80–2.
57. Kiple, *Caribbean Slave*, 18; Wood, *Black Majority*, 82.
58. Kiple and King, *Another Dimension*, 40–1.

he remained safe thereafter, whether he stayed in West Africa or labored in Charles Town. Recent studies suggest that blacks also enjoyed a degree of genetic protection against yellow fever. Although the exact nature of such characteristics remains to be discovered, some sort of genetic factor may be responsible for the relatively mild form of the disease in slaves. Like the blacks who tended Carolina rice fields and Chesapeake tobacco crops, slaves living in Charles Town had important defenses against the imported illness, protection that white Southerners would continually cite as a justification for keeping Africans in bondage.[59]

If their crops survived the various pests and their slaves bore up under the summer onslaught of mosquitoes, coastal plain planters heavily engaged in growing staples soon encountered another ecological consequence of commercial agriculture: soil exhaustion. Depleting the soil had also been a problem for Indians, who had been forced to relocate when their fields no longer produced. Cultivating labor-intensive staples to ship abroad created greater difficulties for colonial farmers. Any variety of tobacco was especially hard on soils, usually depleting a planter's field in only three to four years. An average Carolina indigo crop (which yielded two and a half to three tons of plant per year per acre) removed 118 pounds of mineral matter from the soil and could exhaust a field in only a few seasons. Small wonder that Dr. John Mitchell, a Virginia physician who spent the last twenty-two years of his life in England, described tobacco and indigo as "rank and poisonous weeds, which only grow on rotten soils and dunghills, such as fresh woodlands and will not thrive in any others."[60]

Grains, too, could create problems. Corn, the primary food crop in the colonies, is the most demanding of all grains. As Mitchell explained it, "At the same time, they [colonists] are obliged to plant Indian Corn, which, by its great substance and large spreading root, exhausts the substance of the earth, as much as their staple commodities; and both together deprive the people of the very necessaries of life."[61]

Although such comments would seem to indicate that southern colonists cleared, depleted, and abandoned their fields on a large scale, the exact extent of soil exhaustion during the colonial period varied from region to region and depended on a wide range of environmental and human factors.[62] Bottomland

59. Kiple, *Caribbean Slave*, 19; Wood, *Black Majority*, 91.
60. Quotation from Dr. John Mitchell, *The Present State of Great Britain and North America* (London, 1767), 138, 139. Earle, *Evolution of a Settlement Pattern*, 25; Sharrer, "Indigo Bonanza," 449.
61. Mitchell, *Present State of Great Britain*, 139–40; Cronon, *Changes in the Land*, 150.
62. A primary argument for wide-scale abandonment of southern farmland is Avery Odell Craven's *Soil Exhaustion as a Factor in the Agricultural History of Virginia and Maryland, 1606–1860* (Urbana: University of Illinois Press, 1926). In recent years, Craven's arguments,

tracts, preferred by most tidewater planters, recouped some of their fertility from spring floods that brought fresh deposits of alluvial topsoil. To supplement natural replenishment, Chesapeake farmers called on other methods. Early tobacco planters disdained manure because it lent an unpleasant taste to their crop. Instead, they practiced a three-way system of shifting agriculture. Initially, planters raised tobacco for three to four years until the soil became depleted. Worn tobacco fields were then planted with corn or other grains. Because they were less demanding than tobacco, such grains prospered for several years until they, too, ran short of minerals.

When the old fields no longer yielded sufficient stores of grain, farmers cleared a new plot and allowed the depleted ground to lie fallow. After about twenty years, the fallow field again became suitable for tobacco, though yields were not as high the second time around. This system of shifting agriculture allowed Chesapeake planters to avert chronic soil exhaustion as long as they had enough new forested lands to clear and cultivate while old fields rested. Historians have estimated that a planter needed about twenty acres for each laborer he used to grow tobacco. In addition, planters had to maintain livestock range, cornfields, and woodlands for firewood and building material. Considering those needs, an estimate of fifty acres per laborer may not be excessive.[63]

Geography and the simple techniques used to cultivate tobacco also helped preserve the fields. The relatively level topography of the eastern coastal plain meant that runoff from rains seldom moved fast enough to erode cultivated plots. Moreover, the sandy soils of the region could absorb much precipitation, perhaps as much as two inches an hour. Although some of the earliest colonists along the Chesapeake had brought plows from England, they made only limited use of such devices. The convenient methods of clearing adopted from the Indians left fields that were encumbered by whole trees or at best stumps. Tobacco had to be planted in mounds and hoed by hand in much the same way that Indians tilled corn. The uneven surface of such fields also helped break up and disperse rainwater, thereby preventing severe runoff and the accompanying gullies. For the most part, topsoil probably remained in place, allowing fields to be cultivated as long as they contained sufficient minerals to produce tobacco or corn.[64]

as they apply to the colonial Chesapeake, have drawn criticism from a number of scholars, including Earle (*Evolution of a Settlement Pattern*, 24–30). Recently, historian Jack Temple Kirby has noted more problems with Craven's thesis and suggested that Craven's periodization of soil exhaustion in the Chesapeake needs serious revision. Kirby's ideas are outlined in his essay "Pine to Pine: Chapters of Land Use in the Chesapeake" (Paper delivered at "Forests, Habitats, and Resources: A Conference in Global Environmental History," Duke University, 1 May 1987). I am grateful to Professor Kirby for permission to use his paper in advance of publication.

63. Earle, *Evolution of a Settlement Pattern*, 28–9; Kulikoff, *Tobacco and Slaves*, 47–8.
64. Earle, *Evolution of a Settlement Pattern*, 30.

But Indian farming techniques and field rotation could not keep fields in peak condition forever. Growing populations during the eighteenth century made it difficult for tidewater planters to maintain the minimum fifty acres per worker needed for successful field rotation. More and more frequently, old fields had to be replanted without adequate rest, and tobacco yields began to decline. Seeking new tobacco acreage, planters moved into the Virginia piedmont. Most of those migrating up the major river valleys first took up residence along the bottomlands adjacent to streams. There, the settlers employed many of the same farming techniques as tidewater colonists, girdling trees, hoeing crops, and planting worn tobacco fields with corn. In the hillier piedmont, however, erosion was more extensive, especially as planters moved away from the streams onto the surrounding uplands. Much of the silt that clogged streams and led to disastrous freshets in the tidewater during the middle decades of the eighteenth century, probably washed out of tobacco and cornfields in the piedmont. The ongoing removal of topsoil only compounded the other exhausting qualities of tobacco. By the 1780s the acres available to each worker in the piedmont were also declining, and fresh tobacco lands growing ever more scarce.[65]

Due to increased erosion, more frequent planting of worn fields, and the slow, but steady disappearance of the forests, agriculture in Virginia and Maryland began to change. Although planters continued to grow tobacco as an export crop, they gradually turned more to grains, particularly wheat. Chesapeake farmers had grown some wheat from the earliest days of settlement, and during the first decades of the eighteenth century, Virginians regularly traded wheat to the West Indies and New England. By midcentury, however, ecology and economics combined to make grain production more profitable. During the 1750s several bad harvests in Europe worked to drive the price of American grain high enough to allow planters suitable return for wheat shipped overseas. Moreover, wheat culture was especially compatible with tobacco and corn. Planters sowed wheat in early fall, after tobacco had been harvested, but before the last corn had been gathered. And more importantly, wheat could be grown in fields too depleted to produce profitable tobacco crops. By the 1770s wheat had joined tobacco as an important Chesapeake staple.[66]

Cultivating more wheat did not eliminate the ecological problems inherent in commercial agriculture. Unlike tobacco, wheat was often sown broadcast in broken ground. Consequently, planters had to make more use of plows and draft animals. Farmers intending to plant in the fall usually prepared their

65. Kulikoff, *Tobacco and Slaves*, 48–9, 52; Hall, "Soil Erosion and Agriculture," 76–7, 82–3; Stanley Wayne Trimble, *Man-Induced Soil Erosion on the Southern Piedmont, 1700–1970* (Ankeny, Iowa: Soil Conservation Society of America, 1974), 43–5; Kulikoff, *Tobacco and Slaves*, 53–4.
66. Earle, *Evolution of a Settlement Pattern*, 128–9; Gill, "Wheat Culture in Virginia," 380–2; Kirby, "Pine to Pine," 5.

wheat fields in early summer. Because the plowed plots frequently lay open to the summer storms, the shift to more extensive grain culture in the eighteenth century probably did little to stem erosion.[67]

Well aware of the decreasing supply of suitable farmland, a few eighteenth-century planters in Virginia and Maryland began to study and adopt some of the new conservation techniques used in Europe. If practiced diligently, planters believed, this "new husbandry" would allow prolonged use of plows and cultivation of grain and other staples. Landon Carter was one planter who employed such methods. For Carter, the new husbandry typically involved various schemes of crop rotation, including planting imported clover and other nitrogen-fixing legumes on ground exhausted by corn, wheat, or tobacco. Carter also used imported clover and alfalfa on his worn fields. Over the space of several years, such plants helped restore fertility and check erosion. In addition, Carter began to experiment with the European practice of manuring exhausted land. He had his slaves drive cattle onto worn plots or kept the beasts in pens, where their dung could be easily collected. By century's end, other great planters had found more ways to combat soil depletion. Better plows made it possible to build up ridges in fields to check erosion. Contour plowing on hillsides also helped control rainwash. Some farmers filled existing gullies with trash or straw and then covered them with topsoil for planting. Such practices were essential if planters intended to continue cultivating an area that had been farmed for the better part of two centuries.[68]

Farther south, exhaustion of coastal plain soils was a slower process. The first permanent colonists in North Carolina grew tobacco and corn north of Albemarle Sound and probably used techniques like those employed in Virginia. Over the next hundred years, tobacco agriculture spread south to bottomlands along the Tar, Neuse, and upper Cape Fear rivers.[69] But because eastern North Carolina attracted relatively few overseas immigrants, both white and black populations grew slowly. In 1700 (a point at which soil exhaustion was already a problem along the lower reaches of Chesapeake rivers), North Carolina was home to less than ten thousand whites and fewer than five hundred blacks. Virginia's population, by contrast, included over fifty-six thousand whites and more than five thousand blacks. In 1730, when Chesapeake planters were moving onto new tobacco lands in the piedmont, well over three times as many whites and more than nine times as many blacks lived in Virginia

67. Gill, "Wheat Culture in Virginia," 384–5.
68. Kirby, "Pine to Pine," 5–6; Arthur R. Hall, *Early Erosion Control Practices in Virginia* (United States Department of Agriculture Miscellaneous Publication no. 256, 1937), 9–18.
69. H. Roy Merrens, *Colonial North Carolina in the Eighteenth Century* (Chapel Hill: University of North Carolina Press, 1964), 121–33. Merrens bases the spread of tobacco agriculture on locations of tobacco warehouses in these regions.

as in North Carolina.[70] Because they had access to fewer slaves and indentured laborers, North Carolina tobacco planters devoted fewer acres to the exhausting weed. Even if farmers depleted their small plots, they must have had enough fresh land at their disposal to minimize the effects of soil depletion.

From the mid 1730s to the mid 1760s, North Carolina's population increased dramatically. By 1767 about 124,000 whites lived in the colony; the black population climbed from under 6,000 to 41,000. Few of the white immigrants arriving during the middle decades of the century brought slaves with them. The overall growth in the number of slaves stemmed from established planters acquiring additional black labor and from natural increase within the existing slave population. As those who already owned blacks bought more, the slave population of the tobacco region tended to become concentrated on the larger plantations, a trend that suggests North Carolina slaveowners were becoming more like their neighbors to the north.[71] Acquiring more slaves offered the wealthiest North Carolina planters the potential to farm more intensively, and soil depletion from tobacco and corn might have become more noticeable, especially in the northeastern quadrant of the colony, which had been settled longest.

But even if tobacco and corn took a heavier toll locally, the crops still did not have the same steadily exhausting effects as in Virginia and Maryland. North Carolina's lack of good harbors and easily navigable rivers forced colonists there to take much of their tobacco to Virginia ports. Tobacco prices fluctuated greatly throughout the eighteenth century, and when prices were low, shipping costs made it economically impractical to send large crops overland. As late as 1772, North Carolina's tobacco exports were only about 2 percent of Virginia's and 5 percent of Maryland's total exports. Even if twice that amount went overland to Virginia (a popular contemporary estimate), North Carolina colonists still produced only about one-tenth as much tobacco as Chesapeake planters. Because their tobacco acreage remained comparatively small, North Carolinians did not have to search for new staples to plant on exhausted ground. Planters in the northeastern part of the colony did grow wheat during the eighteenth century, but grain cultivation in the region seems to have stemmed more from the demands of the European market than from chronic soil exhaustion.[72]

70. Peter H. Wood, "The Changing Populations of the Eighteenth-Century South: An Overview, By Race and Subregion, From 1685 to 1790," in Peter H. Wood, G. Waselkov, and M. Thomas Hatley, eds., *Powhatan's Mantle* (Lincoln: University of Nebraska Press, forthcoming).

71. Marvin L. Michael Kay and Lorin Lee Cary, "A Demographic Analysis of Colonial North Carolina with Special Emphasis upon the Slave and Black Populations," in Jeffrey J. Crow and Flora J. Hatley, eds., *Black Americans in North Carolina and the South* (Chapel Hill: University of North Carolina Press, 1984), 72–3, 90–3; Merrens, *Colonial North Carolina*, 80.

72. Merrens, *Colonial North Carolina*, 114–20, 240 nn. 62, 63.

From the lower Cape Fear south to the Altamaha River, coastal plain planters made extensive use of slave labor to grow rice. Although not as exhausting as corn, rice can deplete soils of certain organic material, especially nitrogen. Rice planters, however, enjoyed a built-in natural hedge against exhaustion. The water that periodically covered the inland swamps contained alluvial soil as well as decaying leaves and other vegetable matter that helped maintain a measure of the field's fertility. As William Stephens, secretary of the Georgia colony, explained it "Water diffuses itself variously among these Low Lands, part of which it covers, & a great part not; and when it returns leaves a richness behind it and makes it very productive." An untimely flood could destroy the rice, but Stephens marveled that most planters did not fret if the plants lay "a foot or more under water for a time," its adaptation to such fertile swampy ground being "a peculiar Quality" of the grain.[73]

Even so, rice yields declined after a period of intensive cropping. When that happened, planters usually did not employ any sort of fertilizer. (Applying manure was difficult because the water tended to wash it away.) Instead, rice growers simply moved to another swampy tract while the old plot rested. As white and slave populations grew during the first half of the eighteenth century – the number of blacks in South Carolina went from 2,800 to 40,600 between 1700 and 1745 – planters slowly began to use up the best inland tracts. The mid eighteenth-century shift to the tidal swamps probably resulted in part from the search for fresh ground. Such problems were most extensive in South Carolina, where rice had been cultivated longer. But planters along the lower Cape Fear might also have faced the problems of depleted land by the time of the American Revolution.[74]

The use of dikes and trunks in the tidal swamps allowed planters more control over the amount of water in their fields and afforded more options in controlling soil exhaustion. When yields declined, planters could flood an old field and allow it to lie underwater for several seasons. During such fallow intervals, some planters used the artificial ponds to breed fish. During his travels in the southern colonies in 1765, John Bartram saw an old rice field that nourished "pike, gar, mullet, trout [bass] mud fish, bream, carp pearch [and] silver roach." The fish, in turn, attracted "prodigious numbers of white large heron and gannets." A period of rest and the additional organic matter deposited by birds and fish eventually made it possible to replant such fields with

73. Quotation from Coulter, *Journal of William Stephens*, vol. 1, 245–6. D.H. Grist, *Rice*, 3d ed. (London: Longman Group, 1959), 185.
74. Heyward, *Seed from Madagascar*, 42; Wood, "Changing Population"; Clifton, "Golden Grains of White," 370–1.

rice. The old ground was not as productive as newly cleared swamps, but it required much less labor to bring under cultivation.[75]

By the 1750s many rice planters in the Carolinas and Georgia also grew indigo, potentially a much more exhausting crop than rice. Indigo grew best in higher, well-drained tracts that lay in the mixed hardwood forests of the coastal plain. Because indigo fields generally had to be plowed, most of the stumps and trees had to be removed from the plot. Therefore, cultivating the plants not only depleted the soil of minerals, but also encouraged erosion on the more undulating terrain. It may have been erosion, not indigo's mineral requirements, that inspired Dr. John Mitchell's belief that the plants would grow only in newly cleared woodlands. But indigo's need for higher ground might also have worked to limit the plant's exhausting effects. Encouraged by parliamentary bounties, low-country planters who held enough slaves to produce indigo in quantity used the crop to diversify their agriculture, growing the plants on land ill suited for rice. Thus, soil exhaustion attributable to indigo must have been sporadic and spotty. Moreover, what one contemporary writer called the "golden days of indigo" were relatively short-lived. Parliament reduced the sixpence-per-pound bounty of the 1740s to fourpence in 1765; when the American Revolution ended such assistance, it became even less profitable to devote fresh lands to the plants.[76]

While farmers in the coastal plain were learning to cope with soil exhaustion, Europeans were slowly populating the southern backcountry. In some of these "back parts," farmers might hold title to several hundred acres, but the rigors of clearing heavily forested oak and hickory lands initially worked to keep cultivated tracts small. Geographer Robert D. Mitchell estimates that in the early years of settlement, "the average farm" in the Shenandoah Valley had only about ten to twelve acres of cleared land. Like settlers elsewhere, upland farmers frequently planted corn in fields still encumbered by stumps and girdled trees. Even in fertile clay and limestone soils, maize yields declined after several plantings. But in some parts of the Carolina piedmont, Europeans used the Indian method of planting beans and corn together in mounds, a practice

75. John Bartram, "Diary of a Journey Through the Carolinas, Georgia, and Florida From July 1, 1765, to April 10, 1766," *Transactions of the American Philosophical Society* new series, 23 Part 1 (December 1942), 13–14. (Freshwater trout could not survive in the warm climate of the low country. Bartram probably saw bass in the pond. The silver roach is a European fish. Bartram's use of that term might also refer to some American fish, although silver roach could have been imported from Europe.) Clifton, "Golden Grains of White," 370–1.

76. Quotation from Dr. Alexander Garden to Charles Whitworth, 27 April 1757, in James Edward Smith, ed., *A Selection of the Correspondence of Linnaeus and Other Naturalists*, 2 vols. (New York: Arno, 1928), vol. 1, 383; Bonner, *History of Georgia Agriculture*, 18; Hall, "Soil Exhaustion and Agriculture," 79–80.

that helped replenish nitrogen. Other farmers used a simple system of field rotation, first planting corn and then peas or beans. As the trees and stumps decayed, backcountry colonists with appropriate plows could follow beans with wheat. In the meantime, another field could be cleared for corn.[77]

Like their coastal plain counterparts, settlers in the uplands also sought to sell surplus produce, either to nearby colonists or for export abroad. Over the last half of the eighteenth century, a number of cash crops worked their way into the backcountry. Eastern Virginia planters who held acreage in the northern Shenandoah Valley employed tenants to plant tobacco in the fertile western ground. By 1800 William Tatham could write that the best tobacco lands "in their natural state in Virginia are the light red, or chocolate colored mountain lands; the light black mountain soil in the coves of the mountains and the richest low grounds." Another crop that became commercially important in the Valley was hemp. Encouraged by bounties from the Virginia government, planters in other parts of the colony also experimented with the fiber-producing plants. But hemp grown in the Valley generally seemed to be of a higher quality than that grown in the east. From the Shenandoah Valley south across the North Carolina piedmont, many backcountry farmers grew wheat and ground flour for local sale and export. Indigo, with its adaptation to higher ground, also found a home in parts of the South Carolina and Georgia up-country, where settlers grew it in tandem with corn and other food crops.[78]

As in the coastal plain, commercial farming in the backcountry led colonists there to use more land. (In the Shenandoah Valley, the amount of cleared land rose from about 10 percent of a farm's total acreage to between 20 and 25 percent over the course of the century.) Yet, for a variety of reasons, soil exhaustion was less of a problem in the backcountry than in the east. Even when grown commercially, neither hemp nor wheat were extremely taxing on soils.[79] Transportation problems also worked to keep tobacco and indigo crops small. Traveling interior rivers meant negotiating hazardous shoals and waterfalls; going overland was difficult due to poor roads. Like eastern North Carolina planters, colonists in the interior found it impractical to grow large quantities of crops that were difficult to get to market. Moreover, some of those

77. Mitchell, *Commercialism and Frontier*, 136; Hall, "Soil Erosion and Agriculture," 76–8.
78. Quotation from Herndon, *William Tatham*, 5. Mitchell, *Commercialism and Frontier*, 127–8, 178–81, 162–5, 172–8; Merrens, *Colonial North Carolina*, 111–19; Hall, "Soil Erosion and Agriculture," 74–5.
79. Mitchell, *Commercialism and Frontier*, 177, 164. Hemp did not prove as exhausting as other crops because growers frequently used a process called "dew rotting" to separate the fiber from the stalk. The stalks were cut and spread on the field in late fall until the gum and woody parts of the stalk began to rot and separate from the fiber. The decomposed matter left behind helped maintain the field's fertility. See James F. Hopkins, *A History of the Hemp Industry in Kentucky* (Lexington: University of Kentucky Press, 1951), 53–5.

who settled the backcountry were adept farmers who knew how to limit exhaustion and erosion. German settlers, in particular, experimented with clover and alfalfa, which helped replenish soil and hold it in place.[80]

Perhaps most important, early backcountry settlers made only limited use of slave labor. The expense of acquiring slaves limited their use by tenants on Valley tobacco farms. Many of the colonists who migrated from Pennsylvania to other "back parts" did not hold slaves; indeed, some of the various religious sects objected to slavery. In 1765 the North Carolina governor, William Tryon, noted that "as you penetrate into the Country few Blacks are employed," a trend he attributed to the poverty of settlers coming from "the Northward Colonies." In South Carolina up-country, slave populations increased rapidly during the 1760s as settlers there began to step up production of indigo and other commercial crops. But compared to the low country, inland slave populations were still small. By 1768 only some 8 percent of South Carolina slaves labored in the interior. With fewer slaves, backcountry colonists farmed less intensively and left fewer depleted fields. Outside piedmont Virginia and a small part of north central North Carolina, extensive erosion (one indicator of abandoned exhausted farmland) was minimal during the colonial period.[81]

Like Indian farming, colonial agriculture altered the composition of the southern forest. Abandoned tracts provided an ideal environment for old-field trees. Depending on topography and soil composition, old upland tracts might sprout stands of sassafras or eastern red cedar. But in the Virginia coastal plain and piedmont, where soil exhaustion was most extensive, the most common old-field trees were loblolly pines. Unlike its delicate cousin, the longleaf pine, the loblolly usually produces an abundant seed crop that is carried by wind into open fields and clearings. Robert Beverley discovered that if a Virginia planter cleared land along the major rivers, "he will certainly find that the Pine is the first Tree that will grow up again, tho' perhaps there was not a Pine in that Spot of Ground before." Dr. John Mitchell condemned loblolly pines as "the most pernicious of all weeds," noting that "they have a wing to their seed, which disperses it everywhere with the winds, like thistles, and in two or three years forms a pine thicket, which nothing can pass through or live in." François André Michaux noted that "this species exclusively occupies lands that have

80. Hall, "Soil Erosion and Agriculture," 74–5; Merrens, *Colonial North Carolina*, 119; Bridenbaugh, *Myths and Realities*, 141.
81. Quotation from William S. Powell, ed., "Tryon's 'Book' on North Carolina," *North Carolina Historical Review* 34 (1957), 411. Mitchell, *Commercialism and Frontier*, 127–8, 130–1. Jeffrey J. Crow, *The Black Experience in Revolutionary North Carolina* (Raleigh: Division of Archives and History, 1977), 5–6; Rachel N. Klein, "Ordering the Backcountry: The South Carolina Regulation," *William and Mary Quarterly*, 3d ser. 38 (1981), 663–5; Trimble, *Man-Induced Soil Erosion*, 42, 44. Further exhaustion and erosion of piedmont soils after the American Revolution stemmed primarily from the intensive cultivation of cotton in South Carolina and Georgia.

been exhausted by cultivation, and amid forests of Oak, tracts of 100 or 200 acres are not infrequently seen covered with thriving young pines." Just as the diminishing longleaf forest attested to the importance of the naval stores industry, flourishing loblolly thickets became a legacy of colonial agriculture.[82]

Europeans settling from Maryland to Georgia brought not only new crops, but new animals as well. From 1611, when English ships carried "one hundred Kine and other Cattell" to Jamestown, European livestock were crucial to the welfare of South Atlantic colonists. In every colony, cattle and hogs (sometimes along with sheep and goats) provided much needed meat for malnourished and sickly settlers. But livestock soon became much more than simply a convenient source of animal protein. By the mid seventeenth century, some Virginia planters had developed sufficient herds to sell cattle to other mainland colonies and the West Indies. Before South Carolinians began to grow rice, they augmented income from naval stores and the Indian trade with profits from the sale of cattle and hogs to Barbados.[83]

As settlement spread inland, the livestock trade continued to grow. During the first half of the eighteenth century, southern cattlemen regularly drove herds from the inner coastal plain to Charles Town, Norfolk, and other seaports. By the 1760s cattle keepers from North Carolina, the Virginia piedmont, and the Shenandoah Valley sold their stock in Fredericksburg and Petersburg. Throughout the last decades of the century, other backcountry drovers took their herds north through the Shenandoah Valley to Philadelphia, where cattle also brought good prices, especially during the Seven Years War and the American Revolution. Once the beasts arrived safely in the port towns, cattle and hogs could be slaughtered on the spot and the meat prepared for local sale or export. As the author of *American Husbandry* observed, a colonist "falling to the business of breeding cattle" could find the profit from his enterprise "exceeding great."[84]

82. Quotations from Robert Beverley, *History and Present State of Virginia*, 134; Mitchell, *Present State of Great Britain*, 152, 153; and François André Michaux, *The North American Sylva: Or a Description of the Forest Trees of the United States, Canada, and Nova Scotia*, trans. J. Jay Smith, 5 vols. (Philadelphia: Rice, Rutter, and Company, 1865), vol. 3, 123. For general discussions of forest succession in old fields, see W. D. Billings, *Plants and the Ecosystem*, 3d ed. (Belmont, Calif: Wadsworth Publishing Company, 1978), 105–6; and Stephen H. Spurr and Burton V. Barnes, *Forest Ecology* (New York: Ronald, 1973), 491. Landon Carter once found a runaway slave hiding in a thicket of red cedars on the edge of a cleared field. (Greene, *Carter Diary*, vol. 1, 289–90.)

83. Quotation from John Smith, "The Generall Historie of Virginia, New-England, and the Summer Isles . . .," in Barbour, *Complete Works of Smith*, vol. 2, 241. Bonner, *History of Georgia Agriculture*, 30–1; Wesley N. Laing, "Cattle in Early Virginia," (Ph.D. diss., University of Virginia, 1952), 1; Wood, *Black Majority*, 32–3.

84. Quotation from Harry J. Carman and Rexford G. Tugwell, eds., *American Husbandry*, (New York: Columbia University Press, 1939), 241. Laing, "Cattle in Early Virginia," 159, 163; Mitchell, *Commercialism and Frontier*, 147–8.

As the trade in livestock escalated, some colonists used cattle to claim or exploit land without actually settling it. In the early eighteenth century, planters granted new tobacco lands in the Virginia interior had to "prove" such claims either by cultivating three acres out of fifty or by raising livestock on such acreage until it could be cultivated. Generally, the second option was easier, especially for the Chesapeake planter, who frequently dispatched an overseer and a few head of cattle to claim his new land. South Carolinians also took an interest in backcountry herding. South Carolina planters and Charles Town merchants sometimes acquired cattle and kept the beasts on a parcel of unowned or open range in the inner coastal plain. There the herds could graze and multiply until the speculators decided to have the stock driven to market. In the last half of the eighteenth century, backcountry colonists brought even more cattle to the interior. But for most of the colonial period, eastern planters and speculators probably had as much to do with the backcountry livestock industry as did small farmers and frontier herders.[85]

Both cattle and hogs convert a relatively low percentage of the food they eat into meat suitable for human consumption. Like modern ranchers, colonists found it too expensive to feed their animals solely on corn or other grains and depended on natural forage. Due to the difficulties involved in clearing forests for pastures, most planters and herders simply branded their stock and turned them out into the surrounding forests, fields, and swamps. As John Brickell described it, "The Planters make Penfolds adjacent to their Habitations, wherein they milk the Cows every Morning and Evening; after which, they turn them into the Woods, where they remain feeding all Day." Cattle could browse low-hanging vegetation in the forests or graze savannas and old fields. Hogs could fatten on acorns and other nuts. Colonists did pen sheep to protect those meek animals from predators. Some eighteenth-century planters, seeking to recover manure, corralled cattle on worn fields or kept the beasts in stalls. For the most part, however, livestock roamed the southern woods as freely as the indigenous animals.[86]

Like agriculture and the forest industries, the southern livestock trade could not have flourished without skilled slave labor. On the large plantations along the Chesapeake, planters relief on slaves to see to the daily needs of their herds.

85. Laing, "Cattle in Virginia," 100–1, 104; Gary S. Dunbar, "Colonial Carolina Cowpens," *Agricultural History* 35 (1961), 126, 128–9; Meinig, *Atlantic America*, 184.
86. Quotation from Brickell, *Natural History*, 51. Arnold Stricken, "The Euro-American Ranching Complex," in Anthony Leeds and Andrew P. Vayda, eds., *Man, Culture, and Animals* (Washington: American Association for the Advancement of Science, 1965), 223; John Solomon Otto, "Livestock-Raising in Early South Carolina, 1670–1700: Prelude to the Rice Plantation Economy," *Agricultural History* 61 (1987), 18; Clarence L. Ver Steeg, *Origins of a Southern Mosaic: Studies of Early Carolina and Georgia* (Athens: University of Georgia Press, 1975), 115–16. Even Landon Carter, practitioner of the "new husbandry" and collector of manure, seems to have believed his cattle bred more often if he allowed them to roam the woods freely (Greene, *Carter Diary*, vol. 2, 697).

In the backcountry, blacks probably played even more prominent roles. Many of the first Africans imported to South Carolina probably knew much about handling livestock. In some parts of West Africa, blacks had raised cattle on open range for generations, experience that made them experts in horsemanship and herding. Slave owners who dealt in cattle put such talents to good use. In the inner coastal plain of South Carolina, planters had their slaves erect "cowpens" near savannas or other suitable grazing and forage. Typically a cowpen included a parcel of cleared land, a large corral for cattle, smaller enclosures for hogs and horses, rough-hewn shacks, and a garden plot. Because cowpens frequently had to be located in regions far removed from a planter's other holdings, he relied on slaves to manage the herds. Slaves drove the stock into the forests to locate the best range and rounded them up when the owner decided it was time for a drive or sale.[87]

Although this system of "woods ranching" freed settlers from the laborious task of clearing and enclosing pastureland, the practice created other problems. In the spring, the native grasses available in the savannas and woodlands offered superb forage, perhaps allowing cattle to gain as much as two pounds per day. But as the year wore on, the grasses became scarcer and less palatable. During the fall and winter, a typical range-fed cow or bull might lose as much as two hundred pounds, and many cattle died from exposure. As one observer noted, "The Cattle of Carolina are very fat in Summer, but as lean in Winter, because they can find very little to eat, and have no cover to shelter them from the cold Rains, Frosts, and Snows, which last sometimes 3 or 4 Days."[88]

Cattlemen not only lost stock to intemperate weather, but also to the surrounding forests and swamps. Left to fend for themselves in the southern woods, livestock frequently reverted to the wild. Hogs, among the most prolific of domesticated beasts, were probably the first to return to nature. Wild pigs were "infinite" in Virginia by 1614 and "of a prodigious increase" in South Carolina by 1682. By the end of the seventeenth century, wild cattle and horses were so numerous in eastern Virginia that cattle hunting and horse hunting became great sports among young men. But as John Clayton wrote, the cattle were "difficult to be shott, having [like other wild beasts] a great acuteness of smelling."[89]

87. Laing, "Cattle in Virginia," 68–9; Wood, *Black Majority*, 30, 105; Otto, "Livestock-Raising," 23; Dunbar, "Carolina Cowpens," 126.

88. Quotation from Peter Purry, "A Description of the Province of South Carolina," in Bartholomew R. Carroll, ed., *Historical Collections of South Carolina*, 2 vols. (New York: Harper Bros., 1836), vol. 2, 132; John T. Cassady and W. O. Shepherd, "Grazing on Forested Lands," in United States Department of Agriculture, *Grass: Yearbook of Agriculture 1948* (Washington, D.C.: United States Department of Agriculture, 1948), 469–70.

89. Quotations from Ralph Hamor, *A True Discourse of the Present Estate of Virginia, and the success of the affaires there till the 18 of June 1614* (London, 1615), 23; Joel Gascoyne, *A True Description of Carolina* (London, 1682), 2; and Berkeley and Berkeley, *John Clayton*, 106. Crosby, *Ecological Imperialism*, 173–4; Laing, "Cattle in Virginia," 78–9.

The colonists from New England who attempted to settle along North Carolina's Cape Fear River in 1663 left behind cattle when they abandoned the colony. As other settlers moved in, wild livestock increased. John Brickell witnessed "great Droves" of cattle "feeding promiscuously on the Savannahs amongst the Deer" and observed "great Numbers" of feral bulls and cows breeding in the woods. Later colonists, who sought to confine woods-reared cattle, found the beasts impossible to tame. In the summer of 1737 Georgia's Trustees authorized the purchase of a hundred steers from South Carolina. Colonists near Savannah drove the animals onto a peninsula and surrounded them with a new fence. But the cattle, "being exceedingly wild," soon destroyed the enclosure and escaped into the woods. Only about half could be brought back to domesticity.[90]

Along the South Atlantic, as in other colonies of North America, free-roaming livestock attracted predators. Full-grown, healthy cattle (especially those that were half-wild) probably enjoyed some of the same "horns and hooves" protection against predators as the native buffalo, but young or weak animals were fair game. Black bears soon developed a taste for young pigs and poultry. Panthers preyed on small swine and calves. Domestic animals that wandered into swamps might be attacked by alligators who lay half-hidden in the dark water. In some regions, those reptiles regularly took chickens, geese, and pigs. (The omnivorous swine, however, sometimes got a measure of late revenge by eating dead alligators.) Rattlesnakes, too, occasionally killed horses and cattle.[91]

Even more dangerous were the wolves that stalked southern herds at night and sometimes invaded cowpens. Wolves were a problem throughout the region, but ecological tensions between those native carnivores and imported livestock are best illustrated by the tribulations of the Salzburger settlers of Georgia. The Salzburgers were Lutherans who emigrated from the mountains of Salzburg and settled at Ebenezer, some twenty-five miles up the Savannah River. The new colonists barely got their herds started before the wolves showed up. One particularly gruesome encounter occurred in December 1735. Pastor Johann Martin Boltzius, spiritual and secular leader of the Salzburgers,

90. Quotations from Brickell, *Natural History*, 52; and William Stephens, *A Journal of the Proceedings in Georgia*, 2 vols. (1742; reprint, Ann Arbor, Mich.: University Microfilms, 1966), vol. 1, 417. Powell, *Countie of Albemarle*, xxvi.

91. As suggested below, one of the best regions in which to observe the effects of predators on livestock is early Georgia. For examples of the predators listed here, see: Coulter, *Journal of William Stephens*, vol. 2, 158; "Johann Martin Bolzius Answers a Questionnaire on Carolina and Georgia," trans. and ed. Klaus G. Leowald, Beverly Starika, and Paul S. Taylor, *William and Mary Quarterly*, 3d ser. 14 (1957), 230; George Fenwick Jones and Renate Wilson, eds., *Detailed Reports on the Salzburger Emigrants who Settled in America . . . Edited by Samuel Urlsperger*, 8 vols. to date (Athens: University of Georgia Press, 1968–), vol. 5, 80; Kristian Hvidt, ed., *Von Reck's Voyage: Drawings and Journal of Philip Georg Friederich von Reck* (Savannah, Ga.: Beehive Press, 1980), 37.

described it this way. "Late yesterday evening we heard bellows and cries coming from the calf-pen as if the calves were being hurt. When the men of the watch ran to see about it they found a wolf sitting on a calf, in whose flesh it had already eaten several holes." The carnivores continued to attack Salzburger stock all through the winter. As Boltzius noted in January, "When the nights are cold and bright with stars, we can hear such horrible howlings in the evenings all around our place that we are sure a great many of them are around." Even when the settlers relocated to New Ebenezer, a site that promised better farmland, they still found that "the wolves not only howl terribly from quite close during the cold nights, but have also either eaten or injured calves, hogs, and poultry."[92]

Like most Europeans, Boltzius and the Salzburgers had an almost pathological fear of wolves and might have exaggerated the extent of the depredations. But it also seems likely that wolf populations increased during the early years of colonization. Indians and colonists hunting deer frequently left the skinned carcasses in the woods, providing a ready source of food for the scavenging carnivores. And as Boltzius and the Salzburgers found out, livestock also furnished new nourishment, especially in the winter, when other food supplies may have been scarce. Even if the animals were no more plentiful than before, cattle and hogs attracted the packs to settled regions and cowpens, making the predators seem more numerous and fueling settlers' imaginations.[93]

Like colonists elsewhere, those in the English South dealt with predators in the same way they sought to control squirrels and crows: by offering bounties for their slaughter. Colonists seeking the rewards employed a variety of techniques to kill the marauding beasts. Some hunters set traps rigged with guns so that a wolf taking the bait discharged the weapon and, in effect, committed suicide. In his inimitable style, William Byrd II told of settlers who dug "abundance of Wolf-Pits, so deep and perpendicular, that when a wolf is once tempted into them, he can no more scramble out again than a Husband who had taken the leap can scramble out of Matrimony."[94]

Colonists also enlisted Indians in the cause. Virginia settlers first rewarded the natives with trade goods and later, after the eastern tribes had been subjugated, assigned Indians a set number of wolves' heads to be delivered

92. Jones, *Detailed Reports of the Salzburger Emigrants*, vol. 2, 219, vol. 3, 15. For background information on the Salzburgers and Boltzius, see Leowald et al., "Bolzius Answers a Questionnaire," 218–22 and Bonner, *History of Georgia Agriculture*, 22–3.
93. Cowdrey, *This Land, This South*, 49; Cronon, *Changes in the Land*, 132.
94. William Byrd II, *Histories of the Dividing Line Betwixt Virginia and North Carolina*, ed. William K. Boyd (1929; reprint, Mineola, N.Y.: Dover, 1967), 94; Hening, *Statutes at Large of Virginia*, vol. 1, 199, vol. 3, 141; Thomas Cooper and David J. McCord, eds., *The Statutes at Large of South Carolina*, 10 vols. (Columbia, S.C.: A. S. Johnston, 1836–9), vol. 4, 726; and *Acts of Assembly Passed in the Province of Maryland From 1692 to 1715* (London, 1723), 68. Legislation placing bounties on predators is summarized in Cowdrey, *This Land, This South*, 49–50.

as tribute. Attempting to reduce the number of wolves in the backcountry, colonial legislators imposed fines on hunters who left deer carcasses in the forest. As one North Carolina statute explained it, the rotting meat attracted "wolves, bears, and other vermin which destroy the stocks of the inhabitants of this province." In Georgia, too, Boltzius planned similar action, noting in 1736 that the Salzburgers would be "making arrangements for the gradual extinction of such harmful animals in our region and for the greater safety of their livestock."[95]

Like other hunting regulations, laws designed to deal with predators proved difficult to enforce. Both Indians and colonists sometimes delivered wolves' heads from distant parts of the colonies or took their trophies to the counties that promised the greatest rewards. Thus, colonial officials sometimes paid for the death of predators that had been no threat to their particular area. Clerks who dispensed the bounties also had to remove the ears or tongue from every head they received to make sure the government did not pay twice for the same wolf.[96]

But in spite of such difficulties, the increased hunting pressure, combined with deforestation and habitat destruction, eventually produced the desired effect. Even as Boltzius made plans to deal with Georgia's howling beasts, predators were already becoming scarce in those regions settled earlier. In 1724 Hugh Jones reported that Virginians faced "no danger of wild beasts in traveling." Bears, he noted, had been exterminated "for the sake of their flesh and skins," while wolves were now "much destroyed by virtue of a law which allows good rewards for their heads." Fourteen years later, John Brickell wrote that those same beasts were disappearing from North Carolina due to "Planters continually destroying them as they hunt and travel in the Woods."[97]

If woods ranching contributed indirectly to the decline of predators, livestock had a more immediate impact on vegetation. Cattle, hogs, sheep, and goats all graze selectively, eating more palatable plants first. Initially, some of the tastiest forage could be found in Indian cornfields. Wherever Europeans settled, Indians frequently killed cattle and hogs that ate or trampled their grain, creating another source of tension between natives and colonists.[98]

95. James Iredell, *The Public Acts of the General Assembly of North Carolina* (New Bern: Martin and Ogden, 1804), 70; Jones, *Detailed Reports of the Salzburger Emigrants*, vol. 3, 33–4. For laws concerning Indians and wolves, see Hening, *Statutes at Large of Virginia*, vol. 2, 236, 274.

96. Hening, *Statutes at Large of Virginia*, vol. 2, 236, vol. 6, 153; *Acts of Assembly in Maryland*, 68; William Kilty, ed., *Laws of Maryland* (Annapolis, 1800; microfilm Research Publications, Inc., New Haven, Conn.), chs. 4 and 8.

97. Hugh Jones, *The Present State of Virginia*, ed. Richard L. Morton (Chapel Hill: University of North Carolina Press, 1956), 85; Brickell, *Natural History*, 265.

98. For examples, see Alexander S. Salley, ed., *Journal of the General Council of South Carolina August 25 1671–June 24, 1680*, 2 vols. (Columbia, S.C.: Historical Commission of South Carolina, 1907), vol. 1, 54–5. William Cronon (*Changes in the Land*, 129–31) offers a detailed analysis of the problems between colonists, Indians, and livestock.

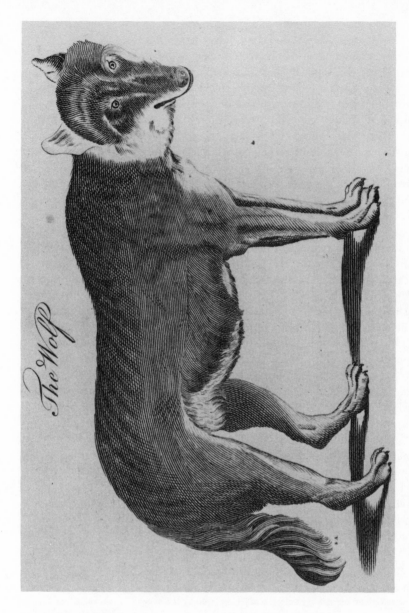

The Wolf

Figure 6.4. The bane of colonial cattlemen. From *Encyclopedia or Dictionary of Arts, Sciences, and Miscellaneous Literature* (Philadelphia, 1798), Vol. 4, Pl. cxix. Reproduced by courtesy of Colonial Williamsburg Foundation Library, Special Collections.

Livestock ranging the forests also affected Indian life in other, more subtle, ways. Cattle, horses, hogs, and goats all competed with deer for browse and mast. Such competition was especially keen in the pine forests and the mixed hardwood vegetation of the coastal plain. By increasing pressure on the natural food supply, livestock may have contributed to the decline of southern deer herds. In areas where large herds of stock used the open range, as in inland South Carolina, those deer that did survive alongside cattle and hogs may have been small and malnourished. Indeed, the proliferation of Carolina livestock – which made it difficult for the Yamasees to acquire enough deerskins to pay off traders – might have been one reason those natives chose to go to war against the colony in 1715.[99]

Colonists, of course, were not sensitive to the delicate ecological interplay between deer, livestock, and forest vegetation. But European settlers did notice that their animals were destroying a number of indigenous plants and trees. In the longleaf pine forests, goats ate the tufts of pine seedlings. In older pine forests, cattle selectively browsed the undergrowth of oak and other hardwoods. Hogs, however, did the most damage in the pinelands. Pigs not only gorged themselves on the none-too-plentiful longleaf mast, but also went after the spongy, tender roots of the smaller trees. In the sandy soil where the trees grew, a hungry hog could dig out and devour the long pine roots, thereby killing the young trees. In certain regions of the South, forest-reared hogs are still known as "piney-woods rooters," a term that probably originated during the colonial period.[100]

At least two prominent up-country plants (both of which must have been important for deer) fell victim to overgrazing. The wild beans, or "peavines" (possibly onetime escapees from Indian fields), and perhaps several other native legumes eventually became extinct as cattle moved into the inner coastal plain and piedmont. The most dramatic destruction of vegetation, however, occurred in the canelands. Because cane did not become dry and brittle in winter, it made excellent forage. As one colonist noted, the plant "bears a long green leaf in

99. Neil W. Hosley, "Management of the White-tailed Deer in its Environment," in Walter P. Taylor, ed., *The Deer of North America* (Harrisburg, Pa.: Stackpole, 1956), 210–11. Richard L. Hahn, "The 'Trade Do's Not Flourish as Formerly': The Ecological Origins of the Yamasee War of 1715," *Ethnohistory* 28 (1982), 350.

100. Robert S. Campbell, "Forest Grazing in the Southern Coastal Plain," *Proceedings of the Society of American Foresters* (1947), 262–4; W. D. Boyer, "Grazing Hampers Development of Longleaf Seedlings in Southwestern Alabama," *Journal of Forestry* 65 (1967), 336–8; Charles Mohr, *Timber Pines of the Southern United States* (Washington, D.C.: Government Printing Office, 1897), 62; W. W. Ashe, "The Forests, Forest Lands, and Forest Products of Eastern North Carolina," *North Carolina Geological Survey Bulletin Number 5* (Raleigh, 1894), 57. On the origin of the "piney woods rooter," see Stephen J. Pyne, *Fire in America: A Cultural History of Wildland and Rural Fire* (Princeton, N.J.: Princeton University Press, 1982), 147.

winter, on which cattle delight much to feed; and where that is plentiful, cattle keeps themselves in very good plight, till grass springs again."[101]

Hogs, too, foraged in the canebrakes, seeking out the tender nodules of the plant's root system. The Moravians of Wachovia observed that cane began to grow scarce after eleven years of continuous grazing. By century's end, Governor John Drayton told his readers that

> At the first settlement of this state, the vallies of the middle and upper country, then in the possession of the Indians, encouraged a plentiful growth of cane. But since the whites have spread themselves over the same, with their herds of cattle and hogs, the canes in these narrow swamps and vallies, are kept so closely cut down, by the continual browsing of cattle, as to have nearly extirpated them.[102]

In the piedmont, livestock also contributed to erosion problems. Cattle grazing selectively tended to congregate along streams, in clearings, and under shade trees. Such "patch grazing" resulted in the trampling of smaller plants and ground cover. If cattle continued to return to the favored area, their hooves compacted the topsoil, destroying its crumblike structure and reducing its capacity to absorb rainwater. During intense storms and prolonged rains, heavily grazed patches like heavily farmed fields became subject to sheet erosion, which took away the topsoil.[103]

At least one colonial government sought to curtail overgrazing problems with legislation. In 1766 North Carolinians passed a law aimed at South Carolina ranchers and speculators who were building cowpens across the border in the northern colony. The law required cattlemen to provide a hundred acres of land for every ten cattle or ten acres per animal. Like most other conservation legislation, the law probably had little immediate effect. Modern studies suggest that cattle in woodlands may require at least twenty to thirty acres per animal to stay healthy and avoid overgrazing their habitat. Overgrazing and erosion probably remained endemic problems throughout the colonial period, especially in the most heavily used parts of the inner coastal plain and piedmont. In upland Virginia, François André Michaux saw forests that

101. "Interview with James Freeman," in Merrens, *Colonial South Carolina Scene*, 49; Dunbar, "Carolina Cowpens," 127.
102. John Drayton, *A View of South Carolina. As Respects Her Natural and Civil Concerns* (Spartanburg, S.C.: Reprint, 1972), 62; Fries, *Records of the Moravians*, vol. 2, 564; Hall, "Soil Erosion and Agriculture," 57; Ralph H. Hughes, "Fire Ecology of Canebrakes," *Proceedings of the Tall Timbers Fire Ecology Conference* 5 (1966), 153.
103. Vinson L. Duvall and Norman E. Linnartz, "Influences of Grazing and Fire on Vegetation of Longleaf Pine Bluestem Range," *Journal of Range Management*, 20 (1967), 246; E. A. Johnson, "Effects of Farm Woodland Grazing on Watershed Values in the Southern Appalachian Mountains," *Journal of Forestry* 50 (1952), 109–13; Spurr and Barnes, *Forest Ecology*, 233–4.

exhibited "a squalid appearance, occasioned not only by the sterility of the soil, but by the injury they are continually sustaining from the cattle which range through them at all seasons, and which in winter are compelled, by the want of herbage, to subsist upon the young sprouts and the shoots of the preceding year."[104]

Seeking to improve the often meager forest range, South Atlantic farmers turned to a tactic used by Indians: seasonal burning. In bottomlands, planters fired low-lying areas to regenerate cane and marsh grasses for forage. Those with large holdings might also set ground fires in small areas to facilitate the growth of other grasses. The most extensive burning, however, took place in the pinelands and backcountry. For some of the immigrants who settled the region, burning to improve livestock range was a long-standing cultural tradition. In Europe, their ancestors had fired oak forests and heathlands. After observing the ways in which Indians used fire, the settlers adapted broadcast burning to the open woods and savannas of the South. John Brickell reported that colonists in North Carolina set fires "every March to burn off the old Grass in their Fields and Woods, as the Heath is burnt off the Mountains of Ireland, by the Farmers in those Places."[105]

Seasonal burning by Europeans produced many of the same effects as Indian-set fires, but because colonists set fires more systematically, changes in the forest pattern became more striking. For colonists raising livestock, as for Indians hunting deer, the most important result of the fires was the new growth that flourished after the burn. Native grasses provided high-quality forage, enabling colonists to drive their animals through the woods to market or to the coveted grazing grounds of canebrakes and savannas. Open woodlands made it easier for ranchers and slaves to maneuver their horses among the herds and to walk barefoot (or in moccasins) through the forest in search of half-wild cattle and hogs. Like Indians, woods ranchers found that regular burning reduced the hordes of insects that plagued colonists, crops, and cattle. Seasonal ground fires also worked to drive away predators. The thickets of berries that sprang up after the burn attracted marauding bears into areas where they might be killed quickly and in quantity. Because wolves preferred older forests, they were less likely to venture into the newly burned, open terrain. The grassy forest floor discouraged deadly rattlesnakes and copperheads, which thrived in the thick underbrush of unburned woods.[106]

104. Quotation from Michaux, *North American Sylva*, vol.1, 37. Walter Clark, ed., *The State Records of North Carolina*, 30 vols. (Goldsboro, N.C., 1904), vol. 23, 676–7; Hall, "Soil Erosion and Agriculture," 59–60. Dunbar, "Carolina Cowpens," 127.

105. Quotation from Brickell, *Natural History*, 84. Pyne, *Fire in America*, 148. Landon Carter was one planter who fired marshes and canebrakes (Greene, *Carter Diary*, vol. 1, 372).

106. H. L. Stoddard, "The Use of Fire in the Pine Forests of the Deep Southeast," *Proceedings of the Tall Timbers Fire Ecology Conference* 1 (1962), 32–4.

Although widespread burning offered cattlemen a number of advantages, it also increased the odds of wildfire. William Stephens reported that one fire kindled by Georgia colonists burning the woods raged for more than five days, destroying a number of houses and outbuildings. To protect themselves from wildfire. some colonists removed all trees and undergrowth near their houses, creating a "yard" of packed clay that served as a private firebreak. Some older houses in rural parts of the southern piedmont still have "dirt yards" that serve as modern reminders of the long tradition of woodsburning.[107]

Colonial governments sought a more systematic remedy to the problem of wildfire. By the end of the eighteenth century, virtually all the American states had legislation governing controlled burning. Noting that "the frequent burning of the woods" proved "extremely prejudicial to the soil" and "destroyed fences and other improvements," the North Carolina legislature in 1777 made it unlawful for any resident to set a woods fire without first giving notice to his neighbors. Adjacent property owners had to be informed two days in advance of the burn and those firing the woods were required to keep the blaze from crossing property and fence lines. By 1782, colonists caught violating the law faced a penalty of twenty-five pounds sterling for each offense, the stiffest "fire fine" recorded during the colonial period – a belated, but stern, warning to careless backcountry burners.[108]

Some agricultural writers frequently criticized such continual woods burning, arguing that colonists would be better served by planting pastures and hayfields. Penning cattle in pastures and feeding them hay in winter would not only improve the quality of the herds, but also allow colonists to use manure collected from confined livestock. But unlike settlers farther north, southern colonists frequently found it difficult to plant pastures like those of England. In the Middle Colonies and New England, imported livestock carried in their digestive tracts seeds of English grasses and legumes. Once the beasts were turned into the northern woods, English grasses often cropped up naturally in the wake of grazing cattle.[109]

Much of the South Atlantic region, however, proved too warm for such ground cover. Along the Chesapeake and in interior uplands, where temperatures were cooler, colonists could grow imported legumes, particularly alfalfa and clover, for forage. And while preaching in the Carolina backcountry in the

107. Coulter, *Journal of William Stephens*, vol. 1, 175–81; Merle C. Prunty, "Some Geographic Views of the Role of Fire in the Settlement Process," *Proceedings of the Tall Timbers Fire Ecology Conference* 4 (1965), 165–6.
108. Iredell, *Public Acts of North Carolina*, 246–7; J. P. Kinney, *The Development of Forest Law in America Including Forest Legislation in America Prior to March 4, 1789* (New York: Arno, 1972), 370. Lillian M. Wilson, *Forest Conservation in Colonial Times* (St. Paul, Minn.: Forest Products History Foundation, 1948), 8.
109. Mitchell, *Present State of Great Britain*, 153–5; Cronon, *Changes in the Land*, 142.

1760s, the itinerant Anglican minister Charles Woodmason distributed "Timothy [another cool-climate species], Burnet, and other grass seeds" along with Bibles, books, and medicine. But to the south and east, such plants were difficult to cultivate. John Brickell seemed to recognize the problems inherent in trying to transplant cool-weather grasses. While he urged prospective North Carolinians to experiment with all sorts of seeds, Brickell suggested settlers pay particular attention to grasses "that have arose and sprung in a warm climate, that will endure the heat of the Sun."[110]

One form of ground cover that could withstand the heat of the southern summer was crabgrass. A single stalk of crabgrass might produce up to 150,000 seeds, which took hold even in the sandy soils of the coastal plain. As Governor Drayton noted, "In good dry land, or where it has been manured, this grass comes up thickly, without being sown." Crabgrass, however, proved a fickle friend and soon took on the status of weed. At first, Carolina cattlemen welcomed it due to "the excellence of its fodder," but because crabgrass matured during the growing season it frequently took up residence in agricultural fields, where it might choke an entire crop.[111]

Another introduced grass that probably created problems in the colonial South is now commonly called panic grass, or barnyard grass. Well-adapted to wet soils, panic grass became the bane of rice planters. In its early stages of growth, panic grass is almost indistinguishable from young rice. And it spreads quickly; a single plant can produce five thousand to seven thousand seeds. Almost before a planter realized it, the grass could take over a field. A thick growth of panic grass could also deplete the plot's fertility, using perhaps 60 to 80 percent of the nitrogen in the soil. During his journey through South Carolina, John Bartram found that "ould rice fields, after they have been planted for some years, is so full of grass that it is next to impossible to keep the rice clean." Hoeing a grass-infested field took up too much time and labor. Usually rice planters who suffered a grass invasion resorted to flooding the tract for several years, which eventually destroyed the bothersome ground cover and helped restore fertility.[112]

Crabgrass and panic grass were not the only problem plants to invade

110. Quotations from: Brickell, *Natural History*, 259; and Hooker, *Journal of Woodmason*, 63. Hall, "Soil Erosion and Agriculture," 61–2; Jones, "Creative Disruptions," 525. For the present range of white clover, see Sellers G. Archer and Clarence E. Bunch, *The American Grass Book* (Norman: University of Oklahoma Press, 1953), 281–3.

111. Quotation from Margaret Babcock Meriwether, ed., *The Carolinian Florist of Governor John Drayton of South Carolina, 1766–1822* (South Caroliniana Library, University of South Carolina, 1943), 11. Le Roy G. Holm et al., *The World's Worst Weeds: Distribution and Biology* (Honolulu: University Press of Hawaii for the East-West Center, 1977), 92–4.

112. Quotation from John Bartram, "Diary of a Journey," 22. Holm et al., *World's Worst Weeds*, 32.

southern fields and forests. Intermixed with the fodder and hay, livestock ate on board European ships were many other Old World weeds that could survive the southern summer. Ecologically adapted to pastoralism, the plants produced myriad seeds that clung to the coats of grazing animals or traveled on the wind into cleared fields. In the orderly colonial fields, weeds soon became a nuisance. Plantain, dock, dandelions, nettles, and many other species well known to European farmers moved in alongside tobacco, wheat, and corn. Even on the generally smaller farms of North Carolina, uninvited plants became a chronic problem, prompting the author of *American Husbandry* to conclude that "There is no greater defect in the husbandry of this province than the foulness of the crops with weeds."[113]

By the end of the eighteenth century, southern settlers were advancing across the Appalachians and into the eastern Mississippi Valley. But east of the mountains, agriculture was changing. Tobacco was still prominent in Virginia and North Carolina, but wheat and dairy products were gradually assuming more important roles. Farther south, new technology, in the form of the cotton gin, had already begun to transform parts of the Carolina and Georgia piedmont into integral parts of the Cotton Kingdom. That kingdom would eventually extend farther west into the Deep South where farmers would also grow rice and sugarcane.[114]

Wherever they went, southern farmers continued to believe that they were improving the woods and fields they occupied. They pointed to the prolifer-ation of domestic animals. They praised the introduction of cash crops and the demise of the foreboding forest. Most of all, they stressed their system of agriculture which seemed better organized and more appealing than Indian farming. When Charles Woodmason took grass seed to the Carolina backcoun-try in 1768, he did so as part of an effort to "make the countryside wear a New face," a face that reflected civility and a higher degree of social organization.[115]

But the innovations of southern colonial agriculture had also created problems for settlers. Single-crop fields made it easier for squirrels, crows, and indigenous insects to obtain food and, periodically, their populations expanded to pest proportions. Invisible organisms responsible for malaria and yellow fever found new habitats in and around colonial settlements. Despite colonists' many and varied efforts at conservation, commercial agriculture inevitably

---

113. Quotation from Carman and Tugwell, *American Husbandry*, 259. Thomas J. Muzik, *Weed Biology and Control* (New York: McGraw-Hill, 1970), 3–4; Crosby, *Ecological Imperialism*, 149–50. I arrived at this short list of European imports by cross-checking plants listed in Wilkinson and Jaques, *How to Know the Weeds* with plants noted in Meriwether, *Carolinian Florist of Governor Drayton*. Some of the weeds had become so widespread in South Carolina that the Governor thought them native to North America.

114. See Cowdrey, *This Land, This South*, 66–75.

115. Hooker, *Journal of Woodmason*, 63.

reduced soil fertility. Domestic animals reverted to the wild or fell victim to indigenous predators. Due to varying topography, climates, and patterns of settlement, the scale of such ecological disruptions varied. Generally the effects of colonial agriculture were most visible in the eastern coastal plain and Virginia piedmont, where early English colonization and larger populations led to more intensive cultivation of land. But by the last quarter of the eighteenth century, those trends were also apparent farther south and west. And the difficulties would not stop there. Later farmers would grow different crops. Eventually they would discover new ways to combat pests, parasites, and soil exhaustion. But like their colonial ancestors, those who continued to farm in the South could never completely escape such problems. A more civil landscape, it seems, had its price.[116]

116. Cronon, *Changes in the Land*, 166–7.

7

Conclusion: Perspectives on land and people, 1800

If we could repeat our semisystematic journey from the South Atlantic coast to the mountains about 1800, what would we see? How would the sights of this second trip differ from the first? With an aerial view, one would still be able to discern the ragged coastline and the basic physiographic divisions of coastal plain, piedmont, and mountains. But during a second walking tour, we would immediately note the changes.

It might be easiest to begin with what we would not see. In spring, the rivers and creeks would hold fewer sturgeon and ocean-going fish. Freshwater fish, too, might be less abundant, although plenty could still be found, both in natural streams and man-made ponds. We might also observe fewer turkeys and wildfowl and, in the appropriate seasons, would surely note the dwindling flocks of Carolina parakeets and passenger pigeons. Buffaloes would be gone from the piedmont and elks confined to the slopes of the Blue Ridge. Beavers, muskrats, otters, and minks also would have diminished. Under the protection of hunting regulations, white-tailed deer might still be visible, though in vastly reduced numbers. Thanks in part to other legislation, wolves, panthers, and bobcats – whose nighttime serenade had chilled the blood of the early inland explorers – would be virtually extinct in and around settled areas. Likewise, black bears could be found seeking solace in the undisturbed forests of the foothills and mountains.

The forests have changed, too. Fewer large live oaks grow on the southernmost barrier islands and across the dunelands. To make room for rice in the freshwater tidal swamps, patches of gum, white cedar, cypress, and other wetlands trees have been removed. During the growing season, the rice fields might appear as shallow, flat pools with sprigs of green sometimes protruding above the waterline. With the water down, it would be easy to glimpse the various weeds and grasses growing in with the crop. A flooded, fallow rice tract would be almost indistinguishable from any other freshwater pond. On higher ground, small patches of mixed hardwoods would have given way to corn and other foodstuffs. In warm weather, the telltale stench of an indigo vat and the attendant flies and mosquitoes might alert us to the presence of that crop – though by 1800 it was declining in importance. Cotton fields in the sea islands and farther inland would stand as harbingers of the next great phase of southern agriculture.

Farther north, the narrowing coastal plain would reflect earlier settlement and long-term field rotation. Here, cultivated fields might sprout tobacco, corn, wheat, peas, beans, oats, barley, or maybe even hemp. Much of the land would still be forested, but throughout the woods, a traveler might encounter numerous old fields covered with weeds and grasses or the ever-present loblolly pines. We could distinguish variations; North Carolina had not been farmed as long and as intensively as Virginia. But even the largest and most well-kept plantation would have its share of plowed fields, woods, and half-grown-over plots. A sprinkling of ramshackle barns, tobacco houses, and outbuildings would suggest some of the ways in which lumber from the surrounding forests had been used. Fences and a growing network of roads would complete a landscape we might well describe as rustic or maybe pastoral.[1]

Farther west, our adjective might shift slightly to bucolic, especially as we moved from piedmont Virginia southward. Here a traveler could also take note of agricultural clearing and forest industries. Selective cutting of oak and hickory would be evinced by sprouting stumps of what were formerly large trees. Tapped for turpentine, burned by periodic fires, and cut for lumber, the vast, open, longleaf pinelands would be giving way (albeit slowly) to tracts of scrubby hardwoods and hardier loblollies. The effects of lumbering are especially noticeable if we chance upon a sawmill, though in summer low water might render it inoperable. Although settlers and even the most astute modern observer might not notice, the forest industries and agricultural clearing have created small pockets around farms, where summers are hotter and winters colder. More noticeable are eroded hillsides, where tobacco and corn have been planted on terrain too steep to slow rainwash.

If certain animals are missed in the forests, others are more prominent around the farms. Bobwhite quail adapted well to the new system of agriculture. And even as beaver and muskrats fell victim to hunters and trappers, the opossum – that hissing, snarling, carrion-eating prehistoric relic – prepared to march side by side with settlers into the next century and beyond. Those animals most visible on the new landscape are imported. As farms replaced forests, cattle, hogs, sheep, and goats supplanted deer, elk, and buffalo. Fewer canebrakes and overgrazed mixed hardwood forests attest to the forage habits

1. Carville V. Earle, *The Evolution of a Tidewater Settlement System: All Hallow's Parish, Maryland, 1650–1783* (The University of Chicago Department of Geography Research Paper no. 170, 1975), 127–30; Rhys Isaac, *The Transformation of Virginia, 1740–1790* (Chapel Hill: University of North Carolina Press for the Institute of Early American History and Culture, 1982), 24–5, 30–42.

of these Old World beasts. Along with livestock have come European grasses, weeds, parasites, and pests – some of which adversely affect the health of farmers, as well as their crops.

Part and parcel of the countryside's new face are the new faces of the human population, white and black, free and slave. Although Indian numbers remain relatively large in the mountains and beyond, many of those east of the Appalachians have been devastated by disease. Some of the smaller bands have simply disappeared, been absorbed into the white population, or joined with other more populous groups. Even those Indians who maintain a degree of cultural identity find their way of life drastically altered. Shortages of game and sporadic outbreaks of disease make it increasingly difficult for Indians to pursue their seasonal activities and sometimes foster starvation or malnutrition. Writing of the Catawbas in 1802, Governor Drayton reported that:

> When South Carolina was first settled by white inhabitants, this nation numbered fifteen hundred fighting men. About the year 1743, it could only bring four hundred warriors into the field; composed partly of their own men, and partly of refugees from various smaller tribes . . . the Wateree, Chowan, Congaree, Nachee, Yamasee, and Coosah. At present, sixty men can scarcely be numbered in the list of their survivors, or two hundred persons in the whole of their nation. And these are scattered about in small villages; and are entirely surrounded by white inhabitants.[2]

What brought the new face and faces to the South Atlantic countryside? Which forces and factors had been most significant in the change? One colonist who was part of the process seems to have been somewhat ambivalent about its causes and results. In his *History and Present State of Virginia*, written in 1705, Robert Beverley noted that "before the English went thither," the colony was a virtual paradise. In this Eden-like land, Beverley observed, Indians had enjoyed "the natural Production" of the country "without the Curse of Industry, their Diversion alone, and not their Labor, supplying the Necessities." Moreover, Beverley chided his fellow Virginians for making "inordinate and unseasonable use" of the land and bringing about unsightly "Alterations," concluding "I can't call them Improvements." What bothered Beverley most, however, was not the European desecration of Virginia. He was far more concerned in 1705 that the changes wrought by colonists had not gone far enough. Virginia was still too unlike England, a failing Beverley blamed on lazy colonists who "spunge upon the Blessings of a Warm Sun, and a fruitfull soil, and grutch the pains of gathering in the Bounties of the Earth." If he lamented

2. John Drayton, *A View of South-Carolina, As Respects Her Natural and Civil Concerns* (1802; reprint, Spartanburg, S.C.: Reprint, 1972), 93–4.

the intrusion on Paradise, Beverley also issued a clarion call for more efficient and extensive exploitation of Virginia's resources.[3]

Beverley's book is instructive in a number of ways. Scholars are now well aware that settlers from the Chesapeake to the Okefenokee were, like colonists everywhere, part of an emerging and expanding world economy, so designated because it was larger than any legally defined European state.[4] It was an economy that stressed the importance of private property, profit, and virtually unrestricted accumulation of goods. It was, in a word, capitalistic. Within that economic system, resources became commodities – articles of value that could be exchanged for other goods or for gold and silver.[5] Explorers searching for commodities found that the South Atlantic region could offer a number of worthwhile goods. Some, such as fish, were also available in Europe or New England and became valuable because they could augment existing food supplies. Other goods, such as timber and furs, were scarce in Europe or the West Indies (though plentiful in other North American colonies) and consequently in demand. Finally, Europeans took an interest in exotic products indigenous to the New World (corn, tobacco, and ginseng) or in commodities that might be acclimatized to the warm southern colonies (sugar, rice, and silkworms).[6] It is hardly surprising that Beverley urged colonists to work the land more intensively. That is why they had crossed the Atlantic in the first place.

Beverley's comparison of Virginia to Paradise also suggests something about English motives. All English churchgoers knew that God had originally given Adam power to control all creatures, commanding him in Genesis 1:28 to "replenish the earth, and subdue it: and have dominion over the fish of the sea, and over the fowl of the air, and over every living thing that moveth upon the earth." Adam, however, had forfeited some of those rights when he rebelled against God. God not only expelled Adam and Eve from Paradise, but also made some soils rocky and infertile. Wild animals became fierce and domestic beasts stubborn. Fleas, flies, and other insects tormented humans at all seasons. Only after the purifying Flood did God see fit to restore man's favored position,

3. Quotations from Robert Beverley, *The History and Present State of Virginia* (1705), ed. Louis B. Wright (Chapel Hill: University of North Carolina Press for the Institute of Early American History and Culture, 1947), 156, 319. Leo Marx, *The Machine in the Garden: Technology and the Pastoral Ideal in America* (New York: Oxford University Press, 1964), 73–88.
4. Immanuel Wallerstein, *The Modern World-System: Capitalist Agriculture and the Origins of the European World-Economy in the Sixteenth Century* (New York: Academic Press, 1974), 15.
5. The basic characteristics of the European world economy, as they applied to New World resources, have been clearly analyzed in William Cronon, *Changes in the Land: Indians, Colonists, and the Ecology of New England* (New York: Hill & Wang, 1983), see especially 20–1, 67–78, 165–9.
6. K. G. Davies, *The North Atlantic World in the Seventeenth Century* (Minneapolis: University of Minnesota Press, 1974), 141–3.

promising Noah that "Every moving thing that liveth shall be meat for you; even as the green herb I have given you all things." But, due to Adam's Fall, such mastery of the natural world would no longer come easily. Soils could be made productive only through arduous labor. Vicious beasts had to be slain and domestic animals forced to the yoke. Nature again existed to serve man, but only if he exerted to the fullest his ascendancy over plants and animals.[7]

One look at Indian subsistence patterns convinced colonists that the natives did not work the land as God commanded. Consequently, it was fitting that Europeans take the country and put it to proper use. Robert Gray, who wrote a 1609 tract justifying the English takeover of Virginia, concluded that "the greater part of the earth was possessed and wrongfully usurped by wild beasts, and unreasonable creatures or by brutish savages." Gray believed colonists had a perfect right to Virginia because Indians had "no particular property in any part or parcell of the country, but only a general residencie there, as wild beasts have in the forest."[8] Throughout the English South and in other colonies as well, Gray's argument or some similar variation became the theoretical justification for replacing Indian subsistence patterns with those dictated by the European market.[9]

Once colonists had taken over land from Indians, the European economy and its attendant theology led South Atlantic settlers to organize and transform the landscape. Certain trees had to be cut in quantity; fields had to be fenced and protected from pests; livestock had to be fattened and marketed; beaver and deer had to be trapped and shot for their skins. As a result, patches of forest had been depleted; soils had been exhausted; livestock overgrazed woodlands; animals began to disappear. The connection between ecology and economics cannot be denied; it is implicit in the very meaning of the terms. Both words derive from the Greek *oikos*, meaning "house" or "place to live." When followed by the Greek suffix *logos*, meaning "discourse," or "study," the word becomes "ecology," which suggests knowledge or understanding of organisms "at home" in the natural environment. "Economics" adds the Greek suffix *nemein*, literally "to deal out" or "manage." Ultimately the ways in which organisms lived "at home" in North America reflected the ways in which European settlers – who became the dominant human organisms in the region – chose to use or manage the homeland. As a planter, Beverley did not question

---

7. Quotations from Gen. 1:28–29, 9:3. For English perceptions of these passages, see Keith Thomas, *Man and the Natural World: A History of the Modern Sensibility* (New York: Pantheon, 1983), 17–18; and Cronon, *Changes in the Land*, 56–7, 63.
8. Robert Gray, quoted in Gary B. Nash, "The Image of the Indian in the Southern Colonial Mind," *William and Mary Quarterly*, 3d ser. 29 (1972), 210; and in W. Stitt Robinson, Jr., *Mother Earth: Land Grants in Virginia, 1607–1699* (Williamsburg, Va.: 350th Anniversary Celebration Corporation, 1959), 3.
9. Cronon, *Changes in the Land*, 56–7.

the connection. He might have felt guilty about alterations in the "garden" and even the changes wrought in Indian life, but he still urged colonists to stop "sponging" and get on with the business at hand.[10]

What Beverley does not seem to have realized is that Europeans could not have affected the "alterations," much less "Improvements," by themselves. Like other works of its genre, Beverley's book reflects the guilt associated with conquest and an emerging nostalgia for "noble savages" and precontact America.[11] To Beverley's mind, Indians lived without effort and consequently had little or no role in changing the landscape of Paradise. Modern scholars know better. Alfred W. Crosby is one historian who has set about correcting such views. Crosby reminds us that when the ancestors of Indians crossed Beringia, they, too, were human invaders of the American environment. As such, their migrations had far-reaching ecological implications, possibly including the extinction of large, prehistoric game animals. Crosby suggests that the disappearance of such beasts left vacant "econiches" in North America. With the arrival of Europeans, livestock moved into the existing void, relatively free of competition from other organisms. That theory may help explain why cattle and hogs multiplied so rapidly in the southern woods.[12]

Crosby's view of Indians as "shock troops – marines – seizing beachheads and clearing the way for a second wave" of human invaders points to other connections.[13] The open fields early colonists coveted and into which some settlers moved had been created by Indian agriculture. The corn on which colonists depended was a crop domesticated by their human predecessors. Savannas that supported livestock and pines that produced naval stores resulted in part from the natives' periodic woods burning. Some Indians employed the ancient practice of driving deer with fire as a means of acquiring skins for European traders. It might even be argued that long before the arrival of Europeans, Indians sensed a serious tension in their relationship with nature – a tension reflected in the countless rituals designed to console the spirits of the animals they hunted and the plants they gathered or cultivated. Were they so unlike Beverley who felt at least a bit uncomfortable with the English invasion of Paradise?

Emphasizing the humanness of both Indians and Europeans suggests another crucial point about environmental change in the southern colonies and elsewhere in colonial America. Economic catch phrases such as "private prop-

10. Ibid., 166–67; Eugene P. Odum, *Fundamentals of Ecology* (Philadelphia: Saunders, 1971), 3, 510–11; *New Webster's Dictionary of the English Language*, 8th ed., s.v. "ecology," "economics."

11. Nash, "Image," 224–6.

12. Alfred W. Crosby, *Ecological Imperialism: The Biological Expansion of Europe, 900–1900* (New York: Cambridge University Press, 1986), 272–80.

13. Ibid., 295.

erty," "unrestricted accumulation," and "capitalism" tend to obscure human motives and rule out cultural interaction, implying that ecological change resulted from abstract forces that, once set loose on the western shore of the Atlantic, quickly steamrolled the land and its original human inhabitants into submission. Historians Richard White and William Cronon have clearly demonstrated the fallacies of such a view. They have shown that Europeans "discovered" forests already inhabited by people with their own well-defined ideas about property and resources. Like Beverley and Robert Gray, most Europeans failed to realize that Indians, including those along the South Atlantic seaboard, understood something of "private property." For Indians, game, fish, crops, clothes, weapons, and other personal goods became the possessions of the particular villages or individuals who invested the necessary labor to acquire or make them. What made the native system different was that it did not encourage continuous stockpiling of goods or money. Indeed, the Indian economy stressed almost completely opposite values: day-to-day subsistence and generosity. As English explorers found out at Roanoke, those values manifested themselves in the practice of gift giving, whereby an Indian "donated" goods or sometimes labor to a friend (or an intended friend) without immediately demanding a specific amount in return. The recipient did, however, incur an obligation to respond in kind at a later date. Articles were not so much traded for profit as exchanged on the basis of reciprocity.[14]

But goods were exchanged in Indian society and that helped facilitate trade. The natives initially welcomed European items with the same enthusiasm explorers and early colonists expressed for exotic New World commodities. Introduced to metal goods in the form of nails and spikes from wrecked Spanish vessels, Indians at Roanoke Island were eager to obtain similar utensils that might make life easier. Due to the value natives attached to ornamental personal property, traders also found a demand for "prestige goods," such as combs, mirrors, and belt buckles. In its early stages, trade was as much a product of New World institutions as of Old.

Whether native demand for European goods would, of itself, have increased depredations on wildlife is a question that will never be answered. It was rendered moot by a particular feature of the American environment: the absence of Old World disease organisms. Unable to counter the lethal microbes with their traditional remedies and seeing relatives perish in unprecedented numbers, the surviving Indians were eventually forced to participate in the

14. Richard White, *The Roots of Dependency: Subsistence, Environment, and Social Change among the Choctaws, Pawnees, and Navajos* (Lincoln: University of Nebraska Press, 1983), 36–47; Cronon, *Changes in the Land*, 58–67; Charles M. Hudson, *The Southeastern Indians* (Knoxville: University of Tennessee Press, 1976), 310–11; John Phillip Reid, *A Law of Blood: The Primitive Law of the Cherokee Nation* (New York: New York University Press, 1970), 123–41.

dominant economic system of the New World. But even when Indians began to supply more commodities for the world market, the trade still reflected much of the natives' precontact way of life. Especially in the mountains and points west, where populations remained larger, Indians showed an uncanny ability to hang on to traditional methods of exchange, incorporating Europeans and their goods into the long-established native culture and economy. In its final form, the Indian trade was the consequence of a long and complex pattern of cultural interaction between Indians and colonists. Although both groups participated willingly, disease and liquor – the effects of which white traders might not have foreseen, but exploited nonetheless – helped tip the balance in favor of the European system.[15]

In the more northerly American colonies and in other temperate regions settled by Europeans, the absence of Old World diseases proved a boon to colonists. To an extent, the same was true from Maryland to Georgia. Diseases such as smallpox, measles, and influenza struck periodically, but were slow to become endemic. The human population was simply not large enough to support the microorganisms for long periods. And settlers could at least battle periodic epidemics with quarantines, variolation, and medicinal plants.[16]

But in the southern colonies it got hot. So hot, William Stephens wrote on one mid-August day, that it rendered him "incapable of much Action" and forced him "to pass over the day in Indolence." Along with the summer heat came humidity. Only those who have spent a steamy night in the inner coastal plain without air conditioning can truly appreciate Stephens's understated note that "the Sultry nights were not less affecting than the day." Under such conditions, natural water supplies along the coast dissipated or became brackish, giving rise to dysentery or salt poisoning.[17] In the hothouse that was the South Atlantic summer, tropical diseases – some of the same maladies that kept Europeans from settling in Africa – cropped up every year to torment colonists. Like other transplanted diseases, they were slow to become endemic and some never did. But their predictable seasonal appearances slowed population growth and lowered life expectancy. Rice fields, mill ponds, sawmills, urban rain barrels, and other trappings of European settlement only helped propagate organisms and vectors.[18]

To get products out of the ground or woods and onto ships, colonists needed other "shock troops." Consequently, the meshing of peoples and cultures was no less important to forestry and agriculture than to trade. As slaves, Indians were also directly involved in the woods and fields. And colonists used tools and

15. White, *Roots of Dependency*, ch. 4.
16. Crosby, *Ecological Imperialism*, 282–4.
17. E. Merton Coulter, ed., *The Journal of William Stephens, 1741–1745*, 2 vols. (Athens: University of Georgia Press, 1959), vol. 2, 136.
18. Crosby, *Ecological Imperialism*, 138.

techniques adopted from the natives throughout the eighteenth century. Most prominently in Virginia, but also in the Carolinas and Georgia, indentured white servants worked the fields and served as human fodder for the disabling and killing warm-weather diseases. But blacks eventually had more impact on production of timber products and export crops. Africans brought with them some of the trappings of their own environment, including both genetic and acquired defenses against malaria and yellow fever, which allowed them to work around flooded fields, ponds, and town cisterns with less risk of infection than either whites or Indians.

Africans, however, contributed much more than disease-resistant labor. Their knowledge of techniques for clearing land and growing rice, as well as their ability to master naval stores and lumber production, played a salient role in sculpting the countryside's new face. Though Governor Drayton probably intended his words more as a defense of South Carolina slavery than as a paean to African culture, he understood that, were it not for slaves,

> the extensive rice fields which are covered with grain, would present nothing but deep swamps, and dreary forests; inhabited by panthers, bears, wolves, and other wild beasts. Hence the best lands of this state, would have been rendered useless; while the pine lands, from their barren natures, although they might maintain the farmer, would have done little towards raising the state to its present importance.[19]

The complexities of the southern climate and disease environment point to still another dimension of ecological change. For Robert Beverley and most other colonists, the land itself was a passive entity, a southern Eden to be "altered" or, preferably, "improved" by their presence. But even as colonists, Indians, and Africans were changing the land, the land was changing them. The role of climate and disease in the evolution of the slave system is only one obvious example of the process. Even with adequate labor, settlers were not always able to acquire the commodities they sought in the coastal plain and piedmont. High costs made it impractical to ship whole trees or unfinished lumber to Europe, encouraging colonists to look instead to the West Indies. Along the Chesapeake, settlers found that the sparsely distributed loblolly and Virginia pines at first made naval stores production difficult. And despite the Crown's best efforts, colonists continued to produce tar and pitch with techniques suited to the local environment and way of life. Likewise, early settlers who came to the South Atlantic coast expecting to grow citrus and sugarcane found their surroundings better suited to corn, tobacco, rice, and indigo. Attitudes about commodities grew out of the Old World economy, but New World climates, forests, and soils helped determine which products

19. Drayton, *View of South-Carolina*, 146–7.

colonists shipped out of their ports. If European economics helped transform South Atlantic ecology, the reverse is also true.

Usually, this reciprocal relationship between colonists and the land they occupied was more subtle. Because all the plants and animals in a given area interacted with each other and with the physical environment, all human actions took place within this larger framework of ecological interaction.[20] The pinelands provide one example of this process. Even in the absence of human influence, pines are only transient residents of southern forests. Without aid from fire or some other clearing agent, pines eventually give way to forests of mixed hardwoods or oaks and hickories. Naval stores production and lumbering only accelerated and altered this natural process of replacement. In similar fashion, colonists or slaves who cleared fields were not simply altering the landscape by introducing new crops. They were setting in motion a series of ecological processes that could affect everything from the forest pattern to local climates and drainage patterns. The exact nature of such alterations varied widely from one locale to another. Clearing a field on a piedmont slope produced conditions not encountered in the more level coastal plain. In any setting – especially the topographically diverse English South – the natural environment within which humans work is at least as important as the cultural and economic background out of which they come.

Moreover, as the landscape around them changed, colonists frequently had to adjust and readjust their goals and methods to correspond to ecological reality.[21] When Virginia and Maryland colonists planted tobacco, the demanding weed exhausted their fields in only a few years. Planters adjusted first by planting corn on the worn tracts and then by allowing them to lie fallow. That worked until the population and labor force grew too large to allow depleted fields adequate time to recover. Colonists then shifted tactics again, growing more wheat and seeking to fill eroded ditches or to replenish their fields with manure. Conservation legislation might be viewed in a similar light. As deer herds decreased, colonial governments tried to curtail and control hunting, even outlawing it for brief periods in an effort to allow animal populations time to recover. Even if less successful than efforts to combat soil depletion, the legislation still sprang from colonists' needs to adjust their way of life to the new demands of the landscape – demands created by the settlers' own patterns of agriculture and trade.

By the time colonists were using manure and passing hunting laws, Indians had long since proven their flexibility in adapting to environmental change.

20. Cronon, *Changes in the Land*, 11–12.
21. Ibid., 13–14. This idea is also neatly summarized in "Indians in the Land: A Conversation between William Cronon and Richard White," *American Heritage* 37:5 (August/September 1986), 20.

The natives had learned new methods for coping with disease; they had ensured their survival by securing an important place within the European world economy. Indians were also adapting to the changing agricultural landscape. By the end of the eighteenth century, most natives east and west of the mountains were keeping livestock.

But like their reactions to other European innovations, Indian acceptance of Old World beasts came slowly and on terms easily comprehensible within the context of native culture. Cherokees, for example, were at first reluctant to eat pork because they believed that by consuming the animal's flesh, they would take on its disgusting habits and appearance. Hogs also resembled opossums, whose consumption was prohibited by certain religious beliefs. In similar fashion, Choctaws generally did not eat four-footed carnivores. Consequently, they, too, initially rejected the omnivorous pig, but had few qualms about eating horses that fed on grass and were therefore acceptable. Eventually, however, declining game populations and the drastic alterations in their former subsistence patterns led most Indians to keep pigs, horses, and cattle. When Benjamin Hawkins toured Creek country in 1798 and 1799, he found fields that had been fenced against wandering cattle and canelands that showed the effects of continuous grazing. In the last quarter of the eighteenth century, some Creeks had even acquired black slaves to help tend fields and raise stock. Such alterations in their subsistence patterns increased Indian dependence on Europeans, but the adaptations also allowed the natives to survive in a rapidly changing physical environment.[22]

As the various human populations interacted with each other and with the fields and forests in which they lived, they produced an equally diverse pattern on the land, the pattern that has made it so difficult for modern historians to define and identify the "colonial South." Yet, as historian Clarence L. Ver Steeg has suggested, this very diversity might be a distinguishing factor. Although he wrote primarily of politics and socioeconomic institutions rather than the natural environment, Ver Steeg noted that "one of the bonds that define the South is its quilt-like mosaic, identifiable enclaves that contribute a special quality to the whole."[23]

22. White, *Roots of Dependency*, 99–101; Gary C. Goodwin, *Cherokees in Transition: A Study of Changing Culture and Environment Prior to 1775* (The University of Chicago Department of Geography Research Paper no. 181, 1977), 134–6; Benjamin Hawkins, *A Sketch of the Creek Country in the years 1798 and 1799* (New York: Klaus Reprint, 1971), 29–30; Martha Cordary Searcy, "The Introduction of African Slavery into the Creek Nation," *Georgia Historical Quarterly* 66 (1982), 21–32.
23. Clarence L. Ver Steeg, *Origins of a Southern Mosaic: Studies of Early Carolina and Georgia* (Athens: University of Georgia Press, 1975), xi–xii.

Ver Steeg's argument is also useful in dealing with the physical and cultural environments of Indians, colonists, and slaves. One way to think about environmental or ecological change in the southern English colonies is to visualize not one, but a series of relationships between humans and the land or simply between humans. Those relationships are indeed identifiable: Indians invading and changing the forests to suit their culture and subsistence patterns; Europeans seeking to organize the land to produce commodities for the world economy; cultural and economic interaction between Europeans and Indians; cultural interaction between Europeans and Africans; the exchange of disease organisms between the three continents; the active role of the landscape itself in altering human perceptions, goals, and methods. Each of these relationships was separate and distinct, but also related to, and often occurring simultaneously with, the others. Each was also reciprocal, characterized by merging peoples, beliefs, and technologies. Every colonist, Indian, and slave – from the coastal plain to the mountains, from the Chesapeake to the Okefenokee – became a participant in one or more of these relationships and, as a result, was directly involved in changing the landscape.

Was one factor more important than the others? Perhaps. One can argue that for the southern colonies as for most of the European-occupied world, the expanding economy was the crucial factor in environmental change. After all, it was Europeans who crossed the Atlantic. And it was their economic system in which Indians and Africans became enmeshed. But, given the unfamiliar summer climate, the hazards attending early colonization, and the labor shortage, it also seems clear that the triumph of the world economy along the South Atlantic was never inevitable. And if it is difficult to imagine wide-sweeping ecological change without the innovations of a capitalist economy, it is equally difficult to envision South Atlantic agriculture and forestry without slaves (at least during the eighteenth century) or the deerskin trade without Indians. If the landscape that had emerged by 1800 was a recognizable variation on the values of the European world economy, it was also a decidedly American and, more specifically, a southern countryside – one colored as much by red and black as by white.

Such an eclectic interpretation has its advantages. For one thing, it points up the complex nature of environmental change, especially when three distinct cultures are involved. For another, it takes us still farther away from the notion of early America as an unspoiled wilderness ravaged by Europeans – a refrain still evident in Robert Beverley's history of Virginia. A more comprehensive view suggests that since his arrival in North America, mankind has remained apart from, and altered, the natural world. The innovations brought by colonists changed the nature and scale of those alterations and created a new face on the countryside. But what seems equally striking about the English

South is the ability of human beings of various racial and cultural backgrounds to adapt and survive sweeping ecological change. Instead of decrying the environmental evils of capitalism and pointing accusingly to its colonial origins, perhaps we should focus instead on that remarkable pattern of adjustment. For there – in that uniquely human ability to employ "culture" as a means of environmental adaptation – is hope for our future.

Index

acorns, 55–6
Adair, James, 1, 39–40, 45, 56, 79, 81, 83
agriculture (*see also* erosion; individual crops;
  soil exhaustion): colonial, 105–7, 139–79
  passim; Indian, 37–8, 46–52
Albemarle Sound, 8, 16
alewives, 44
alfalfa, 166, 182
alligators, 28, 148
Alsop, George, 90
Altamaha River, 9, 10, 146, 168
American Husbandry, 115, 134, 184
American Revolution, 94
animals, domestic (*see* cattle; livestock; pigs);
  wild (*see* individual species)
Apalachees, 83
Appalachian Highlands, 10
Appalachian Mountains: as a boundary, 3;
  erosion of, 12, 22; geologic origin of,
  10–12; vegetation of, 22–4
apples, 145
arthritis, 79
aster, white, 50
Atkin, Edmond, 88
Atlantic coastal plain: description, 9; geologic
  origin, 12–3; vegetation, 14–19
Ashley River, 110
Augusta, Ga., 93
Ayllon, Lucas Vásquez de, 7, 71, 156

Bainton, Epaphroditus, 90
Banister, John, 1, 99
Barbados, 117, 144
barberries, 154–5
barley, 187
Barlowe, Arthur, 68, 86
Bartram, John, 135, 168–9, 183
Bartram, William, 41, 43, 99–100, 103, 121
Batts, Thomas, 72
bay, sweet, 19
beans, 37, 50–1, 187
bears, 26–8, 33, 52, 54–5, 100, 110, 148,
  181
beaver, 28, 98–100, 186
beech, American, 15
Berkeley, William, 108, 122

Beverley, Robert, 38, 44, 102, 171, 188–9,
  190, 191, 194, 197
birch, yellow, 23
birds (*see also* individual species): 30–1
bison, prehistoric, 35
black drink, 79, 80
Bland, Edward, 72
Blue Ridge province, 10
bobcats, 26, 186
bobolinks, 149–53
Boltzius, Johann Martin, 175–7
Brahm, (John Gerar) William De, 59, 61, 62,
  63, 105, 135
Brickell, John, 50, 57, 124, 128, 148, 153,
  177, 181, 183
broad arrow policy, 137
broomsedge, 50
bubonic plague, 77
buckeye, red, 46
buffalo, 26, 51, 100, 186
Byrd, William, I, 72
Byrd, William, II, 44, 59, 63, 64, 72, 84, 90,
  92–3, 98, 176

cane, 22, 24, 26, 56, 108, 179–80, 187
canoes, 45, 57
Cape Fear River, 9, 10, 108, 144, 168, 175
Cape Fear valley, 117
Carter, Landon, 112–14, 133–4, 153, 155
castoreum, 99
Catawba River, 10
Catawbas, 72, 89, 188
Catawba valley, 93
Catesby, Mark, 86, 89, 90, 107, 110, 130, 152
cattle, 177, 179; in Georgia, 175–6; and
  Indians, 196; in North Carolina, 172; in
  South Carolina, 173; in Virginia, 172, 173
cedar, Atlantic white, 16, 108, 119–20, 130,
  186
cedar, red. *See* juniper
Charles I (king of England), 122
Charles II (king of England), 122
Charlesfort, 122
Charles Town, 89, 92, 93, 98–9, 110, 144.
  See also yellow fever

Cherokees, 41, 46, 57, 89, 92, 196; belief
    system, 40; disease among, 79, 80, 81, 83;
    population, 39, 82; and seasons, 43; and
    trade, 72, 84, 86, 87–8, 91, 94
Cherokee War, 96
Chesapeake Bay, 8, 13, 56, 59, 71
chestnut, American, 22–3, 24
chestnut, horse, 45–6
Chickasaws, 73, 82–3
chicken pox, 77
chickens, 153, 175
Choctaws, 73, 82–3, 93
clay, white, 84, 86
Clayton, John, 98, 101, 157, 174
clearing (see also deforestation): 46–8,
    105–10, 195
climate: changes in, 112–15; South Atlantic
    region, 14–15, 16, 17, 19–21, 22–3,
    139–40
clover, 166, 182
coastal plain. See Atlantic coastal plain
cockroaches, 154
Cofitachequi, 71, 74, 89
College of William and Mary, 64, 97
Combahee River, 9
conquistadores, 67
copperhead, 28, 181
corn, 48, 49, 107, 121, 147, 187, 191, 194;
    compared to European grains, 140–1;
    cultivated by Indians, 37–8; Indian beliefs
    about, 41. See also soil exhaustion
cotton, 5, 6, 120, 184, 186–7
cotton gin, 5, 6
Cotton Kingdom, 5
cottonmouth, 28
cowpens, 174, 176
crabgrass, 183
crayfish, 45
Creeks, 73, 82–3, 89, 92, 94
Crisp, Edward, 110
Cronon, William, 192
crop rotation, 164, 166
Crosby, Alfred W., 191
crows, 51, 149
Cusabos, 89
cypress, bald, 16, 108, 119–20, 130, 186

Dale, Thomas, 142
dams, 32, 101, 135
Danckaerts, Jasper, 133
Dan River, 10
Davies, K.G., 4
Deep River, 10
deerskins. See trade

deer, whitetail (see also trade): 32, 69, 186;
    and colonial agriculture, 111–12; decline,
    91–4; and Indian agriculture, 54; Indian
    hunting, 52–4; and livestock, 179; original
    range and habitat, 24–6
deforestation (see also clearing): control,
    Crown's efforts to, 137; effects on animals,
    110–11; effects on climate, 112–15; effects
    on drainage, 134–5
diptheria, 77
disease (see also individual diseases;
    medicine), 192–3; absence in New World,
    35, 36, 42; among colonists, 77; European
    and Indian resistance to, 77–8; Indian
    beliefs about, 40–1; among Indians, 70–1,
    76–83 passim, 88; among slaves, 160
Dismal Swamp. See Great Dismal Swamp
dogwood, 50, 78
Drayton, John, 100, 101, 107, 180, 183, 188,
    194
Duché, Andrew, 84
dyes, 56, 145, 159
dysentery, 157, 193

Eddis, William, 96, 97, 132
Edisto Island, 111
Edisto River, 9, 110
elks, 26, 100, 186
erosion, 100, 169, 171; colonial fields, 114,
    164–6; Indian fields, 49, 61
extinctions, 36

Fallam, Robert, 72
fall line, 10, 19. See also forts, fall-line
fences, 106, 121, 130–2, 187
fern root. See seneca root
fertilizer, 105–6, 164, 166, 168
field rotation, 164–5, 187
figs, 139, 145
fire: and beaver ponds, 100; colonists' use of,
    181–2; and deer, 62; Indians' use of,
    59–64; laws governing, 182; lightning,
    17–18; and natural vegetation, 12, 19,
    21–2, 24; and naval stores production, 126
firearms. See guns
firewood, 57–9, 106, 132–4
fish, 30, 36, 38, 135, 186
fishing: colonial, 135; Indian, 44–6; laws
    governing, 135
flea beetle, tobacco (flie), 153
fleas, 62
floods, 100, 115
forests: European perceptions of, 104; of
    South Atlantic region, 13–34 passim

forts, fall-line, 71–2
foxes, 62, 111
frost pockets, 113

Gascoyne, Joel, 83, 104, 110
George III (king of England), 3
gift giving, 69, 86, 192
gin. *See* cotton gin
ginseng, 41, 83–4, 101
glaciers, 13, 14, 35
Glen, James, 147
goats. *See* livestock
grapes, 145
grasses: European, 182–3, 188; native, 61–2,
    181
grasshoppers, 153
Gray, Robert, 190, 192
Great Dismal Swamp, 16, 28, 120
Great Northern War, 123
green corn ceremony, 41
Griffiths, Thomas, 84, 86, 87
gum, black (tree), 17
gum, white (tree), 108
guns, 89–90, 90–1

Hamor, Ralph, 53
Harriot, Thomas, 69–70, 86, 94
Haw River, 10
Hawkins, Benjamin, 94, 196
Hazard, Ebenezer, 128
hemlock, eastern, 23
hemp, 170, 187
herring, 44
Hessian fly, 154
hickory, 16, 21, 24, 50, 107, 131, 187; decline
    of, 119; mockernut, 21; pignut, 15;
    shagbark, 21
History and Present State of Virginia, 188–9
holly, American, 15
honeybees, 154
hornworms, 153
horses, 83, 174, 196
horseweed, 50
humans: characteristics different from
    animals, 32–3; early migrations of, 35
hunting: backcountry, 96–7; colonial, 90; fire,
    53; Indian, 36–7, 41, 52–5, 64, 90–1; laws
    governing, 94–7, 195; prehistoric, 35–6
hurricanes, 32

Ice Age. *See* Pleistocene epoch
Indians (*see also* disease; fishing; fire; hunting;
    individual tribes; trade): 190, 191, 192;
    belief system, 40–2, disappearance of,
    81–3; eating habits, 64–5; economy,

192–3; European images of, 67, 86; initial
    occupation of America, 6, 35–6; language
    groups, 39; population, 38–9; sex roles and
    division of labor, 44; subsistence, 35–66;
    subsistence compared to Europeans, 65;
    summer migrations, 51
indigo (*see also* soil exhaustion): 106, 169,
    186, 194; bounties on, 145; initial culture
    of, 144–5; pests in, 153
influenza, 42, 76–7, 193
Iroquois, 56, 63

James River, 8, 10, 16, 19, 73, 81
James River traders, 72, 92
Jamestown, 71
Jones, Cadwallader, 72
Jones, Hugh, 64, 107, 110, 177
juniper, red, 16

kilns, tar, 127–8, 129

laws, conservation, 195. *See also* fishing;
    hunting; fire; livestock
Lawson, John, 1, 26, 41, 43, 45, 48, 51, 57,
    62, 64, 80, 89, 92, 98, 102, 107, 119, 132,
    134, 141, 148–9
Lederer, John, 72
legumes, wild. *See* beans
lemons, 139
lice, 62
liquor, 87–8, 89, 90, 93, 102–3
live oak. *See* oak
livestock: absence among Indians, 42; in
    backcountry, 173, 174; in Chesapeake
    region, 173; and deer, 179; and erosion,
    180; feral, 174–5, 181; and indigenous
    vegetation, 177–80; kept by Indians, 196;
    laws governing, 180; on open range, 174;
    and predators, 175–7; in South Carolina,
    173; trade in, 172–3
locust (tree), 56
Lucas, Eliza, 145
lumber and lumbering, 116–21, 130, 187

Mad Dog (Creek chieftain), 94
magnolia, southern, 15, 16
malaria (*see also Plasmodium falciparum*;
    Plasmodium vivax): and birth rate, 157–8;
    in Chesapeake region, 157–8; in Georgia,
    159; among Indians, 156; initial absence
    in South Atlantic region, 155–6; and life
    expectancy, 158–9; in North Carolina,
    158–9; resistance among blacks, 160–1; in
    South Carolina, 157, 158; symptoms,
    155–6

mammoth, 35
Manahoacs, 63
maple, red, 17, 22, 50
maple, silver, 56
maple, sugar, 23, 56
marshlands, 15
Martin, Calvin, 79
martins, purple, 148–9
Maxwell, Hu, 59–60
measles, 76, 79, 193
medicine: European, 77–8; Indian, 78–9,
    80–1
mice, 111, 148, 153
Michaux, André, 118
Michaux, François André, 118–19, 127, 181–1
minks, 186
mission system (Spanish), 73, 92
Mitchell, Dr. John, 169, 171
Mitchell, Robert D., 169
Mobile, 73
monoculture, 147–8
Moravians, 50, 148, 180
mosquitoes, 62, 100; *Aedes aegypti*, 161;
    anopheline, 155–6; new habitats for, 159.
    See also malaria; *Plasmodium falciparum*;
    Plasmodium vivax
moss, Spanish, 15, 16
mulberry, 56, 145
Murray, James, 124, 129
muskrats, 28, 148, 101

Nairne, Thomas, 116–17, 145
naval stores (*see also* slaves, black): 137, 187,
    195; in Carolinas, 123; English need for,
    121–2; in Georgia, 124; and longleaf pines,
    123–9; pitch, 121, 122, 123, 124, 128;
    resin, 124; rosin, 121, 124–6; spirits of
    turpentine, 121, 124; tar, 121, 122, 123,
    124, 127–8; turpentine, 122, 123, 124; in
    Virginia, 122–3
Needham, James, 72
Neuse River, 9, 19
Newport, Christopher, 19, 81, 122, 140
New River, 10
North American Sylva, 118
Northampton, County, Va., 74
Northwest Passage, 67
nuts, 55–6

oak, 21, 22, 50, 107, 129, 187; black, 21, 24;
    laurel, 15; live, 15, 16, 32, 120, 132, 186;
    post, 21; red, 21; white, 16, 19, 21, 24,
    118–19
oats, 187

Ocmulgee River, 10
Oconee River, 10
Ogeechee River, 9
Okefenokee Swamp, 2, 3, 15, 108
olives, 139, 146
opossums, 28, 101, 111, 148, 187, 196
oranges, 139
otters, 28, 101, 186
Outer Banks (N.C.), 8, 68
oysters, 30, 63

palmetto, cabbage, 15, 16, 130
Pamlico Sound, 9
Pangaea, 12
panthers, 26, 110, 186
Panton, Leslie, and Company, 94
parakeets, Carolina, 30, 149, 186
Pardo, Juan, 7, 8
Pasquotank River, 8
peaches, 139
pears, 145
peas, 187
peat, 16
Pee Dee River, 9, 10
Pensacola, Fla., 93
Percy, George, 59, 63
Piedmont Plateau: described, 9–10;
    vegetation of, 19–22
pigeons, passenger, 30–1, 52, 55, 101, 110,
    186
pigs (*see also* livestock): 174, 176, 177, 179,
    180, 196
pine (*see also* lumber and lumbering; naval
    stores): eastern white, 23; and fire, 18; as
    firewood, 57–9; loblolly, 17, 21, 50, 171–2,
    187, 194; longleaf, 19, 187, 120–9 passim;
    pitch, 21, 22; shortleaf, 21; table mountain,
    23; Virginia, 21, 22, 50, 194
pitch. *See* naval stores
Plasmodium falciparum, 157
Plasmodium vivax, 155
Pleistocene epoch, 12, 13, 14
plows, 114
pneumonia, 157
poplar, yellow, 21, 23
population: Indian, 38–9, 81–3, 188; North
    Carolina, 166; South Carolina, 168;
    Virginia, 166–7
porcelain, 84
Pory, John, 122–3
Potomac River, 10, 19
Powhatans, 72
Proclamation Line of 1763, 3

quail, 111, 187

rabbits, 111
raccoons, 28, 52
rainfall, in South Atlantic region, 14, 22
Ramsay, David, 100, 111, 120, 132, 133
Rappahannock River, 8, 10
rats, 153
rattlesnakes, 28, 78, 181
Reuter, Christian Gottlieb, 50, 83
rheumatism, 79
rhododendron, 22
rice (see also bobolinks; slaves, black; soil
    exhaustion): 108, 130, 168–9, 186, 194;
    ecological adaptation of, 144; pests in, 153
Ridge and Valley province, 10
Roanoke colony, 71
Roanoke Island, 68, 72, 74
Roanoke River, 10, 90
Rolfe, John, 142
rum. See liquor
rust, blackberry, 155
rust, stem (of wheat), 154–5

St. Lucia, 117
St. Mary's River, 2
salt poisoning, 51, 193
Salzburgers, 175–7
sandhills, Carolina, 17
Santee River, 9, 10, 26
sassafras, 19, 22, 24, 78
Satilla River, 9
Savannah, Ga., 93
Savannah River, 9, 10, 19
savannas, 18–9, 26, 28, 173, 174
sawmills, 117, 121, 135, 159, 187, 193
scallops, 30
scarlet fever, 77
seasonal subsistence, among Indians, 42–3,
    43–55 passim
seneca root, 78, 83
Shakespeare, William, 104
sheep. See livestock
Shenandoah Valley, 82, 23–4, 170
shingles, 119–20, 129
silkworms, 145–6
skunks, 28
slaves, black: in backcountry, 171; importance
    in South Atlantic region, 1–2, 3, 4, 194,
    197; and Indians, 196; knowledge of
    fishing, 46, 135; knowledge of girdling and
    burning, 106–07; knowledge of indigo
    culture, 145; knowledge of rice culture,
    108, 144, 152; in livestock industry, 173–4;
    in lumber production, 119, 121; in naval
    stores industry, 124, 127. See also disease;
    malaria; yellow fever

slaves, Indian, 73–4
smallpox, 74–6, 78, 79, 92, 193
Smith, John, 45, 46, 53, 54, 59, 63, 65, 67,
    79, 86, 101, 140
snakeroots. See seneca root
soil exhaustion, 105, 195; in backcountry,
    169–71; in Chesapeake region, 163–6; and
    corn, 163; by Indians, 49–50; and indigo,
    163, 169; in North Carolina, 166–7; and
    rice, 168–9; in South Carolina, 168–9; and
    tobacco, 163; and wheat, 165–6
soils: Atlantic coastal plain, 14; Appalachian
    mountains, 22; piedmont, 21
de Soto, Hernando, 7, 71
sourwood, 50
South Atlantic region: boundaries, 1–6;
    description, 8–34
spiders, 62, 78
squirrels, 28, 129, 148, 149
Stephens, William, 168, 182, 193
Stockholm Tar Company, 123
Stono River, 110
Strachey, William, 42
strawberries, 19, 50
succession, forest: in colonial fields, 111,
    171–2; in Indian fields, 50, 51, 54, 104
sugarcane, 139, 194
suicide, Indian, 81
Susquehanna River, 3, 8, 13
swamps (see also Great Dismal Swamp;
    Okefenokee Swamp): bottomland, 21;
    clearing 108; inland, 16, 108; origins of, 13
sweat lodge, 79, 80

tar. See naval stores
Tar River, 9
Tatham, William, 170
ticks, 62
tobacco (see also soil exhaustion): 107, 122,
    187, 194, 195; in Chesapeake region,
    142–4, 164; cultivated by Indians, 44;
    decline of, 165; ecological adaptation of,
    142–4; erosion due to, 164; in Georgia,
    106; in North Carolina, 166–7; pests in,
    153; in Shenandoah Valley, 171; supposed
    medicinal qualities of, 142; weeds in, 184
tornadoes, 32
trade: deerskin, 68–9, 71, 72, 89, 90–7; fur,
    68–9, 97–101; between Indians, 69;
    between Indians and colonists, 83–4,
    86–90, 192–3. See also clay, white;
    ginseng; horses; venison
Treaty of Paris (1763), 93
trees (see also individual species): 114–15
Trent River, 9

Tryon, William, 171
turkeys, wild, 31, 43, 51, 54, 55, 101, 129
turpentine. *See* naval stores
Tuscaroras, 72, 92, 98, 102
Tuscarora War, 82
typhoid fever, 157
typhus, 74

variolation, 78, 193
venison, 90
vermilion. *See* dyes
Ver Steeg, Clarence L., 196, 197
Verrazzano, Giovanni da, 7, 38–9, 59, 67

Waccamaw River, 9
walnut, black, 16, 131
wapiti. *See* elk
war, between Indians and colonists: 81, 93,
   97. *See also* Cherokee War; Tuscarora
   War; Yamasee War
Warren, Robert Penn, 1
Wedgwood, Josiah, 84

weeds: imported, 184; indigenous, 37, 50
West Indies, 117–18
Westos, 89, 98, 99
wheat (*see also* soil exhaustion), 105–6,
   165–6, 187, 195
White, John, 18
White, Richard, 192
Whitney, Eli, 6, 7
whooping cough, 77
witch hazel, 56
wolves, 26, 110–11, 175–7, 181, 186
Wood, Abraham, 72
Woodmason, Charles, 183, 184

Yadkin River, 10
Yamasees, 89, 92, 102
Yamasee War, 82, 92, 172
yaupon (*see also* black drink): 15, 16
yellow fever, 161–3
York River, 8
Yuchis, 94

DATE DUE

MAY 0 8 1997			

Ireton Library
Marymount University
Arlington, VA 22207